Lamar

Lamar Archaeology
Mississippian Chiefdoms in the Deep South

Edited by
Mark Williams
and
Gary Shapiro

A Dan Josselyn Memorial Publication

The University of Alabama Press
Tuscaloosa and London

The paper on which this book is printed meets the minimum requirements of
American National Standard for Information Science-Permanence of Paper for
Printed Library Materials, ANSI A 39.48-1984.

∞

Library of Congress Cataloging-in-Publication Data
   Lamar archaeology : Mississippian chiefdoms in the deep South / edited by
Mark Williams and Gary Shapiro.
      p.   cm.
   Bibliography: p.
   Includes index.
   ISBN 0-8173-0466-5 (alk. paper)
   1. Lamar culture   2. Indians of North America—Southern States—
Antiquities.   3. Southern States—Antiquities.   I. Williams, Mark.   II. Shapiro,
Gary.
E99.L25L36   1990
976'.01—dc20

                                                                      89-4941
                                                                         CIP

British Library Cataloguing-in-Publication Data available

Contents

Figures and Tables

Figures

Tables

Part I
Lamar Archaeology

Introduction

From the mountains of east Tennessee to the low hills of north Florida and from the coast of South Carolina to the central Alabama Piedmont lived the Native Americans known to archaeologists as the Mississippian period Lamar people. These were the people encountered in those areas by the Spaniard Hernando de Soto on the first exploration of interior America. Though he hoped these people would be mining gold from the mountains in the way he had earlier seen in Peru, he was sadly disappointed. De Soto and his army left the Lamar area with no gold and wandered almost aimlessly to the west.

What of these Lamar people? Where did this name come from? What was the culture of these people like? What have archaeologists learned in the last 50 years of research upon these now long-gone and mostly forgotten early southerners? What can we glean from historic documents about them at this late date? How did the Creek and the Cherokee emerge from their descendants 150 years after De Soto died?

When De Soto entered what would later become the area of central Georgia, he found Indian societies that differed from those farther south. The houses here had cane roofs instead of the grass thatch the Spaniards had seen earlier. The explorers also recognized that they had entered a different environmental province, one in which Indian towns were strung along the river valleys, where corn was more abundant and the soil contained minerals that encouraged their hopes of finding gold. Perhaps more remarkable than these differences was a change in the behavior of the Indians. In contrast to Florida's Apalachee, who were relentless in their attacks, these Indians were less likely to fight with the Spaniards and even paid tribute to them. Some chiefs saw the explorers as potential allies

3

in their conflicts with other Indian provinces. Others cooperated simply because they feared the ruthless terror tactics employed by De Soto and his troops. Only after having traveled northeast to central South Carolina, then north and west through North Carolina, and finally southwest through parts of Tennessee and into Alabama, did the explorers again encounter fierce resistance from the Indians. At this point in his travels, somewhere in central Alabama, De Soto exited the region today known to archaeologists as the Lamar culture area.

Although they noticed differences in behavior, house construction, village location, and natural environment, none of the De Soto chroniclers mentioned the unique style of Indian pottery in this region. In fact, it is pottery that defines the Lamar area and the Lamar period for the archaeologist. As early as 1903, William Henry Holmes recognized uniformity in the area's pottery and named it the South Appalachian Group (Holmes 1903). During the 1930s, excavations near Macon, Georgia, allowed archaeologists to formally define some of the characteristic pottery types. The pottery was named Lamar for a famous mound site located there. As more excavations were conducted in the Southeast, archaeologists began to recognize the broad distribution of Lamar pottery. They found regional variations of the broad Lamar style and in many places applied new type names to indicate these differences. Some examples include Pisgah and Qualla in western North Carolina, Pee Dee in south-central North Carolina and north-central South Carolina, Irene on the Georgia coast, Bull Creek along the Alabama-Georgia border, and Leon-Jefferson in north Florida. All of these regional variants occur within an area that Leland Ferguson (1971) has called South Appalachian Mississippian. This is a subarea of Mississippian culture where for many centuries the Indians decorated their pots with complicated designs stamped into the wet clay (Figure 1).

The Lamar period began relatively late in the history of South Appalachian Mississippian cultures. In most areas, researchers estimate the beginning of the Lamar period at about A.D. 1350, although it extends to some regions only at a much later date. This is the case in north Florida, where Lamar pottery first appears sometime after 1540.

The characteristics of early Lamar stamped pottery include specific stamped designs, such as the filfot stamp and figure nine motifs. Stamping is usually applied in what appears to us as a careless

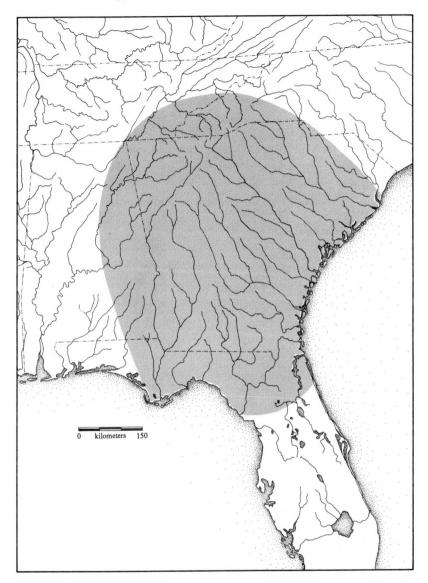

Figure 1. The Lamar Area

fashion, and the designs are often smoothed over and nearly obliterated. The rims of pottery vessels are often embellished with strips
of clay appliquéd around the rim or are folded outward to achieve
the same effect of apparent thickening. These thickened rims are
usually decorated with notches, pinches, or large punctations. Later
in the Lamar period, the Indians applied incised designs to the upper
portion of pottery vessels. Like the stamped designs, the incised
designs vary through time and from region to region, but some common incised motifs include running scrolls and nested lines separated by bull's-eye designs. Many of these variations are illustrated
elsewhere in this book. They are mentioned here only to provide
some boundary definition for our use of the term *Lamar*. Lamar
is the name we conveniently apply to the later South Appalachian
Mississippian cultures that produced certain pottery types. This
usage does not in any way diminish the reality of regional ceramic
variation within the Lamar culture area.

Of course, we are interested in documenting more than just the
variability of pottery within the Lamar area. Research by the con-
tributors to this volume includes studies of site plans, human ecology, and political structure and attempts to reconstruct the ancient
worldview of these people. Individually, these studies are intrinsi-
cally interesting, but together they promise to shed light on issues
of broad anthropological concern. We assume that shared pottery
styles reflect other shared aspects of culture. Although we do not
know the extent to which this is true, it is certain that the relative
uniformity of pottery styles within this broad region indicates some
degree of social interaction among these people. This is what makes
the study of Lamar societies exciting, for they represent a distinctive
segment of Mississippian culture in the Southeast.

Mississippian peoples are generally known for their large villages
set in river floodplains, for their construction of earthen mounds
to support temples and the houses of chiefs, and for their relatively
complex social structures. At a large scale of analysis, we hope to
learn much by comparing Lamar societies with other regional Mississippian cultures. What characteristics are held in common? And
in what ways, other than pottery styles, do Lamar societies resemble one another more than they resemble Mississippian societies
elsewhere? In discovering the unique evolutionary history of Lamar
cultures, we will inevitably document variations in chiefdoms that
may be similar to variations in chiefdoms in other parts of the earth.

For the specific knowledge of local Indian cultures and for the potential contribution to the general study of North American chiefdoms, Lamar societies deserve serious study.

During the last decade, our study region has seen a tremendous increase in archaeological fieldwork and ethnohistoric research. This is due in part to the excellent archaeological salvage work performed by private contract firms and universities. Research on Lamar period societies has received special impetus from renewed interest in the sixteenth-century Spanish explorations of De Soto, Pardo, and De Luna, all of whom came in contact with Lamar cultures. In spite of the accelerated pace of archaeological and ethnohistoric research, there has been no attempt at synthesis since Leland Ferguson's (1971) excellent dissertation. That's why the LAMAR Institute organized a small, informal meeting in 1986.

The LAMAR Institute was founded in 1982 to help coordinate research on these societies and to help educate the public at all levels about these and earlier southeastern Indian cultures. Toward this end, the institute sponsored a two-day conference in Macon, Georgia, on May 9–10, 1986. In order to share their recent contributions, scholars from all the states where the Lamar culture is known to have existed (except North Carolina) attended the conference.

Figure 2. Conference Participants

The participants (Figure 2) felt that others might benefit from the knowledge we shared that weekend, and accordingly, we have assembled the conference papers into this book.

The meeting was organized into two major parts, and this book follows that division. The first part dealt with the various chronologies revised by researchers working in eighteen study regions within the Lamar area. These are presented in Part II, which contains the most complete and detailed set of chronological data yet available for the overall Lamar area.

The second portion of the conference was devoted to individual research topics. Some of these papers present new approaches to the study of Lamar societies; others present new data for theorists to ponder. We hope they will spur further research in the Lamar area, provide ideas that may be useful to researchers of Native Americans in other parts of the New World, and, finally, inform the general public of the various avenues scientists are presently pursuing in their study of the Indian societies that once held sway in the South.

A number of key people, of course, were involved in the success of the conference. Among the many individuals with critical roles, none was more important than Jacqueline Saindon, vice president of the LAMAR Institute. Her tireless efforts made the meeting run as smooth as a burnished plain potsherd!

In the earliest stages of conference planning, there was a strong desire to hold it at Ocmulgee National Monument in Macon, Georgia, the nominal home of the Lamar culture. Through the kind permission of superintendent Sibald Smith, this desire became reality, and we most kindly thank him for his efforts. Sylvia Flowers, also of the Ocmulgee National Monument staff, helped us in innumerable ways and was a constant joy for us to work with. The rangers of the monument staff, particularly Russ Whitlock, gave us a memorable tour of the undeveloped Lamar-type site.

Jim Hawkins, a professional sound engineer from Athens, Georgia, most kindly recorded the entire proceedings on audiotape— fodder for some future historian of southeastern archaeology, no doubt!

Beth Misner and Ken Carleton, archaeology graduate students at the University of Georgia, both aided in many ways. We thank them for their cheerful contributions.

John Whatley of the Central Georgia Chapter of the Society for Georgia Archaeology arranged for us to borrow a number of tables and chairs from his local church to create a roundtable atmosphere. We kindly thank John for his aid. Most of the graphics are by Julie B. Smith. The front cover illustration is by Frankie Snow.

Finally, we wish to invoke the spirits of the late Joseph Caldwell and Charles Fairbanks and meekly hope that they approve of the progress we have made in the recent years.

In conclusion, it is my (Williams) sad task to report that Gary Shapiro, my coeditor, professional partner, and best friend, died on June 24, 1988, shortly after the manuscript for this volume was accepted for publication. He was 33 years old. Gary was a special person who enriched the lives of all those around him with wit, charm, and love. As I write this one year later, I still can't believe that he is gone. While his contributions to Lamar archaeology were substantively important, his unbounded enthusiasm about the worth of this research will continue to motivate those who knew him for years to come. So long, Bro'.

Before embarking on the two main parts of the book, we must explain how the research on Lamar societies presented here came to be; that is, some history of the last 50 years of Lamar archaeology is needed.

Lamar Archaeology: 1987

Beginnings

Whether or not John Basil Lamar ever saw, much less seriously reflected upon, the Indian mounds he owned is unrecorded. In 1862, during the Battle of Crampton's Gap in Maryland, he was killed by a Yankee bullet. His name, however, is forever tied to an Indian culture, a period of time, several Indian ceramic styles, and even a research and public education institute.

Lamar was descended from French Huguenot ancestors who had settled in America two generations earlier. As a planter and plantation owner, he acquired the land on which the famous Lamar site is situated about 1830. The land around the mounds was cleared by the 1840s, and he had ample opportunity to see them. Lamar had attended Mt. Zion school near the Shoulderbone site in Hancock County and then was a student at the University of Georgia. That he had some interest in Indians is indicated by his presentation of a five-piece beaded Cherokee costume to Oliver Prince at Milledgeville in the 1830s (John Walker, personal communication). In his time, he was a state and a federal legislator, as well as the author of several famous humorous sketches, including "Polly Peablossom's Wedding" and "Cornelius Corntassel's First Affair of Honor.'"

At his death, the Lamar mounds were left to his sister, Mary Ann Lamar Cobb. In 1868, they passed to a niece, Mary Ann Lamar. She had earlier been married to her first cousin, Jefferson Jackson Lamar, who was also killed in the Battle of Crampton's Gap. If the Lamar family was short of original female names, this was not the case for their males. Jefferson Jackson Lamar had several brothers, including Lucius Quintus Cincinnatus Lamar (father of a U.S. Supreme Court justice of the same name) and Mirabeau Buonapart Lamar (later governor of Texas).

Mary Ann Lamar's second husband was Dr. Robert M. Patterson. The mounds passed into his hands for most of the remainder of the nineteenth century. At the time of their transfer to the Macon Junior Chamber of Commerce in December of 1933, the mounds (by then known as the Lamar-Patterson mounds) were a part of a large plantation owned by the Gledhill family. The mounds and 40 acres around them were legally transferred to the United States government on March 25, 1935, as an integral part of Ocmulgee National Monument.

Early Days

Several Lamar archaeological sites were excavated before *Lamar* as such was defined. These include some of the excavations on the Georgia coast by Moore (1897), at the Hollywood site by Reynolds (1894), at the Nacoochee site reported by Heye, Hodge, and Pepper (1918), at the Etowah site by Moorehead (1932), at the mound in Dillard, Georgia, by Colburn (1936), and at the Peachtree site by Setzler and Jennings (1941). But it was with the 1930s excavations at Macon that Lamar archaeology really began to come into focus.

Arthur R. Kelly came from Texas to direct the Macon Civil Works Authority archaeological public-relief project in mid-December of 1933. While he was setting up excavations on the huge Macon Plateau site, James A. Ford, who was also hired by the Smithsonian Institution as an archaeologist, began excavations at the Lamar site. Ford immediately began documenting the remains of a vigorous society with distinctive material culture remains. Almost immediately, Ford and Kelly began to apply the name of this site to both the material remains and the people who had made them. Ford left the Macon project in late May of 1934, and work continued at Lamar under Kelly's direction.

Even in the first scholarly account of the excavations, Kelly began generalizing the name *Lamar* to the "Lamar villagers" and the "Lamar type" of flexed burial of the dead (Kelly 1935, 245). The location of this site in the low swamps along the Ocmulgee River south of Macon led Kelly to assume mistakenly that these people were uniquely adapted to a swamp way of life (246). The sites in the floodplains did not flood as often prehistorically as they do at present, and thus the floodplains were not as swampy then as now (Trimble 1974).

By the time his more famous Smithsonian Institution monograph was completed in July of 1937, Kelly had greatly expanded the notion of Lamar (Kelly 1938). Other uses of the term there include: Lamar stamped vessels, Lamar pottery decoration, Lamar pottery complex, Lamar-like pottery traits, Lamar bold incised, Lamar complicated stamped, Lamar occupation, Lamar-like sites, Lamar sites, and Lamar focus (Kelly 1938, 47–51, 68). The last of these refers to the then-current McKern classification scheme for archaeological sites and materials (Willey and Sabloff 1980).

Kelly recognized that the ceramics from the Lamar site were different from those in other Mississippian areas in the Midwest and that there were many other sites in Georgia that yielded pottery of similar form (Kelly 1938, 50–51). He summarized those characteristics that, even today, form the hallmarks of Lamar pottery wherever it occurs (47–50). He also correctly hypothesized that these sites were the ones occupied at the time that De Soto made his entrance into the interior Southeast (57).

In spite of all Kelly did in founding the Lamar concept, he did not discuss the site or materials in an anthropological context. There was almost no discussion of people or society. Perhaps this was appropriate at the time, given the general level of initial discovery and description of the remains, but it helped set the tone for Lamar research for many years to come. Jesse Jennings and Charles Fairbanks (1939) formally described the pottery that Kelly identified with the Lamar people in the 1939 newsletter of the then recently formed Southeastern Archaeological Conference.

During the late 1930s, several other sites with Lamar pottery were excavated in central Georgia. These include the Stubbs mound (Williams 1976), the upper levels of the Mossy Oak site (Padgett 1975), Cowarts Landing (Willey 1939), the Carroll site near Eatonton, Bull Creek at Columbus, and the Irene site at Savannah (Caldwell and McCann 1941). The latter is still the most thoroughly investigated Lamar mound site to date. The Irene report provides a valuable description of what these sites are likely to yield upon excavation.

In 1939, Robert Wauchope conducted an archaeological survey of north Georgia out of the University of Georgia in Athens. He acquired the best data at that time about the size and variety of Lamar sites over that area. His final report, unfortunately, was not published until 1966 and by then served more as a valuable summary than as a spur to new research (Wauchope 1966).

In east Tennessee, many archaeological sites were excavated with WPA labor under the direction of Thomas Lewis and Madeline Kneberg. The most important of these sites was the famous Hiwassee Island site. Although they found only a small amount of Lamar material there, their report of the excavation (Lewis and Kneberg 1946) is the best reported site in the Southeast based upon work in the 1930s.

Middle Period

During World War II, no archaeology was conducted on Lamar sites. Following the war, the archaeology of Georgia was dominated into the 1960s by salvage excavations within several river basins prior to the construction of dams. There was no problem-oriented work aimed at furthering our knowledge of Lamar society.

Charles Fairbanks wrote "Creek and Pre-Creek" in 1947 to summarize all that had been learned from the 1930s excavations in Georgia. He describes a few of the many mound sites around the state that were believed to date to the Lamar period and discusses the problem of ethnic identity and Lamar ceramic styles for the first time. The dating of the earlier pottery of the Etowah period was not understood at that time. Fairbanks mistakenly believed that "Etowah and Lamar are roughly synchronous" (Griffin 1952, 297). He did recognize the wide distribution of Lamar ceramics (and, by extension, culture) and says, "It seems to be the most widespread unit in the Southeast . . ." (295).

The period from 1945 up to 1955 was concerned chiefly with the refinement of the chronology of the Mississippian stamped pottery in north Georgia. Articles by Robert Wauchope (1948; 1950), William Sears (1950; 1952), Charles Fairbanks (1950; 1952), and Joseph Caldwell (1950; 1953; 1955) all were critical in outlining the sequence from late Woodland, to Etowah, to Savannah, to Lamar to historic times. The stratigraphic seriation of this was worked out just as carbon-14 dating was coming available.

By 1955, the Mississippian chronological periods that stand today were set. None of these papers (except Fairbanks 1950) discusses the lifeways of the people during these time periods. Even Fairbanks's comments were limited to the presentation of the then-popular trait lists, with no attempt to provide real social context. The major excavations at the Etowah and Kolomoki sites also took place during this period (Larson, personal communication; Sears 1955).

From 1955 until about 1972, archaeology for the Mississippian period in the Lamar area can best be viewed as "business as usual." By this we mean that excavation on Lamar sites continued as opportunities arose, particularly in the context of salvage archaeology. The goals of such work, however, were merely outlining details of the ceramic variability in time and space as an end in itself. There still was little or no attempt to discuss the societies of the Lamar Indians. Indeed, this period seems to us to be the most stagnant of the periods of research on Lamar in the last 50 years. On the other hand, it was not a period of inactivity. Important salvage excavations took place at several Lamar sites that are now destroyed. Among these were: Arthur R. Kelly and Clemens de Baillou's excavations at Estatoe (1960), Kelly and Robert S. Neitzel's work at the Chauga site (1961), Kelly and associates' excavations at Sixtoe Field (1965), Kelly's work at the Bell Field mound (1970, 1972), and David Hally's investigations at Potts' Tract (1970) and Little Egypt (1979, 1980).

Modern Approaches

Among the more interesting papers to appear near the end of this period were those of Lewis Larson on mortuary practices (1971a) and on the causes of Mississippian warfare (1972). Larson's work grows out of the general advances that took place in American archaeology following the lead of Lewis Binford in the early 1960s (1962). The New Archaeology was aimed at making archaeologists address more anthropologically oriented questions. It was designed to seek general laws about human society and to better use the data available on archaeological sites toward the goal of improving our knowledge of past societies, not just artifacts. This had a strong positive impact on the study of Lamar societies, and all of the papers included in Part III have benefited from this approach.

There have been many researchers interested in the Lamar Indians since 1972. This is partially the result of the increase in the number of archaeologists who have come of age in the wake of the postwar baby boom and partially because of the general increase in awareness and study of the environment and our heritage, which has taken place during the same period. The increased interest is also the result of the evolution of contract archaeology in the wake of federal environmental legislation and the growing sophistication of amateur archaeologists and their contributions. The result of all this is that the quantity of work on Lamar is greater now than ever before. Because much of this new work has been conducted by New Archaeologists, many of the more important works are in the form of doctoral dissertations or master's theses of these young professionals.

These studies are not easily grouped by approach, however. They represent a wide variety of approaches, no one of which is more important than the others in providing an overall better understanding of these Indians.

More Detailed Site Reports

There has been more pressure to publish the results of excavations in a timely manner than ever before. Site excavations are the lifeblood of increased knowledge about the Lamar people. The original excavations at the Lamar site began in 1934 and were sporadically conducted through October 1941. There was no report of that work available until 1973 (H. Smith 1973). Even though this report is a welcome and important addition to our knowledge, the data presented had suffered considerably through 40 years of storage and handling. Indeed, new excavations at that important site are well overdue. The site has two mounds, one rectangular and flat-topped and one round with a spiral ramp leading to a flat summit. The site was surrounded by a palisade and was situated in the floodplain of the Ocmulgee River.

The Stubbs site, located 16 kilometers south of the Lamar site, was excavated in 1936 by Gordon Willey. A site report of this small single-mound Lamar site was prepared by Williams (1975) as his master's thesis. The data from the excavations there were in better shape than that from the Lamar site, and the report is a valuable account of the complete excavation of a small Lamar mound. Stubbs remains the most completely excavated Lamar mound in the Georgia Piedmont.

Excavations at the Little Egypt site in northwest Georgia were conducted in 1968 and 1969 by David Hally. He has completed two site reports on the separate seasons of work there (1979, 1980), and they provide the first detailed descriptions of life in this periphery of the Lamar area. This important two-mound site has tentatively been identified as the main town of the province of Coosa visited by De Soto in 1540 (Hudson et al. 1985).

In 1976, the late Roy Dickens provided important accounts of the excavations at the Warren Wilson and Garden Creek sites near Asheville, North Carolina (Dickens 1976). These had taken place in the 1960s under the direction of Joffre Coe. Dickens recognized differences in the material from this area and from central Georgia and named the North Carolina variety Pisgah.

In east Tennessee, several recent site reports will measurably contribute to the study of Lamar and related cultures. These include, among others, the work of Gerald Schroedl at Chota-Tanasee (1985), William Baden at Tomotley (1983), and Richard Polhemus at Toqua (1985b).

The Cemochechobee site on the lower Chattahoochee River was excavated in 1977 (Schnell et al. 1981). The only part of the site excavated consisted of the mound area eroding into the river. This report is one of the best to date describing the construction of a Georgia Mississippian mound. Although the site was mostly constructed prior to the Lamar period, it is an invaluable published report on Lamar antecedents along the Chattahoochee River.

Excavated in 1977 and 1978, the Dyar mound was located on the Oconee River in the central Georgia Piedmont. A report has been prepared by Marvin Smith (1981), excavator of the single-mound site. Smith conducted extensive work in the village and the mound and helped develop the refined Oconee Valley ceramic chronology.

Also excavated in 1977 was the Joe Bell site, located at the junction of the Oconee with the Apalachee River. This nonmound late Lamar site was excavated by Mark Williams. His dissertation provides a complete site report, as well as much new information about lifeways in the important seventeenth century in the interior of the South (Williams 1983). This was the first report since the report of the Irene site (Caldwell and McCann 1941) to provide excavation information on almost all of a single site rather than the small-scale testing typical of most earlier excavations.

The Rucker's Bottom site along the Savannah River was excavated from 1980 to 1982 in three separate seasons. The report on these excavations was published in 1985 by David Anderson and Joseph Schuldenrein (1985). This important nonmound site was quite large, and the majority of the site was excavated. The report is an invaluable detailed account of the site plan. The date for the site is primarily the Savannah period and earliest Lamar period.

The Beaverdam Creek site, located also along the piedmont portion of the Savannah River, was excavated in 1980 and 1981, with Jim Rudolph in charge (Rudolph and Hally 1985). This Savannah period single-mound site was badly disturbed by looters before the professional work. A tremendous amount of information is presented in this report, and it will remain a standard reference for years to come.

In the piedmont portion of the Oconee River, Williams has led student excavations each summer from 1983 through 1987. Lamar mound sites investigated include the Scull Shoals site, the Shinholser site, the Shoulderbone site, and, with Gary Shapiro, the Little River site. Site reports are available on all of these projects.

In recent years, there have been major excavations and publications of three sixteenth- to seventeenth-century Spanish missions. These include the work of Stanley South at Santa Elena on Parris Island on the South Carolina coast (South 1982), David Hurst Thomas at Santa Catalina de Guale on St. Catherines Island on the Georgia coast (Thomas 1987), and Gary Shapiro at San Luis de Talimali in Tallahassee, Florida (Shapiro 1987). All of these detailed and extensive reports present views of sites occupied by Lamar people (again based upon the pottery) near the end of their history.

Chronological Refinements

From the first introduction of the notion of Lamar until the introduction of carbon-14 dating in 1950, there was no clear idea of the period of time represented by Lamar. Kelly (1938) believed that most of the period was pre–De Soto, but how long was unclear to him. In this era, it was typical for researchers to underestimate the age of chronological periods (Ford and Willey 1940). In the post–carbon-14 era, it became clear that all archaeological periods known for the Southeast were older and of longer duration than originally estimated.

In most regions, researchers accept A.D. 1350 as the beginning date for Lamar, but there are exceptions. In some cases, such as the Apalachee province of north Florida, Lamar pottery appears at a late date, in this case sometime after 1540. For most of the time

from 1950 until 1975, the Lamar period remained a monolithic
300-year temporal unit, not clearly subdivided at all. One of the
greatest advances of the last 10 years has been the subdivision of
Lamar into smaller units of time using pottery traits. The system
adopted to implement this refinement is that of Phillips (1970),
which consists of defining *phases* within the Lamar *period* as finer
space-time units.

Rather than summarize all the new data here (Part II of this book
presents this in great detail), we wish to comment on a few of the
positive aspects of these refinements. First, it is remarkable how
well some of the criteria used to subdivide Lamar phases in one
area work in other areas. For example, similar changes in pottery
rim modifications and incised design motifs may be observed in
sites along the Atlantic coast and the Georgia Piedmont (cf. Braley,
and Smith and Williams in this volume). This illustrates the high
degree of ceramic similarity over the huge South Appalachian area
and emphasizes the active and ongoing communication across this
vast area during the Lamar period. This insight to Lamar period
society remains to be examined in detail.

We are beginning to define phases that approach the length of
human lives for some parts of the Lamar area. This has had the
salutary effect of getting us ever closer to discussing the lives of
real people. New questions of inter- and intravalley relationships
are now being examined. Indeed, the chronological refinements for
the Lamar area have probably been as important in understanding
these people anthropologically as any other advances introduced by
the New Archaeology.

There will be a limiting factor on the degree of chronological refinements for Lamar, but we do not believe that the end has been
reached. Phases of 50 years' duration or less may be possible for
the entire area.

Geographical Studies

One valuable contribution of New Archaeology has been to force
archaeologists to look beyond their own research methods to other
fields of inquiry. Many archaeologists began to realize that geographers had developed methods and approaches to examine the ways
people distributed themselves over the landscape. Settlement pat-

tern studies allowed archaeologists for the first time to begin conceptualizing their archaeological cultures as real-world entities with defined spatial boundaries.

Leland Ferguson's dissertation (1971) applied a broad-scale geographical approach to describing and defining what we now call, in his words, South Appalachian Mississippian. He recognized the distinctiveness of these societies, as opposed to those Mississippian societies in the rest of the prehistoric eastern United States. Indeed, as the first attempted summary of the vast Lamar area, his work really laid the direct foundation for the information presented in this book.

Dissertations by Chung Ho Lee and Charles Pearson both applied models essentially borrowed from geography to Lamar settlement data. Lee's (1977) work was on the Lamar sites in the piedmont portion of the Oconee Valley in Georgia. He was able to show that there were clusters of sites by size and importance within the valley and its tributaries. These were suggested as potentially autonomous social or political units within the universe of Lamar sites. Lee's work was hampered by the then lack of refined Lamar chronology, but the method is a useful one.

Pearson (1979) applied similar reasoning to the Mississippian sites on Ossabaw Island on the Georgia coast. He emphasized classification by site size and dramatically demonstrated that the mound sites were not the typical site type in Lamar societies. The importance of the hundreds of small sites, formerly thought to be insignificant, in understanding the total adaptation of the population to the landscape dates from the works of Pearson and Lee.

Environmental Studies

The study of settlement patterns leads naturally to the search for correlations between archaeological and environmental variables. This approach has led to new studies in Lamar archaeology.

Lewis Larson (1980) examined in detail the Georgia coastal environment, particularly as opposed to that of the inland south Georgia piney woods. His attempts to understand Lamar adaptations to these two areas has, among other things, led to our finally examining the vast unknown area of south-central Georgia (Snow 1977).

Gary Shapiro (1983) approached the Lamar societies of the Oconee Valley from an environmental perspective in his dissertation. He discusses adaptations by the Indians to different areas along the river, such as bottomlands and rapids, and shows that settlement models developed for the lower Mississippi River (logically) can be modified to help understand Mississippian societies in the southern piedmont. He further developed a measure of site permanence, site specialization, and group size to help begin our understanding of the smaller sites that make up Lamar settlement systems.

Political Studies

An understanding of the political aspects of Lamar societies has been developing over the years in a complex manner. One of the first important steps was the 1962 publication by Elman Service of a model for the evolution of human social systems from simple to complex. This included the notion of chiefdom-level sociopolitical organization as a distinct stage between tribal-level and state-level societies around the world. For years, researchers in the Southeast, particularly John Swanton, had been constrained to force the southeastern Indian societies at the time of first European contact into one or the other of these categories, usually into the notion of a tribe.

That the Lamar societies best fit Service's notion of a chiefdom is widely accepted. One of the best studies showing this in detail is the dissertation of Chester DePratter (1983). He has carefully extracted early historic accounts of the Indians and has shown how these chiefdoms operated in some detail. His essentially nonarchaeological study has tremendous archaeological importance for understanding the politics of Lamar chiefdoms.

Perhaps the first real attempts to define a political unit per se on the basis of archaeological information is that of M. Smith and Kowalewski (1980) for the piedmont portion of the Oconee River in north Georgia. Their work was based upon the recognition of equal spacing for mound centers within that area. In the years since 1983, Williams and Shapiro have followed up their lead by obtaining the necessary data to examine this concept. In a series of papers, they have found that the growth of the Oconee Province was far more complex than initially thought. Their study is still under way but represents an attempt to apply chronological refinements to the study of Lamar politics.

Historical Studies

DePratter's 1983 study clearly showed that there is much to be gained by analyzing the available historic documents in detail. Charles Hudson has been a leader of this new analysis of the historical record. Further, with Marvin Smith and Chester DePratter, he has attempted to use new information to more accurately reconstruct the routes of the early Spanish explorers in the interior of the Southeast (Hudson, Smith, and DePratter 1984). Second, and more importantly, he has insisted that these route reconstruction attempts are important to gaining a better understanding of the southeastern societies contacted, rather than simply solving the puzzle of these routes themselves.

One of the most valuable historical studies that has resulted from this lead is a dissertation and recent book by Marvin Smith (1987). He studied the early historic societies of the Southeast and outlined the rapid and dramatic decline in the chiefdoms within the Lamar area. His study effectively combined both archaeological and historical data to gain information that could not have been revealed by either source alone.

Daily Life Studies

On the level of attempts to discuss the daily life of Lamar Indians, Mark Williams (1983) attempted to combine a detailed traditional site report with a traditional ethnographic point of view in his dissertation. He examined the form, use, meaning, and function (sensu Ralph Linton) of parts of the society. This was most extensively undertaken with the data on the ceramics as containers from the small nonmound Joe Bell site.

There have been many other attempts to understand the role of Lamar ceramics as containers in recent years. David Hally (1983a; 1983b; 1984) has attempted to determine the range of vessel forms and uses for Lamar peoples in northwest Georgia. Under his guidance, Gwyneth Duncan (1985) has conducted similar studies on the Lamar materials from the Tugalo site in northeast Georgia for her master's thesis. Shapiro (1984) also studied Lamar containers as an indicator of the use and function of small Lamar sites in the Oconee Valley.

There is still much room for studies of all sorts in this area designed to present quasi ethnographies of these archaeologically known Lamar societies. Several of the papers presented in Part III of this book directly address this concern. This kind of work is especially important if we are to tell the public what life was like in the Lamar towns and homesteads.

Belief System Studies

There is no doubt that this is the most difficult area for us to probe. There is also no doubt that it is one of the most fascinating. Charles Hudson has used the myths of the Cherokee as a basis for several fascinating lectures on the beliefs and worldview of the Lamar people. This approach is essential to a more complete and satisfying understanding of these people. His paper in this volume is typical of that important approach.

The only archaeologist in recent years who has attempted to seriously address the beliefs of the Indians, primarily with reference to their construction of mounds as sacred centers, is Vernon J. Knight, Jr. (1981; 1986). In his dissertation (1981), he detailed the nature of mound use as it related to the worldview for these people. His work is exciting and should lead others to deal with this most interesting side of Lamar societies.

The Future

Progress on Lamar and pre-Lamar Mississippian societies is progressing at an ever- increasing rate. Some of the current major trends include:

1. Tremendous increase in recognition of the need for extensive surveys to locate Lamar sites of all sizes and types over large contiguous areas.
2. Recognition of the huge number of small Lamar sites (possible homesteads) present throughout the Lamar area and complete excavation of some of them.
3. Continued refinements in our basic chronologies.
4. Acquiring basic data of site size and internal chronology from the remaining untested mound centers and large sites.

5. Recognition of the importance of sixteenth-century historic documents for reconstructing Lamar society in all its complexity.

6. Wide acceptance of chiefdom models derived from ethnographic analogues for understanding South Appalachian Mississippian.

7. Increased study of man-land relationships over the entire area.

8. Greater emphasis on timely publication of detailed excavation reports.

While all of these trends are important, and we urge that all of them continue unabated, there remain some research areas that require new effort. First, the geographical coverage of detailed research over the range of Lamar societies is uneven. While some areas have received a tremendous amount of research, others have barely been visited. This is no one person's fault. Usually, the areas researched are determined by factors beyond our control, such as the exigencies of contract archaeology. On the other hand, we should shortly be in a position to identify and target for work those critical areas where our knowledge is particularly weak. One such area, for example, is western South Carolina. Another, Georgia's Flint River, is just now receiving the attention it deserves by John Worth.

We should continue to pursue the definition of archaeological, and perhaps social, phase boundaries through intensive survey and chronological refinement. There should be a finite number of phases represented in time and space for the Lamar area, but even with the eighty-plus described in this volume, we are less than halfway there.

There should be more studies on the organization of food production by ancient Lamar societies. There apparently was no single area-wide strategy for obtaining food in the Lamar area. What were the different strategies and what factors, environmental and otherwise, were at play?

Trade played a vital role in the expansion of Lamar society and the maintenance of communication among different parts of the area. Yet trade as a research topic for Lamar studies has barely been broached. Indeed, interactions of all sorts need to be examined in the context of adjacent chiefdoms. What types of interaction took place, and can we see the results of these interactions archaeologically?

We need a clearer understanding of chiefly power and its transmission through space and time. We must understand how chiefdoms came into existence and how and why they collapsed. At the same time, we caution all researchers to stay firmly grounded in the need of the public to know what the Lamar Indians were like. Clearly, it profits us little to do all this work if it is not used to educate those who funded the work in the first place.

Part II
Time and Space

Introduction

This section summarizes the chronological periods and phases that have been defined to date for the research area. Some of this information was first defined many years ago, but much of it has been only recently worked out and was presented for the first time at the conference. Many of the phases represent archaeological units of time as short as 75 years. Twenty years ago, the briefest time unit researchers had was probably no shorter than 300 years.

The chronologies presented here are based almost entirely upon changing ceramic attributes. The attributes primarily involve variations in the rims and in incised and stamped decorations on the exterior of vessels. Many of these stylistic changes are remarkably consistent across a wide area. At this level of analysis, the use of traditional named ceramic types is of increasingly less importance. Indeed, their use seems to be rapidly declining in this area. One of the original reasons for the conference was to provide an opportunity for archaeologists from the many areas where Lamar ceramics are found to bring along representative sherds from their areas for all of the participants to examine side by side. This was an unequivocal success. Not all areas that have Lamar (or related) pottery are represented, however. Notably absent are materials from North Carolina.

We hope that this section can be used for some years to come as a new basis for the Mississippian chronology in this part of the Deep South. We recognize that it is long and complex and is bound to be modified in the future. Few, if any, researchers will (or need) learn all of the phase names for all of the areas. The important thing is that all archaeologists in this broad region of the southeastern United States are explicitly using these outlines to organize their studies of the birth, growth, and decline of the Indian chief-

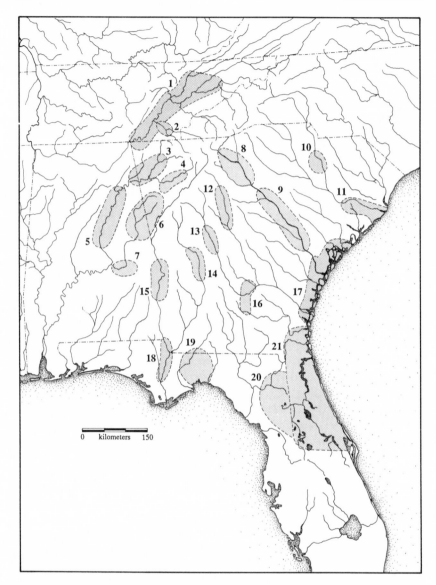

Figure 3. Areas of Chronologies

doms that were once dominant there. The obvious question of why there should be such ceramic consistency over an 800-kilometer-wide area remains to be adequately addressed. The areas for which chronologies are presented are mapped here in Figure 3.

The Lamar period, as presently understood, begins at about A.D. 1350. The chronological charts and phases that follow start at the very beginning of the Mississippian period at an arbitrary date of A.D. 950. This was done for completeness within the Mississippian period as usually understood and because it is clear that chiefdoms were present in some of these areas before Lamar. Those phases clearly within the definition of Lamar are so noted in brackets after the phase name and dates on the phase characteristics charts. Many earlier phases are assigned in the same manner to the earlier Etowah and Savannah culture periods. Some phases are assigned to other culture periods such as Dallas or St. Johns. Several of the historic phases are described as "Lamar derived" when the ceramics for those phases are related by history but have lost some important characteristic of Lamar ceramics as usually defined, such as complicated stamping.

The unevenness in the reporting of phase characteristics in this section is a result of two things. First, there is a good deal of variation in the amount of work in the different areas, and thus the details available differ. Second, as part of the difficulties of communication, not all researchers knew in advance the kind of analyses researchers in other areas were conducting. While we have attempted to even this out somewhat, it was not possible to make all the data from all areas exactly equivalent. Additionally, a few Lamar phases are known to have been defined since 1986, but these are not included in this compilation. Both of these problems are problems to be handled in some future Lamar conference.

Regional Chronologies

REGIONS:		SUBMITTED BY:
1	East Tennessee River	Richard R. Polhemus
2	Hiwassee River	Richard R. Polhemus
3	Upper Coosa River	David J. Hally
4	Lake Allatoona	W. Dean Wood
5	Middle Coosa River	Vernon J. Knight, Jr.
6	Upper Tallapoosa River	Vernon J. Knight, Jr.
7	Lower Tallapoosa River	Vernon J. Knight, Jr.
8	Upper Savannah River	David J. Hally
9	Central Savannah River	David G. Anderson, David J. Hally, James L. Rudolph
10	Wateree River	Chester B. DePratter and Christopher Judge
11	Lower Santee River	David G. Anderson
12	Piedmont Oconee River	Marvin T. Smith and Mark Williams
13	Middle Ocmulgee River	Mark Williams
14	Middle Flint River	John E. Worth
15	Middle Chattahoochee River	Frank T. Schnell
16	Lower Ocmulgee/Upper Satilla Rivers	Frankie Snow
17	Georgia/South Carolina Coast	Chad O. Braley Morgan R. Crook
18	Lower Chattahoochee/Upper Apalachicola Rivers	John F. Scarry
19	Tallahassee Hills	John F. Scarry
20	North-Central Florida	Jerald T. Milanich
21	East Florida	Jerald T. Milanich

30

	EAST TENNESSEE	HIWASSEE	UPPER COOSA
1800-			
1750-	Overhill Cherokee		
1700-			
1650-	————————		————————
1600-	Late Dallas	————————	
1550-	————————		Barnett
1500-		Mouse Creek	————————
1450-	Middle Dallas	————————	Little Egypt
1400-	————————		————————
1350-	Early Dallas	Dallas	
1300-	————————		
1250-	Late Hiwassee Island		
1200-	————————		Bell Field?
1150-			
1100-			
1050-	Hiwassee Island		
1000-	————————		
950-	Martin Farm		

	LAKE ALLATOONA	MIDDLE COOSA	UPPER TALLAPOOSA
1800-	Galt	Late Childersburg	
1750-	————————————	Early Childersburg	Tallapoosa
1700-		————————————	————————————
		Woods Island	
1650-	???	————————————	Atasi
1600-		Late Kymulga	————————————————
1550-	————————————	Early Kymulga	
1500-	Brewster	————————————	Avery
1450-	————————————	???	
1400-	Stamp Creek	————————————————	
1350-	————————————	Savannah/ Wilbanks	???
1300-	Savannah/ Wilbanks		
1250-		————————————————	
1200-	————————————	Etowah II-III	Etowah II-III
1150-			
1100-	Etowah I-IV	————————————————	
1050-		West Jefferson	
1000-	———————————— Woodstock		???
950-			

	LOWER TALLAPOOSA	UPPER SAVANNAH	CENTRAL SAVANNAH
1800-			
	Tallapoosa	————————————	
1750-			
	————————————		
1700-		Estatoe	
	Atasi		
1650-		————————————	
		???	
1600-	——		
	??		
1550-	————————————		
		Tugalo	
1500-			
	Shine II		
1450-		——	
1400-	————————————		Rembert
		Rembert	
1350-			————————————————————
1300-	Shine I	————————————————————	Hollywood
1250-		Beaverdam	————————————————————
1200-		————————————	
1150-		Jarrett	
1100-		————————————	
1050-			
1000-			
950-			

	WATEREE	LOWER SANTEE	PIEDMONT OCONEE
1800-			
1750-		Ashley	
1700-			
1650-	Daniels		Bell
1600-			
1550-			Dyar
1500-	Mulberry	Pee Dee	Iron Horse
1450-			
1400-	McDowell		Duvall
1350-	Town Creek		Scull Shoals
1300-	Adamson	Jeremy	
1250-	Belmont Neck		
1200-			Stillhouse
1150-			
1100-		Santee II	
1050-			Armor
1000-			
950-			

	MIDDLE OCMULGEE	MIDDLE FLINT	MIDDLE CHATTAHOOCHEE
1800-			
			Lawson Field
1750-	————————		
	Ocmulgee Fields		————————
1700-	————————		
			Blackmon
1650-	???		
			————————
1600-	————————		
			Abercrombie
1550-		————————	
	Cowarts		Stewart
1500-		Lockett	————————
1450-		————————	
			Bull Creek
1400-	————————	Thornton	————————
1350-		————————	
1300-	Stubbs	???	
1250-		————————	
1200-		Brunson	
1150-		————————	
1100-	————————		
1050-			
1000-			
950-			

	LOWER OCMULGEE/ UPPER SATILLA	GEORGIA/SOUTH CAROLINA COAST (BRALEY)	GEORGIA/SOUTH CAROLINA COAST (CROOK)
1800-			
1750-		English Colonial	San Marcos/ Altamaha
1700-		———————————————	———————————————
1650-		Altamaha II	Irene/ San Marcos
1600-	———————————————	———————————— Altamaha I/ Sutherland Bluff	———————————————
1550-	Square Ground		Irene
1500-		Pine Harbor	
1450-	———————————————		———————————————
1400-	Pre– Square Ground	Irene II (Pipemaker's Creek)	
1350-		——————————————— Irene I	
1300-		———————————————	
1250-		Savannah II	Savannah
1200-		——————————————— Savannah I	
1150-		———————————————	
1100-			
1050-		St. Catherines	
1000-			———————————————
950-			Wilmington

	LOWER CHATTAHOOCHEE UPPER APALACHICOLA	TALLAHASSEE HILLS	NORTH CENTRAL FLORIDA
1800-			
1750-		San Luis	Seminole
1700-			Potano II
1650-			Potano I
1600-			
1550-		Velda	
1500-	Yon		
1450-			Alachua
1400-			
1350-			
1300-	Sneads	Lake Jackson	
1250-			
1200-			
1150-			Hickory Pond
1100-	Cayson		
1050-			
1000-			
950-			

EAST FLORIDA
1800-

1750-

1700-
          Timucua

1650-

1600-
          ─────────────

1550-   St. Johns
            IIc
          ─────────────
1500-

1450-
          St. Johns
            IIb
1400-

1350-

1300- ─────────────

1250-

1200-

1150-

          St. Johns
1100-   IIa

1050-

1000-

950-

Phase Characteristics

East Tennessee River Richard R. Polhemus

Phases:

Martin Farm ?–A.D. 975

    Ceramic attributes:
      Temper is shell and limestone.
      Plain pottery predominates.
      Distinctive plaited cord marking is present.
      Vertically grooved vessel necks are present.
      Plugged loop vessel handles are present.
    Architectural attributes:
      Flexed-pole single-set and wall trench construction is
        common.
      Square or rectangular form occurs.

Hiwassee Island A.D. 975–1200 [Etowah related]

    Ceramic attributes:
      Plain pottery predominates.
      Cord marking is present but rare.
      Stamped pottery is more common.
      Red filming is present.
      Red on buff painting is present.
      Plugged loop vessel handles are present.
      Lug handles are present but rare.

Coarse-weave fabric marked "salt pan" is present.
Architectural attributes:
Flexed-pole single-set and wall trench construction occurs.
Rectangular, square, or (rarely) circular form occurs.

Late Hiwassee Island A.D. 1200–1300 [Etowah related]

Ceramic attributes:
Plain pottery predominates.
Cord-marked pottery is present in small quantities.
Red filming is present.
Red on buff painting is present.
Some stamping is present.
Plugged flattened loop handles on vessels are present.
Tongue-shaped lug handles are present.
Fabric marked "salt pan" is present.
Architectural attributes:
Flexed-pole single-set construction occurs.
Rectangular, square, or circular form occurs.

Early Dallas A.D. 1300–1400 [Dallas]

Ceramic attributes:
Cord marking is common.
Four-peaked rims are present on some jars.
Fabric marked "salt pan" is present.
DeArmond Incised is absent.
Not much other incising is present.
Small amount of red filming is present.
Appliqué strap and lug handles on vessels are present.
Burnished black pottery is absent.
Negative painting is present.
Architectural attributes:
Rigid single-set construction occurs.
Square form is present.

Middle Dallas A.D. 1400–1525 [Dallas]

Ceramic attributes:
   Cord marking is common (up to 40 percent).
   Burnished black pottery, primarily in bowl form with
      appliqué fillet, is present.
   Effigy pottery is more common than in later phases.
   DeArmond Incised is present.
   Four-peaked rims are present on some jars.
   Fabric marked "salt pan" is present.
   Appliqué strap and bifurcated lug handles on vessels are
      present.
   Negative painting is present.
Architectural attributes:
   Rigid single-set construction occurs.
   Trench entryways occur on some buildings.
   Square form is present.

Late Dallas A.D. 1525–1625 [Dallas]

Ceramic attributes:
   Cord marking is less common.
   Plain and black burnished pottery is more common.
   Effigy pottery is more stylized.
   Incising is less well executed.
   Laurel Incised is more common.
   Fabric marked "salt pan" predominates, but plain "salt pan"
      is present.
   Appliqúe strap and bifurcated lug handles are present.
Architectural attributes:
   Rigid single-set construction occurs.
   Trench entryways are frequent.
   Square form is present.

Hiwassee River Richard R. Polhemus

Phases:

Mouse Creek A.D. 1450–1575 [Lamar related]

Notes:

Mouse Creek, as here utilized, is restricted to those sites on the Hiwassee River displaying all characteristics utilized by Lewis and Kneberg to originally define the Mouse Creek focus or culture. These include ceramic traits, burial patterning, architecture, and distinctive artifact types. Those sites located outside the Hiwassee Valley and attributed to the Mouse Creek culture by others lack one or more of these characteristics and, in the east Tennessee Valley at least, represent a terminal Mississippian late Dallas phase or perhaps a later Mouse Creek variant that resembles Mouse Creek in some characteristics but should not be confused with the originally defined Mouse Creek culture.

Ceramic attributes:

Plain and black burnished surface treatment predominates.

Cord marking is virtually absent (less than 1 percent).

Rectangular fine line incised is present on jars and strap handles.

Appliqué strap and bifurcated lug handles on vessels are present.

Effigy forms, frequently on burnished black pottery, are present.

Effigy elements, like Middle Cumberland Culture and in contrast to Dallas Culture, frequently face toward vessel interior.

Plain "salt pan," sometimes with leaf impressions, is present.

Architectural attributes:

Mound construction is absent.

Rigid single-set construction with recessed floor and wall trench entryways occurs.

Square form is present.

Burial attributes:

Extended burial position predominates.

Adult burial outside of primary structure limits in cemetery-like groupings.

Other attributes:
  Deer and elk astragali dice are present.
  Pebble form edge-ground tools are present.
  Dumbbell-shaped ear ornaments are present.

Upper Coosa River David J. Hally

Phases:

Little Egypt A.D. 1400–1500 [Lamar]

Notes:
  Little Egypt (9MU102) is the best collection.
  The best collections are stored at the Department of Anthropology, University of Georgia, Athens.
Ceramic attributes:
  Shell tempered accounts for 65 percent.
  Grit tempered accounts for 35 percent.
  Lamar Complicated Stamped accounts for 10 percent.
    Motifs: filfot cross, concentric circle, figure eight, nested rectangles.
  Simple stamping is present.
  Lamar Incised accounts for less than 1 percent.
    Motifs: simple broad line designs with two or three parallel lines encircling bowl rims, interrupted by pendant festoons and loops.
  McKee Island Cord Marked accounts for 7 percent.
  Rudder Comb Incised accounts for 1 percent.
  Dallas Negative Painted accounts for less than 1 percent.
  Dallas Incised accounts for 2 percent.
  Dallas Filleted accounts for 1 percent.
  Dallas Plain accounts for 63 percent.
  Lamar Plain accounts for 8 percent.
  Lamar Coarse Plain accounts for 10 percent.
  "Salt pans" are present.
  Early narrow forms of folded and pinched rims are present.
  Rectilinear complicated stamped motifs are slightly more common than curvilinear motifs.

Barnett A.D. 1500–1625 [Lamar]

Notes:
   Little Egypt (9MU102) and Potts' Tract (9MU103) are the best
      collections.
   These collections are stored at the Department of Anthropol-
      ogy, University of Georgia, Athens.
Ceramic attributes:
   Shell tempered is less frequent and accounts for 26 percent.
   Grit tempered accounts for 74 percent.
   Lamar Complicated Stamped is present.
      Motifs: concentric circles, bisected oval, figure eight, filfot
         cross.
   Simple stamping is present.
   Lamar Incised accounts for 9 percent.
   Increased number of lines and more complex designs.
      Motifs: spiral, concentric U's, pendant festoon, guilloche,
         interlocking scroll.
   Dallas Incised accounts for 2 percent.
   Dallas Filleted accounts for less than 1 percent.
   Dallas Plain accounts for 24 percent.
   Lamar Plain accounts for 34 percent.
   Lamar Coarse Plain accounts for 21 percent.
   Late wide forms of folded and pinched rims are present.
   Rectilinear complicated stamped motifs are slightly more com-
      mon than curvilinear motifs.

Lake Allatoona W. Dean Wood
(after Joseph Caldwell)

Phases:

Woodstock ?– A.D. 1000

   Ceramic attributes:
   Curvilinear and rectilinear complicated stamping is present.
      Clean, bold execution.
      Motifs: oval, rounded diamonds with straight line fillers, line
         block.
   Incising is present.
   Rims are rounded or rolled.
   Temper is small to medium grit and quartz, often with mica.

Etowah I–IV A.D. 1000–1200 [Etowah]

Ceramic attributes:
Rectilinear complicated stamping is primarily present.
  Clean execution.
  Motifs: nested diamonds, line block, concentric polygons, filfot cross.
Painted pottery is present.
Burnished plain pottery is present.
Incised pottery is present.
Rims are rounded or rolled.
Temper is small sand and grit.
Shell and limestone temper is present, but rare.

Savannah/Wilbanks A.D. 1200–1350 [Savannah]

Ceramic attributes:
Curvilinear complicated stamping, with some rectilinear, is present.
  Heavily executed usually, although some neatly done.
  Motifs: concentric circles (some with crosses in center), figure eight, figure nine, scroll.
Rims are rolled or rounded.
Temper is medium sand or grit (shell tempering is rare).
Thicker than Savannah sherds?

Stamp Creek A.D. 1350–1450 [Lamar]

Ceramic attributes:
Rectilinear and curvilinear complicated stamping is present.
  Fair to poor execution quality.
  Motifs: bold Etowah-like diamond, line block, filfot cross, concentric circles combined with straight lines.
Incised pottery is absent.
Rims have nodes along appliqué strip.
Temper is small grit and quartz.

Brewster A.D. 1450–1520 [Lamar]

Ceramic attributes:
   Complicated stamping is indistinct and very poorly executed.
   Incised bowls appear.
   Rims are pinched or notched along appliqué strip.
   Temper is large and abundant quartz.

Galt A.D. 1750–1838 [Lamar derived]

Notes:
   Named after the Galt Ferry site.
Ceramic attributes:
   Check stamping is present.
   Rectilinear complicated stamping is present.
   Roughened and brushed pottery is present.
   Incised pottery is absent.
   Rims are pinched or notched on appliqué strip.
   Temper is large and abundant quartz.
   Bluish white and red exteriors are common.

Middle Coosa River Vernon J. Knight, Jr.

Comments:
   The Mississippian period in the middle Coosa Valley, circa
   A.D. 1100–1500, opens with an Etowah II–III complex, followed
   by an extremely sparse showing of Wilbanks/Savannah, as occurs in northern Georgia. No good candidate for the late Mississippian period has been yet identified. The overall frequencies
   of Mississippian sites known for the region suggest initially
   small and declining populations during the period, for reasons
   unknown.

Phases:

Etowah II–III A.D. 1100–1250 [Etowah]

Notes:
   Only a few small site components are present.

Sites are distributed largely in the northern segment of the middle Coosa Valley.

All known components are in floodplain environments.

Ceramic attributes:

Pottery is indistinguishable from that of northern Georgia.

Etowah Complicated Stamped is the main diagnostic ceramic type.

Savannah/Wilbanks A.D. 1250–1400 [Savannah]

Notes:

This phase was identified from uncertain context at the Sylacauga Water Works site (1TA115).

Nature of Middle Mississippian occupation in the region remains an open question.

Ceramic attributes:

Only a few sherds of Wilbanks Complicated Stamped pottery are known.

Kymulga A.D. 1500–1650 [Lamar]

Notes:

Nine site components have been identified.

Seven appear to be compact villages.

All are located in Talladega County.

Ceramic attributes:

Domestic assemblage resembles roughly contemporaneous Barnett phase of the upper Coosa.

Pottery represents a combination of Lamar and late Dallas (McKee Island) characteristics.

Differences compared to Barnett phase include:

1. The prevalence of clay/grog tempering.
2. The importance of brushing after about A.D. 1600.
3. Apparent differences in motif frequencies in incised pottery.

Most pottery is plain.

Tempered is clay/grog, shell, sand/grit, or any combination.

Complicated stamping is Lamar-like.

Brushing is present.

Relatively bold incised pottery, sometimes burnished, is
   present.
Modeled effigy adornos are present.
Well-made clay pipes are common.
Lithic attributes:
Small triangular arrowheads are present.
Greenstone celts are present.
Stone pipes are present.
Mortars and hammer stones are present.
European attributes:
European (probably Spanish) trade goods are moderately abun-
   dant.
Glass beads in several varieties are present.
Various brass ornaments are present.
Iron knives, celts, horseshoes, bracelets, and a sickle are
   known.

Woods Island A.D. 1650–1715 [Lamar derived]

Notes:
Morrell (1965) published a report on the type site, 1SC40.
Only a few other site components are known.
Ceramic attributes:
Grit-tempered pottery is absent.
Complicated stamping is absent.
It is difficult to distinguish from Childersburg phase assem-
   blages in small collections.
European (English) trade goods are abundant.

Childersburg A.D. 1715–? [Lamar derived]

Notes:
Childersburg site (1TA1) remains the only published excavated
   component (DeJarnette and Hansen 1960).
Definition was based on upper Creek material culture of the
   colonial period in the middle Coosa Valley.
Spatial distribution is very restricted and confined to a portion
   of the middle Coosa Valley.
Other known sites of the phase are numerous.

Ceramic attributes:
  Pottery is almost exclusively shell and clay/grog tempered.
  McKee Island Plain is present.
  McKee Island Incised is present.
  McKee Island Brushed is present.
  Contemporaneous upper Creek sites of the nearby Piedmont
    Plateau do not yield shell- or clay/grog-tempered pottery in
    abundance.
European trade goods are relatively abundant.

Upper Tallapoosa River Vernon J. Knight, Jr.

Phases:

Etowah II–III A.D. 1100–1250 [Etowah]

Notes:
  Only a few small site components are present.
  Sites are distributed largely in the northern segment of the mid-
    dle Coosa Valley.
  All known components are in floodplain environments.
Ceramic attributes:
  Pottery is indistinguishable from that of northern Georgia.
  Etowah Complicated Stamped is the main diagnostic ceramic
    type.

Avery A.D. 1400–1600 [Lamar]

Ceramic attributes:
  Lamar Plain:
    Plain is the dominant type.
    Rims are usually unmodified.
    Notched and noded rim decorations are present but not im-
      portant.
    The dominant rim decoration at 1RA28, the pinched appli-
      qué fillet, is not reported in the Avery (9TP64) sample.
  Lamar Bold Incised:

Dominant motif on bowls is the curvilinear scroll or guilloche.

Appliqué "button" decoration is absent.

Reed punctations, absent at Avery (9TP64), occur on only a single vessel at 1RA28.

Lamar Complicated Stamped:

It occurs in the same proportion as Lamar Bold Incised.

Bowls occur exclusively with obliterated, mainly curvilinear stamping.

Pinched or appliqué pinched decoration is the rule, although unmodified rims occur.

Check stamping is absent.

Atasi A.D. 1600–1715 [Lamar derived]

Notes:

This material is identical to the Atasi phase material from the lower Tallapoosa and is described in that section. It is present only in the southern part of the upper Tallapoosa area.

Tallapoosa A.D. 1715–1835 [Lamar derived]

Notes:

This material is identical to the Tallapoosa phase material from the lower Tallapoosa and is described in that section.

Lower Tallapoosa River Vernon J. Knight, Jr.

Comments:

This material is from Knight (1985b).

Phases:

Shine I A.D. ?–1400

Shine II A.D. 1400–1550 [Lamar]

Ceramic attributes:
  Plain pottery accounts for 85 percent.
  A small amount of the pottery is shell tempered.
  Lamar Complicated Stamped accounts for 10 percent.
  Check Stamped is present.
  Bold incising accounts for 3 percent.
  Flaring rim bowls and cazuelas occur.
Other attributes:
  Small triangular and lanceolate projectile points occur.
  Knobbed ear pins, perforated buttons, and plain gorgets of marine shell occur.

Atasi A.D. 1600–1715 [Lamar derived]

Ceramic attributes:
  Complicated stamped is absent.
  Brushed and cob-marked pottery become common.
  Incising is bold, trailed, and widely spaced.
  Flared rim vessels are common.
  Some cazuela bowls are present.
  Shell tempering is present along with sand and grit tempering.
Other attributes:
  Small triangular projectile points are present.
  European trade goods are present.

Tallapoosa A.D. 1715–1837 [Lamar derived]

Ceramic attributes:
  Chattahoochee Brushed is the dominant type.
  Cob marking diminishes in popularity.
  Incising becomes narrower.
  Kasita Red Filmed is added to the ceramic inventory but is rare.
  Shell tempering almost disappears.
  Vessel shapes are essentially the same as in the Atasi phase.
Other attributes:
  A few triangular projectiles are still present.
  Trade goods are very common.

Upper Savannah River David J. Hally

Phases:

Jarrett A.D. 1100–1200 [Etowah]

Notes:
Tugalo (9ST1) and Chauga (38OC47) are best collections.
These collections are stored at the Department of Anthropology, University of Georgia, Athens.
Ceramic attributes:
Tempering is exclusively grit.
Etowah Complicated Stamped accounts for 47 percent.
Motifs: one-bar diamond (17 percent), two-bar diamond (48 percent), three-bar diamond (3 percent), cross-bar diamond (6 percent), ladder-base diamond (17 percent), line block (9 percent).
Savannah Check Stamped accounts for 4 percent.
Etowah Red Filmed accounts for 2 percent.
Etowah Plain accounts for 43 percent.
Etowah Burnished Plain accounts for 3 percent.
Cob marking on necks of stamped jars accounts for less than 1 percent.
Collared rims on stamped jars accounts for less than 1 percent.

Beaverdam A.D. 1200–1300 [Savannah]

Notes:
Beaverdam (9EB85) and Rucker's Bottom (9EB91) are the best collections.
These collections are stored at Mound State Monument, Moundville, Alabama.
Ceramic attributes:
Tempering is exclusively grit.
Etowah Complicated Stamped accounts for 1 percent.
Motifs: one-bar cross diamond (14 percent), two-bar cross diamond (55 percent), herringbone (31 percent).
Savannah Complicated Stamped accounts for 1 percent.

Motifs: concentric circles (64 percent), filfot cross (19 percent), two-bar concentric circles (11 percent), one-bar cross concentric circles (3 percent), keyhole (2 percent).
Savannah Check Stamped accounts for 9 percent.
Savannah Plain accounts for 74 percent.
Savannah Burnished Plain accounts for 12 percent.
Cob marking on necks of stamped jars accounts for 3 percent.
Collared rims on stamped jars accounts for 2 percent.

Rembert A.D. 1300–1450 [Lamar]

Notes:
Phase was named for the Rembert site (9EB1).
Rembert (9EB1) and Rucker's Bottom (9EB91) are the best collections.
Rembert collection is stored at the Department of Anthropology, University of Georgia, Athens.
Rucker's Bottom collection is stored at Mound State Monument, Moundville, Alabama.
Ceramic attributes:
Tempering is exclusively grit.
Lamar Complicated Stamped accounts for 50 percent.
Motifs: concentric circles, figure-eight, figure-nine, filfot cross, line block.
Lamar Incised accounts for less than 1 percent.
Motifs: simple broad line designs with two or three parallel lines encircling bowl rims, with pendant festoons and loops.
Lamar Plain accounts for 34 percent.
Lamar Burnished Plain accounts for 8 percent.
Lamar Coarse Plain accounts for 6 percent.
Check stamping accounts for 1 percent.
Cob marking accounts for 1 percent.
Cord marking accounts for 1 percent.
Rims on jars are either:
1. Unthickened and frequently decorated with cane punctations and rosettes.
2. Thickened and decorated with punches, notches, or cane punctations.

Tugalo A.D. 1450–1600 [Lamar]

Notes:
   Phase was named for the Tugalo site (9ST1).
   Tugalo (9ST1), Estatoe (9ST3), and Chauga (38OC47) are the
      best collections.
   All three collections are stored at the Department of Anthropol-
      ogy, University of Georgia, Athens.
Ceramic attributes:
   Tempering is exclusively grit.
   Lamar Complicated Stamped accounts for 62 percent.
      Motifs: difficult to identify but include concentric circles,
         figure-nine.
   Lamar Incised accounts for 8 percent.
      There are a greater number of lines.
      Motifs: concentric circles, oval with brackets, line-filled tri-
         angle.
   Simple stamping is present.
   Check stamping (1 percent) is absent from Tugalo, 1 percent
      at Estatoe.
   Lamar Plain accounts for 12 percent.
   Lamar Coarse Plain accounts for 16 percent.
   Lamar Burnished Plain accounts for 1 percent.
   Red filming accounts for less than 1 percent.
   Rims of jars are thickened and decorated with pinches, notches,
      and cane punctations at bottom of rim.

Estatoe A.D. 1650–1750 [Lamar]

Notes:
   Phase was named for the Estatoe site (9ST3).
   Tugalo (9ST1), Estatoe (9ST3), and Chauga (38OC47) are the
      best collections.
   All three collections are stored at the Department of Anthropol-
      ogy, University of Georgia, Athens.
Ceramic attributes:
   Tempering is exclusively grit.
   Lamar Complicated Stamped accounts for 68 percent.
      Motifs: difficult to identify but include concentric crosses,

line block, concentric circles, figure-nine, keyhole.
Simple stamping is present.
Lamar Incised accounts for 4 percent.
  Motifs: same as Tugalo phase.
  This may be mixed from other components.
Check stamping accounts for 6 percent.
Lamar Plain accounts for 11 percent.
Lamar Coarse Plain accounts for 7 percent.
Lamar Burnished Plain accounts for 4 percent.
Red filming accounts for less than 1 percent.
All jar rims are modified in one of following ways:
  thickened and pinched, rolled, L-shaped, filleted strip.

Central Savannah River David G. Anderson, David J. Hally, and James L. Rudolph

Comments:
  Apparently, this area was completely abandoned by 1400–50 and was not reoccupied until very late in the historic sequence. No phase names have been applied to the sparse post–A.D. 1600 occupations. This abandoned area was part of the "desert" through which De Soto traveled in the spring of 1540. The phases here are based upon Hally and Rudolph (1986), as published after the Lamar Conference.

Phases:

Hollywood A.D. 1250–1350 [Savannah]

Notes:
  This is partially equivalent to the Beaverdam phase listed above in the upper Savannah. It is named after the Hollywood site in Richmond County, just south of Augusta.
Ceramic attributes:
Savannah Check Stamped is very common.
Filfot-stamped motif is very common.
Diamond-stamped motifs are infrequent.
Cane punctation on upper vessel wall and cane-punctated nodes are common.

Rembert A.D. 1350–1450 [Lamar]

Notes:
See the description above in the Upper Savannah area.

Wateree River Chester B. DePratter and
  Christopher Judge

Phases:

Belmont Neck A.D. 1200–1250 [Etowah]

Notes:
Phase was named for the Belmont Neck site (38KE6).
All the best collections are stored at the South Carolina Institute of Archaeology and Anthropology, Columbia.
Ceramic attributes:
Tempering is fine to medium sand.
Some tempering is coarse sand/fine grit.
Complicated stamping accounts for 43 percent.
  Motifs: predominantly concentric circles, undefined concentric curvilinear forms, Etowah cross-bar diamond present but rare.
Incising is absent.
Plain accounts for 31 percent.
Burnished plain accounts for 9 percent.
Simple rims account for 86 percent.
Notched rims account for 7 percent.
Reed punctations below lip are in low frequency.

Adamson A.D. 1250–1300 [Savannah]

Notes:
Phase was named for the Adamson site.
All the best collections are stored at the South Carolina Institute of Archaeology and Anthropology, Columbia.
Ceramic attributes:

Tempering is medium sand to medium grit.
Complicated stamping accounts for 23 percent.
  Motifs: predominantly filfot cross, line block.
Plain accounts for 45 percent.
Burnished plain accounts for 14 percent.
Rim forms include: simple (53 percent), notched (13 percent),
  punctations below lip (13 percent), rosettes (3 percent).
Lip punctation is rare.
Zoned punctation below lip is rare.
Riveted lugs are present.
Fabric marking is present.

Town Creek A.D. 1300–1350 [Lamar]

Notes:
Phase was named for the Town Creek site.
Ceramic attributes:
  Tempering is medium sand to medium grit.
  Complicated stamping accounts for 30 percent.
    Motifs: filfot cross, line block.
  Plain accounts for 30 percent.
  Burnished plain accounts for 19 percent.
  Rim forms include: simple (43 percent), segmented appliqué
    strips (17 percent), punctated appliqué strips (13 percent), ro-
    settes (8 percent), nodes (4.5 percent).

McDowell A.D. 1350–1450 [Lamar]

Notes:
Phase was named for the McDowell site.
All the best collections are stored at the South Carolina Insti-
  tute of Archaeology and Anthropology, Columbia.
Ceramic attributes:
  Tempering is medium sand to medium grit.
  Complicated stamping accounts for 45 percent.
    Motifs: filfot cross.
    Stamping is bolder and motifs are larger.

Mulberry A.D. 1450–1550 [Lamar]

Notes:
  Phase was named for the Mulberry site.
  All the best collections are stored at the South Carolina Institute of Archaeology and Anthropology, Columbia.
Ceramic attributes:
  Complicated stamping is present.
  Lamar-like incising is present.
  Segmented or punctated appliqué rim strips are present.
  Vertical ticks are present on vessel shoulders.

Daniels A.D. 1550–1675 [Lamar]

Notes:
  Phase was named for the Daniels site.
  All the best collections are stored at the South Carolina Institute of Archaeology and Anthropology, Columbia.
Ceramic attributes:
  Sloppy "exploded" stamping is present.
  Wide appliqué rim strips are present.
  Thick vessel walls are present.

Lower Santee River David G. Anderson

Phases:

Santee I

Ceramic attributes:
  V-shaped cross simple stamping is present.
  Lip treatment is infrequent.
  Cord-marked pottery is present.
  Fabric-marked pottery is present.
  Both types are present in both sand and crushed-sherd temper.

Santee II ?– A.D. 1200

Ceramic attributes:
V-shaped cross simple stamping with stamped lips are common.
Stamping sometimes is noted on interior just below lip.
Heavy parallel cord marking (sherd tempered) is a minority type.

Jeremy A.D. 1200–1400 [Savannah]

Ceramic attributes:
Curvilinear complicated stamping is present.
  The stamping is well executed.
  Concentric circles form the most common motif.
Rims are typically unmodified.
Check stamping is present.
Fine parallel and cross-cord marking is also present.

Pee Dee A.D. 1400–1550 [Lamar]

Ceramic attributes:
Curvilinear and rectilinear stamping is present.
  The stamping is well executed.
  Motifs: arc-angle, filfot cross, scroll (rarely with land width greater than 2 millimeters).
Rim treatment includes unmodified and modified (circular hollow reed punctations, rosettes) forms.
This is similar to "classic" Pee Dee series.

Ashley A.D. 1550–1760 [Lamar]

Ceramic attributes:
Complicated stamping is bold, carelessly applied designs, often poorly carved and crude in appearance.
Folded and/or finger-pinched rim strips are present.

Piedmont Oconee River Marvin T. Smith and Mark Williams

Phases:

Armor A.D. 950–1100 [Etowah]

Notes:
Phase was defined at the Dyar site (9GE5).
All the collections are stored at the Department of Anthropology, University of Georgia, Athens.
Ceramic attributes:
Ladder-base diamond motif predominates.
Red filming is absent.
Loop handles are rare.

Stillhouse A.D. 1100–1250 [Etowah]

Notes:
Phase was defined at the Dyar site (9GE5).
All of the collections are stored at the Department of Anthropology, University of Georgia, Athens.
Ceramic attributes:
Good quality Etowah stamping is present.
Filfot cross design is absent.
Ladder-base diamond motif is virtually absent.
Rectilinear stamping is more common than curvilinear stamping.
Red filming is present.
Check stamping is present.
Cob marking is present.
Rim adornos (duck and owl) are present.

Scull Shoals A.D. 1250–1375 [Savannah]

Notes:
Phase was named for and defined at the Scull Shoals site (9GE4).

All the collections are stored at the Department of Anthropology, University of Georgia, Athens.
Ceramic attributes:
Complicated stamping is sloppier.
Diamond motif is continued.
Filfot cross motif is common.
Curvilinear stamping is very common.
Incising is absent.
Cob marking is present but rare.
Cord marking is present but rare.
Rim modifications are extremely rare.
Red filming is present.
Lithic attributes:
Small triangular projectile points are common.

Duvall A.D. 1375–1450 [Lamar]

Notes:
Phase was defined at the Dyar site (9GE5).
All the collections are stored at the Department of Anthropology, University of Georgia, Athens.
Ceramic attributes:
Morgan Incised (fine line crosshatched incised) is present.
Stamping is rarer than in previous phases.
Cane punctation on narrow folded rims is common.
    Punctation is approximately 5 millimeters in diameter.
    They occur in one, two, or three rows on the rim folds.
Narrow pinched or folded/appliqué rims (approximately 10 millimeters) occur.
Rim effigy adornos occur.
Lithic attributes:
Flaked stone is almost completely absent.
Projectile points are absent.

Iron Horse A.D. 1450–1520 [Lamar]

Notes:
Phase was defined at the Scull Shoals site (9GE4).

All the best collections are stored at the Department of Anthro-
pology, University of Georgia, Athens.
Ceramic attributes:
Stamping is more common.
Bold incised (less than 2 millimeters) motifs have two to four
lines.
Morgan Incised (fine line crosshatched incised) occurs.
Medium width (14–15 millimeters) pinched or folded appliqué
rims occur on jars.
Cane-punctated rims are present but rare.
Lithic attributes:
Flaked stone is almost completely absent.
Projectile points are absent.

Dyar A.D. 1520–1580 [Lamar]

Notes:
Phase was named for and defined at the Dyar site (9GE5).
All the best collections are stored at the Department of Anthro-
pology, University of Georgia, Athens.
Ceramic attributes:
Bold incised (less than 2 millimeters) motifs with four or more
lines occur.
Wide (17–20 millimeters) pinched folded/appliqué rims occur
on jars.
Stamping is common.
Lithic attributes:
Flaked stone is almost completely absent.
Projectile points are absent.

Bell A.D. 1580–1670? [Lamar]

Notes:
Phase was named for and defined at the Joe Bell site (9MG28).
All the best collections are stored at the Department of Anthro-
pology, University of Georgia, Athens.
Ceramic attributes:
Stamping is present but rare (less than 1 percent).

Incised motifs with multiple (up to thirty or more) fine incised (less than 1 millimeter) lines occur.

T-shaped rims occur.

Widest (approximately 20 millimeters) pinched folded/appliqué rims occur.

Lithic attributes:

Flaked stone is almost completely absent.

Projectile points are absent.

Middle Ocmulgee River Mark Williams

Comments:

This chronology was worked out in 1975 largely on the basis of Williams's analysis of materials from the 1936 excavations at the Stubbs mound. It badly needs to be reworked in light of new information from other regions. For example, it is now clear that his original definition of Stubbs phase includes a mixture of materials from Savannah and early Lamar contexts. Stratigraphic separation was impossible for the sample from Stubbs. Clarification of the middle Ocmulgee chronology will require new excavations, as there are no sufficiently documented extant collections.

Phases:

Stubbs A.D. 1100–1400 [Lamar]

Notes:

Phase was named for and defined at the Stubbs site.

All of these collections are stored either at the Southeast Archaeological Center in Tallahassee, Florida, or at Ocmulgee National Monument in Macon, Georgia.

Ceramic attributes:

This includes mixed Savannah and early Lamar materials.

Bold incising makes first appearance but is very rare.

Sherds are sandier and thinner than in the subsequent Cowarts phase.

Notched lips are present and reflect the Savannah component.

Unmodified jar rims also reflect the Savannah component.

Stamping is common.

Cowarts A.D. 1400–1600 [Lamar]

Notes:
   Phase was named for the Cowarts Landing site.
   All of these collections are stored either at the Southeast Ar-
      chaeological Center in Tallahassee, Florida, or at Ocmulgee
      National Monument in Macon, Georgia.
Ceramic attributes:
   This includes "Classic" Lamar of the 1930s, as defined by Kelly
      (1938).
   Stamping is common.
   Bold incising is more common.
   Incised sherds commonly have black surfaces.
   Sherds contain more grit temper.
   Sherds are thicker than in Stubbs phase.
   Pinched rims are more frequent.

Ocmulgee Fields 1685–1715 [Lamar derived]

Notes:
   Phase was defined at Macon Plateau site (9BI1).
   Phase represents the Creek Indians' moving into this area from
      east Alabama.
   Phase seems to be identical to Blackmon phase material from
      the lower Chattahoochee.
Ceramic attributes:
   Stamping is absent.
   Fine line, poorly executed incising is common.
      Ocmulgee Fields Incised is the type name.
      Incising usually occurs on bowls.
   Brushed pottery is most common type.
      Walnut Roughened is the type name.
      Brushing usually occurs on jars.
   Red-filmed pottery is present but rare.
   Lips are often flattened.
   Small strap handles often occur on jars.

Middle Flint River John E. Worth

Comments:

This section is based upon Worth's 1988 University of Georgia thesis. The work was not conducted until after the conference but has been included here for completeness. Worth concluded that this stretch of the Flint River was abandoned during the Savannah period, a very unusual situation when compared with all of the other chronologies presented in this section. Interestingly, the upper Flint Valley appears to have been completely abandoned at or just after the De Soto trip through the area.

Phases:

Brunson A.D. 1150–1225 [Etowah]

Notes:

Worth actually divides this phase into early and late subdivisions, based upon increasing Savannah Stamped and decreasing ladder-base diamonds. Because of the ladder-base diamonds, he assigns the entire phase to a pre-Savannah, Etowah period context. Despite his arguments to the contrary, it seems likely that at least some of the occupation dates to the Savannah period as usually defined. The percentages given here are means from his two subsections. The collections are all at the Department of Anthropology, University of Georgia, Athens.

Ceramic attributes:

Etowah Complicated Stamped accounts for 18 percent.

Ladder-base diamonds are present.

Savannah Complicated Stamped accounts for 8 percent.

No filfot cross is present.

Etowah Red Filmed accounts for 2 percent.

Plain accounts for 72 percent.

No check-stamped, cob-marked, or simple stamped sherds are present.

Thornton A.D. 1325–1450 [Lamar]

Notes:
  The collections are at the Department of Anthropology, University of Georgia, Athens.
Ceramic attributes:
  Complicated stamped accounts for 30 percent.
  Plain accounts for 60 percent.
  Vessel paste is coarse grit temper that creates a rough, bumpy surface.
  Some shell tempering is present.
  Sherds are thicker than in Brunson phase.
  Lugs, strap handles, and rim adornos are present.
  Folded rims are narrow and always pinched.
  Cane-punctated rims are not present.
  Incising is absent.
  Cob marking, check stamping, and net marking are present but rare.

Lockett A.D. 1450–1550 [Lamar]

Notes:
  The collections are at the Department of Anthropology, University of Georgia, Athens.
Ceramic attributes:
  Incised pottery is added to the inventory.
  Most incised sherds have few incised lines.
  Shell-tempered incised is present.
  Wider rim folds are present.
  Pinches on rims are smaller.
  Cane punctation of the rim is common.

Middle Chattahoochee River Frank T. Schnell

Phases:

Bull Creek A.D. 1400–1475 [Lamar]

Notes:
   Phase was named for the Bull Creek site at Columbus.
   The best collections are stored at the Columbus Museum,
      Columbus, Georgia.
Ceramic attributes:
   Complicated stamping predominates (approximately 60 per-
      cent).
   Plain is the next most common (approximately 35 percent).
   Incising and punctating occur (less than 4 percent).
   Rim pinching and noding are the most common rim forms.
   Reed punctating is rare.
   Coarse red-tinted grit tempering is present.
   Mercier Check Stamped occurs.
   Negative painted dog effigies occur (four known).
Architectural attributes:
   Square houses are present.
   Individual post houses are present.
   Central roof supports occur.
   Unknown form with daub occurs.
Burial attributes (from 9ME1):
   74 percent have no grave goods, 2 percent extended, 22 percent
      semiflexed, 76 percent flexed, 12 percent oriented W-E, 17
      percent oriented S-N, 7 percent oriented SW-NE, 24 percent
      oriented SSE-NNW, 22 percent oriented NW-SE, 15 percent
      oriented E-W, 2 percent oriented N-S.

Stewart A.D. 1475–1550 [Lamar]

Notes:
   The best collections are stored at the Columbus Museum, Co-
      lumbus, Georgia.
Ceramic attributes:
   Plain pottery accounts for approximately 55 percent.

Complicated stamping is the next most common (approximately 20 percent).

Incising and punctating are present (approximately 15 percent).

Coarse grit tempering is present.

Mercier Check Stamped occurs.

Architectural attributes:

Square and rectangular houses occur.

Individual post houses occur.

Central roof supports are present.

Whole-cane wattles with clay daub are present.

Burial attributes:

Two are known (one from top of Mound A at Rood's Landing).

Extended burials are present.

Grave goods are absent.

Abercrombie A.D. 1550–1625 [Lamar]

Notes:

Phase was named for the Abercrombie site.

The best collections are stored at the Columbus Museum, Columbus, Georgia.

Ceramic attributes:

Plain (smoothed, burnished, and polished) predominates.

Incising and punctating is more common than complicated stamping.

Complicated stamping is less common.

Shell tempering is common.

Architectural attributes:

Possibly semisubterranean structures are present.

Individual post houses are present.

Whole-cane wattles on interior of daub with a split-cane daub surface reinforcement are present.

One structure had a baked clay floor.

Burial attributes:

Extended and flexed burials occur.

Shallow and deep graves occur.

Grave goods more likely with children and youths.

Shell ornaments are the most common grave goods.

Sixteenth- and seventeenth-century Spanish trade goods are found with some burials.

Blackmon A.D. 1625–1715 [Lamar derived]

Notes:
> This phase is to be identified with the Apalachicola province of early Spanish documents. This description is from Knight and Mistovich (1984).

Ceramic attributes:
> Shell tempering is common.
> Shell-tempered Ocmulgee Fields Incised is present.
> Walnut Roughened pottery is present.
> Kasita Red Filmed is present.
> Grit-tempered–type Chattahoochee Brushed is absent.

Lawson Field A.D. 1715–1835 [Lamar derived]

Notes:
> This represents the amalgamation of material resulting from the formation of the Creek Confederacy after the Yamassee War of 1715. This description is from Knight and Mistovich (1984).

Miscellaneous:
> All sorts of English trade material are present on these sites.

Ceramic attributes:
> Ocmulgee Fields Incised is present.
> Chattahoochee Brushed is present.
> Kasita Red Filmed is present.
> Coarse and fine plain pottery is present.

Lower Ocmulgee/Upper Satilla Rivers
Frankie Snow

Phases:

Pre–Square Ground ?–A.D. 1450 [Savannah/Lamar]

Notes:
> The best collections are stored at South Georgia College, Douglas.

Ceramic attributes:
Jars without decorative rim strips occur.
Clearly impressed filfot stamping is present.
Bowls are rare.
Some bowls are plain.
A few bowls are bold incised and have hollow reed punctation.

Square Ground A.D. 1450–1600 [Lamar]

Notes:
The best collections are stored at South Georgia College, Douglas.
Forty sites are known.
The distribution extends from the confluence of the Oconee and Ocmulgee rivers westward 50 kilometers to near Jacksonville, Georgia, then south to the Satilla in Atkinson County, Georgia.
Lamar ceramics are rare south of the Satilla River.
Seventeen Mile River near Douglas has several sites usually associated with hammocks.
Ceramic attributes:
Jars remain the major vessel type.
A marked increase in the frequency of bowls occurs.
Bold line incising is the common mode of decoration.
It is confined to a zone near the rim.
Solid punctations frequently are combined with incising.
Complicated stamping is present beneath the incised zone.
Motif is described as a "square ground."
Considerable variation exists.
Filfot cross motif is rare.
A fold or fillet of clay is placed around the rims of jars.
Base of fold is pinched to produce an undulating effect.
Some jars with sharply flared rims occur.
Shallow platelike pots with interior incising near the rim are present.
Incising on jar exterior surfaces are absent.
Both jars and bowls are burnished or well smoothed on interior.
Tempering is grit.
Stemmed clay pipes are common.
Pot handles are rare.

Georgia/South Carolina Coast Chad O. Braley

Comments:

Chad Braley and Morgan R. Crook generally agree on the ceramic attributes defining the sequence on the Georgia coast. They disagree on the dates and phases. These differences are made clear on the chronological charts. The authors agree with the dates used by Braley (based partly on the works of Caldwell and DePratter) because they are much more closely aligned with all of the dates from the interior. The characteristics listed here are those supplied by Braley.

Phases:

Savannah I A.D. 1150–1200

Ceramic attributes:
Large jars with check stamping are present.
Cord marking is present.
Carinated bowls with plain surfaces are present.

Savannah II A.D. 1200–1300 [Savannah]

Ceramic attributes:
Large jars with complicated stamping are present.
Check stamping is present.
Noded rims occur.
Carinated bowls with plain surfaces are present.

Irene I A.D. 1300–1350 [Lamar]

Ceramic attributes:
Large jars with plain surfaces are present.
Reed-punctated rims are present.
Noded rims are present.

Irene II (Pipemaker's Creek) A.D. 1350–1450 [Lamar]

Ceramic attributes:
  Large jars with appliqué rim strips or segmented rim strips are
     present.
  Small jars incised with simple scroll motifs are present.
  Carinated incised bowls, bold with decorative elements consist-
     ing of two or three lines, are present.

Pine Harbor A.D. 1450–1575 [Lamar]

Ceramic attributes:
  Large jars with reed-punctated appliqué rim strips occur.
  Small jars with intricate incised motifs occur.
  Bold incising is present.
  Punctation is present.
  Carinated bowls with multiple-line incising are present.

Altamaha/Sutherland Bluff A.D. 1575–1700 [Lamar]

Ceramic attributes:
  Large jars occur with wide folded rims, reed punctating, recti-
     linear complicated stamping or cross simple stamping.
  Small jars occur with narrow incised lines, red filming, and
     punctation.
  Carinated bowls occur with narrow incised line, bold incised
     lines, or punctation

Lower Chattahoochee/Upper Apalachicola Rivers John F. Scarry

Phases:

Cayson A.D. 1000–1200 [Fort Walton?]

Ceramic attributes:
  Check stamping is present.
  Cob marking is present.
  Zoned punctation ispresent.
  Fort Walton Incised is present.
  Wakulla Check Stamped is present.
  Alachua Cob Marked is present.
  Lake Jackson Incised is present.
  Cool Branch Incised is present.

Sneads A.D. 1200–1400 [Fort Walton]

Ceramic attributes:
  Stamping is absent.
  Zoned punctation is present.
  Ticked rims are present.
  Loop handles are present.
  Lug handles are present.
  Fort Walton Incised is present.
  Lake Jackson Incised is present.

Yon A.D. 1400–? [Lamar]

Ceramic attributes:

  Stamping is present.
  Bull's-eye motif is present.
  Bold incising is present.
  Curvilinear incising is present.
  Folded rims are present.
  Pinched rims are present.

Lamar Complicated Stamped is present.
Point Washington Incised is present.

Tallahassee Hills John F. Scarry

Phases:

Lake Jackson A.D. 1100–1500 [Fort Walton]

Notes:
> Phase was named for the Lake Jackson site northwest of Tallahassee, Florida.
>
> Most of the best collections are at the Florida Bureau of Archaeological Research, Tallahassee.

Ceramic attributes:
> Grog tempering predominates.
>
> Zoned punctation is present.
>
> Rectilinear incising is present.
>
> Stamping is absent.
>
> Wakulla Check Stamped is absent.
>
> Lake Jackson Plain is common.
>
> Lake Jackson Incised varieties Lake Lafayette and Winewood are present.
>
> Marsh Island Incised varieties Columbia and Marsh Island are present.
>
> Fort Walton Incised varieties Cayson and Sneads are present.
>
> Cool Branch Incised variety Cool Branch is present.
>
> Andrews Decorated beakers are present but rare.
>
> Lug and loop handles are common.
>
> Jars, collared bowls, and cazuela bowls occur.

Velda A.D. 1500–1633 [Lamar]

Notes:
> Phase was named for the Velda site northeast of Tallahassee, Florida.
>
> The best collections are at the Florida Bureau of Archaeological Research, Tallahassee.

Ceramic attributes:
  Curvilinear incising is present.
  Rectilinear incising is present.
  Folded rims occur.
  Punctated rims occur.
  Lamar Complicated Stamped variety Early is present.
  Leon Check Stamped is present.
  Point Washington Incised is present.
  Collared bowls are no longer present.
  Cazuela bowls, unrestricted bowls, and flaring rim jars are present.

San Luis A.D. 1633–? [Lamar]

Notes:
  Phase was named for the mission of San Luis de Talimali in Tallahassee, Florida.
  Most of the collections are at the Florida Bureau of Archaeological Research, Tallahassee.
Ceramic attributes:
  European ceramics (majolica and olive jar) are present.
  Aboriginal copy pottery is present.
    This includes ring bases and plate forms.
  Lake Jackson Plain is present.
  Lamar Complicated Stamped variety Jefferson is present.
  Leon Check Stamped is present.
  Mission Red Filmed is present.
  Ocmulgee Fields Incised is present.

North-Central Florida Jerald T. Milanich

Phases:

Hickory Pond ?–A.D. 1250

Ceramic attributes:
  Some pottery is tempered with clay lumps.
  Cord-wrapped paddle stamped accounts for 45–70 percent.
  Fabric-wrapped paddle stamped is present.

Alachua A.D. 1250–1600

   Ceramic attributes:
      Pottery is sand tempered.
      Cob-marked pottery becomes more common.
      Fabric-wrapped paddle stamped is absent.
      Cylindrical pots and small bowls are common.
   Small triangular projectile points are common.

Potano I A.D. 1600–1630

   Phase named for the historic Potano Indians in this area.
   Spanish artifacts appear in village sites.
   Ceramic attributes:
      Ceramics are very similar to those in the Alachua phase.
      Pottery is sand tempered.
   Small triangular projectile points are common.

Potano II A.D. 1630–1710 [Lamar]

   Ceramic attributes:
      Ceramics are apparently imported complicated stamped wares
         from Georgia.
      Plain pottery is most popular during this phase.
      Pottery is sand tempered.
   Decrease in the number of lithic tools and points.

Seminole A.D. 1710–? [Lamar derived]

East Florida Jerald T. Milanich

Phases:

St. Johns IIa ?–A.D. 1300 [St. Johns]

Ceramic attributes:
St. Johns Check Stamped occurs in villages and mounds.
Burial mounds increase in use.
Late Weeden Island pottery and copies occur in some mounds.
Some pottery caches occur in mounds.

St. Johns IIb A.D. 1300–1520 [St. Johns]

Notes:
Some Fort Walton and Safety Harbor pottery and Southeastern
Ceremonial Complex objects occur in mounds.
Mississippian "influences" are present.
Ceramic attributes:
St. Johns Check Stamped pottery is present.

St. Johns IIc A.D. 1520–1565 [St. Johns]

Notes:
Burial mounds are still present.
European artifacts occur in some mounds.
Severe population reductions due to European diseases occur.
Ceramic attributes:
St. Johns Check Stamped is present.

Various Timucua (St. Johns complex into San Marcos) A.D. 1565–?

Part III
Case Studies

Introduction

The papers presented in this section illustrate the wide range of approaches being explored by those currently studying Lamar societies. We begin with a series of papers (by Snow, Braley, Langford and Smith, and Elliott) that present important basic data on variability in Lamar material culture and settlement patterns. Although his study area is just outside the boundary of Lamar pottery distributions, Polhemus demonstrates a relationship between Dallas phase architecture and social structure that should be of direct interest to students of Lamar cultures. Papers by Nance and by Shapiro also deal with settlement patterns, but from an environmental perspective. Williams and Shapiro consider some important environmental and political factors that may influence site relocation. This leads directly to papers by Scarry and by Anderson that highlight the importance of understanding Mississippian political structure. The final paper, by Hudson, demonstrates the importance of trying to understand the Indians' worldview. Perhaps more importantly, it does so in a style that immediately gives us a startling glimpse of what the lives of Lamar Indians must have been like—a glimpse that gives us hope for eventual understanding of the original inhabitants of the Deep South.

1. Pine Barrens Lamar

Frankie Snow

Introduction

Late Lamar sites that contain European artifacts dating to the sixteenth and early seventeenth centuries have been located deep in the Pine Barrens section of south Georgia. That area includes the lower Ocmulgee River and upper Satilla River drainages. This site distribution reflects a post–De Soto location of at least a portion of the province of Tama. Spanish documents of the seventeenth century make numerous reference to their visits to this province of Tama (Lawson 1987). Most previous archaeological literature has treated the south Georgia area as one of minimal significance during the Mississippian period. As we shall see, however, the area was not devoid of occupation during this time and had an interesting Lamar occupation. As a further note of introduction, most of the data reported here was located by the author in the wake of massive commercial pine tree harvesting and land preparation activities over much of south-central Georgia during the last several years.

Since there are earlier Mississippian components in the area, a few comments must be made about the ceramics of Lamar and pre-Lamar Mississippian people in south Georgia. No radiocarbon dates are available for most of these Mississippian occupations, and the chronological placement of the various groups of Mississippian people is inferred from adjacent areas where radiometric determinations have been made. Spanish majolica of a known manufacturing date is present with some late Lamar ceramics and serves as a time marker for the Square Ground Lamar occupation that I reported on previously (Snow 1977).

Early Mississippian

Sites bearing cord-marked ceramics represent the most frequently occurring type and are known from over 700 sites located in the area. It is likely that at least some of these sites date to the early Mississippian time period (A.D. 1000–1300). While the unimaginative cord-marked ceramics are not like most traditional Mississippian ceramic styles, the close association of Ocmulgee I cord-marked sites with river floodplains suggests that these people may have practiced agriculture. Limited botanical analysis from one large cord-marked site in Telfair County (9TF2), however, failed to locate any cultigens (Bracken et al. 1986).

Temple mounds associated with Mississippian sites in south Georgia are present, but they are not common. Several mounds are located just west of the principal area of concern in this chapter. Just southwest of Albany, Georgia, along Chickasawhatchee Creek, is a flat-topped mound measuring approximately 27 meters by 37 meters by 4 meters in size. Another mound, very similar in size but located on the west side of the same creek, was destroyed a few years ago. These two mounds are probably the ones Swanton (1939) referred to during his De Soto route study as being on Pine Island. A visit to the destroyed mound revealed a surface scatter of Fort Walton ceramics. An earlier walk-over survey along Chickasawhatchee Creek revealed twenty-one Fort Walton sites, with the largest measuring more than 10 hectares in extent.

Closer to the present study area, a flat-topped structure is located at the Fish Trap Cut site on the lower Oconee River; another mound is present nearer the river. The occupation period of these mounds is unidentified, although simple stamped, cord-marked, and check-stamped ceramics are present in an adjacent dirt road. Recent investigations in South Carolina have demonstrated that simple stamped pottery was in use as late as A.D. 1000 (Anderson et al. 1982). Flat-topped mounds do not necessarily equate to Mississippian occupation in south Georgia, however. The large middle Woodland "temple mound" at Kolomoki is obviously pre-Mississippian (Sears 1956).

Etowah period Mississippian sites extend down the Ocmulgee River to the area of Hawkinsville. The Etowah midden at Sandy Hammock (9PU10), located just south of the confluence of Mosquito Creek and the Ocmulgee River, was exposed in the river access road and in potholes on the site. Ceramics include: Etowah

Complicated Stamped, Etowah Line Block, and Etowah Plain. Red
paint adorns the rim and interior of some bowls. A common motif
is the intersecting double-barred concentric circles. Also present
are single intersection barred diamonds and line block motifs. At
Lind Landing (9WL7) on the Ocmulgee River, near its confluence
with the Oconee River, Etowah Complicated Stamped ceramics
occur in a Savannah occupation associated with check-stamped and
cob-marked pottery. On the upper Altamaha River, grit-tempered
ceramics occur that bear crude attempts at Etowah motifs. The
paste of these sherds also differs from that of the fine sand-tempered
Etowah vessels. These sites probably derive from Savannah II occupations.

Early Lamar

Early Lamar sites are recognized in the area by the presence of
well-impressed filfot cross designs on jar forms, which have plain
flared rims that lack the classic Lamar decorated rim strip. When
present, bowls are usually undecorated. An early Lamar shell midden was exposed during reforestation activities at site 9JD78, located along the upper Altamaha River. Sherds were mostly early
Lamar Complicated Stamped jar forms; however, some plain bowls
and a few early Lamar Incised examples were located. The incised
motifs on these bowls differ from later incised types in the number
of lines used to construct the design. Three or four incised lines
were employed in this early Lamar type, while the later Square
Ground Lamar variety frequently contains up to fourteen incised
lines. When punctations are present with the early incising, they
are made with a hollow reed. This contrasts with the late variety,
in which solid punctations are far more common than hollow punctations. The most common complicated stamped motif at site
9JD78 is the filfot cross; however, a few recognizable Savannah
Complicated Stamped motifs are present (see Table 1).

Occasionally, Lamar ceramics that must have been produced elsewhere are seen in the south Georgia area. An incised jar from the
Turnpike Creek site in Telfair County has been located with an
atypical incised motif and clay node rim treatment similar to some
coastal Irene rim forms. Another similar jar with a typical coastal
Irene filfot stamp design was found on the River Trail in Wheeler
County (Snow 1978).

Table 1   Sherd Count from Lamar Shell Midden at Site 9JD78

Plain 75
Lamar Bold Incised 25
Lamar Complicated Stamped 86
Complicated stamped (Savannah motif) 14
Cord marked 12
Simple stamped 1
TOTAL 213

Square Ground Lamar

The major Mississippian occupation of the Pine Barrens area occurred during the late 1500s and early 1600s by people who made
what can be called Square Ground Lamar designs (Figure 4). Square
Ground Lamar stamped motifs occur below the ten- to twelve-line
incised zone on flat-bottomed bowls and over the entire surface of
jars (Figure 5). The motif is referred to as a "square ground" design
because of its resemblance to the layout of the square ground in
historic villages, as described by the early naturalist William Bartram (Van Doren 1955) and others. The design found on these ceramics is described as a central dot that may stand alone or may have
one or more concentric circles about it. Four lines radiate from the
central dot element and may be seen as pointing to the cardinal
directions. The four quadrants formed by these lines are usually
filled with chevrons (Snow 1977). Wauchope (1966, 82, Figure 37,
m–q) illustrates similar designs from north Georgia. It is likely that
the square ground motif is quite widespread (Anderson et al. 1986,
43, Figures d–e).

The Square Ground Lamar ceramic assemblage has been recovered from over forty sites extending from the lower Ocmulgee River
to the upper Satilla River (Figure 6). Sites with square ground motifs
are often found near known Indian trails marked on original land
lot survey maps. Several sites, such as the village at Lind Landing
(9WL7), are strategically situated near the confluence of the Oconee
and Ocmulgee rivers. Not only do trails following the rivers con-
verge here, but overland routes do as well. The Spanish referred
to this area as La Tama, a region that encompassed an area from
the forks up the Ocmulgee and Oconee rivers to Macon and Mil-

Figure 4. Square Ground Lamar Sherds

Figure 5. Square Ground Lamar Stamped Motifs

ledgeville, respectively. In 1597, a Spanish soldier, Gaspar de Salas, and two Franciscan fathers, Pedro Fernandez de Chozas and Francisco de Verascola, visited La Tama and gave a general description of what they saw. The Tallahassee Trail also connects the area with the Gulf Coast and the lower Savannah River region.

Swanton (1946) comments that the earliest references to the Hitchiti suggest that a group of that tribe was located on the lower Ocmulgee. The Square Ground Lamar pottery may equate with these Hitchiti people. Swanton also points to the Yamassee as having once been there prior to their move to the lower South Carolina area. Some archaeologists consider *Yamassee* to be a term applied to Indians who inhabited a large area of the interior Georgia coastal plain, rather than to a specific group of people.

We will now briefly look at some of these late Lamar sites and their ceramics. Lind Landing (9WL7), mentioned above, is located in the Ocmulgee River swamp, less than 100 yards north of the river. During periods of high water, the site appears as an island. Because of its location near a river confluence, food resources present in the extensive floodplain systems of both the Oconee and Altamaha rivers were also available within 6 kilometers of the site. Frying Pan Lake, a slough adjoining the river, lies within a kilometer to the southwest along the edge of a river terrace. Quin Lake, a river cutoff channel, lies within a kilometer to the northwest along

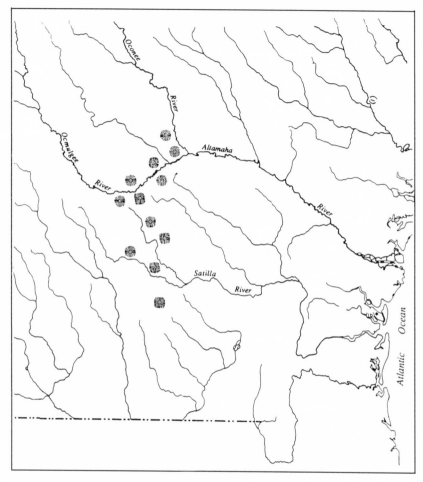

Figure 6. Square Ground Lamar Distribution

the edge of a river terrace. Late Lamar ceramics were recovered along this terrace after it had been bulldozed and planted in pine trees. Oaky Bluff, where hickory and oak trees still provide large crops of nuts, lies immediately downstream. Cypress domes were also apparently utilized as food resource areas by these people. Lamar ceramics at nearby Moses Lake and McEachin's Wood Landing are examples of small satellite sites of the village at Lind Landing. The Indian trail that paralleled the Altamaha and Ocmulgee rivers from the coast at Darien to the Macon area passed along high ground 2 kilometers to the north of the site (Snow 1978). The Lind Landing site was bulldozed in 1986 and exposed midden features along a 100-meter stretch of the presumed orientation of the village. Gray clay layers were visible in two areas in the face of plow cuts. They may represent the remains of clay hearths located within Lamar houses. A cluster of carbonized corncobs, exposed by reforestation activities, was also discovered. Years earlier, a firebreak was cut into a Square Ground Lamar midden here and exposed a large quantity of ceramics and food remains—including corn, beanlike seeds, river mussels, and deer bones. A fragment of metal (from one of the features) and a blue glass bead both indicate Spanish contact at Lind Landing.

Coffee Bluff, near the Ocmulgee River in Telfair County, is the location of another recently bulldozed Lamar site. Reforestation activities exposed five refuse middens in alluvial mud adjacent to a sandy interfluve where the village was located. One of these areas (midden 1) appeared to be a house mound with daub, food remains, and Lamar ceramics visible on the surface. Spanish contact was established by one sherd of lead-glazed Columbia Plain majolica recovered from the surface of this house mound. The approximate time interval for the manufacture of this style of Columbia Plain is 1580 to 1630 (Calvin Jones, personal communication). Midden 3 included fragments of a small incised vessel with handles that is similar to the type known as "gravy boat" bowl, a possible copy of a Spanish style.

A sample of several thousand Lamar sherds from these exposed middens provides information on incised design variability and preference for particular motifs (Figure 7). Two basic designs found are the scroll, with several variations of the motif occurring 65 percent of the time, and the loop, with only two subvariations known and constituting 28 percent of the incised motifs. A variety of miscellaneous designs made up the remaining 7 percent of the motifs. The use of punctation occurred on one out of ten reconstructed incised vessels. The use of punctation within the incised motif may be a useful trait in separating this variant of Lamar from the more northern varieties. The incorporation of punctation in the incised motif is reminiscent of Fort Walton Incised pottery in southwest Georgia.

Sherds from Lamar jars recovered from the middens at Coffee Bluff (9TF115) show pinched rim folds around the vessel lip. Both rim strips and the bodies of jars were complicated stamped with the square ground motif. Data derived from an analysis of 3,000 sherds recovered from five Square Ground Lamar sites show that 15 percent are Lamar Incised, 45 percent are Lamar Square Ground Complicated Stamped, and 40 percent are Lamar Plain (Table 2).

A cache of four broken Lamar smoking pipes was recovered from Coffee Bluff. Three were typical perishable stem types; however, a fourth one was a larger elbow type with a flange around the bowl.

Another late Lamar site, known as the Bloodroot site (9JD81), was recently bulldozed in Jeff Davis County on an 11-meter-high bluff overlooking the Ocmulgee River. Pike Creek (shown as "Pipe" Creek on the original land lot survey field notes) enters the river immediately below the site. An 1889 Corps of Engineers map shows rocky shoals within the river at the base of the bluff. These shoals apparently supported a large population of river mussels, which were heavily exploited by the inhabitants on the bluff, judging from the surface scatter of these shells across the site. Also important to this site was the adjacent Tallahassee Trail, which crossed the Ocmulgee River at Burkett's Ferry near the mouth of Pike Creek.

A scatter of ceramics at this site consisted of typical Lamar Incised and Square Ground Lamar Complicated Stamped sherds similar to those found at Coffee Bluff. Two areas contained visible concentrations of house daub. Partial removal of the upper 30

Table 2   Sherd Counts from Selected Square
Ground Lamar Sites

SITE NAME AND NUMBER	INCISED	COMPLICATED STAMPED	PLAIN
Lind Landing, 9WL7 (F1)	255 (20%)	776 (62%)	229 (18%)
Lind Landing, 9WL7 (F2)	42 (14%)	170 (58%)	80 (27%)
Lind Landing, 9WL7	109 (14%)	447 (57%)	226 (28%)
Bloodroot, 9JD81 (F1)	90 (16%)	256 (44%)	216 (38%)
Bloodroot, 9JD81	154 (16%)	451 (45%)	390 (39%)
Coffee Bluff, 9TF115 (F1)	41 (15%)	143 (54%)	82 (31%)
Corn Cob, 9JD9	59 (10%)	263 (44%)	280 (47%)
Lamar, 9CF46	37 (13%)	154 (53%)	100 (34%)
Coffee State Park 9CF1	51 (15%)	203 (61%)	80 (24%)

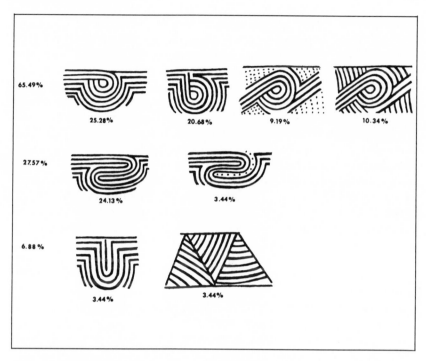

Figure 7. Square Ground Lamar Incised Motifs

centimeters of soil in one of the daub concentrations exposed stains
probably attributable to house posts. A second daub concentration
remains unexcavated. Trash middens were located southwest of
each daub concentration. Food remains were well preserved. While
no evidence of corn was found here, clusters of charred corncobs
occur on nearby late Lamar sites. Among the potsherds in the trash
midden were two reconstructible vessels, an incised cazuela and
a small plain bowl with a flared lip. Included in the trash midden
were two copper finger rings, probably Spanish in origin. One bears
perforations. Similar finger rings are reported to occur at Spanish
mission sites in north Florida (Calvin Jones, personal communication) and at the Santa Catalina de Guale mission on St. Catherines
Island on the Georgia coast (David Hurst Thomas, personal communication). Pinellas-like triangular projectile points were recovered
from the house floor.

The Satilla Area

Within the Pine Barrens area south of the Ocmulgee Valley, late Square Ground Lamar sites occur along the upper reaches of the Satilla River drainage in association with a hammock-type environment. These hammocks are especially prevalent along extensive sand ridges that occur on the eastern side of the Seventeen Mile River. Wharton (1978) describes this area as presenting a remarkable array of natural environments, including the best example of a mature bay forest that he has found. In terms of quantities of soil nutrients, such as calcium, magnesium, potassium, and phosphorus, Monk (1968) found that bay heads exceeded southern mixed hardwood, cypress head, flatwood, and sandhill soils. However, he also found that they were more sterile and acidic than mixed swamp soils. In any event, based on nutrient availability, the soils found in patches along Seventeen Mile River present the second most desirable area for occupation in south Georgia, trailing only the Ocmulgee River swamp system.

It is important to note that these more southerly Square Ground Lamar sites occupy a fringe area along an Indian trail that later became known as the Blackshear Road. This road, which runs from Augusta to St. Augustine, passes through the heart of this Lamar area (Myer 1928). The southernmost known Square Ground Lamar site occurs on the Atkinson-Clinch county boundary at the junction of forks in Kenard's Trail. As one traveled southward along the road, the Spanish region of Florida was approached. South of the Satilla River were Timucuan-speaking peoples, whose ceramic inventory differed from that of Lamar people. Excavations at St. Augustine have uncovered a quantity of nonlocal aboriginal ceramics. In addition to the aboriginal San Marcos or Altamaha assemblage, some pottery sherds that appear identical to those of the Square Ground Lamar assemblage have been recovered (Piatek 1985, 84, Figure 1).

Altamaha Series

People who made a pottery assemblage that developed out of the Square Ground Lamar ceramics formed the next occupation along the lower Ocmulgee River. Their ceramics resembled the Altamaha ceramics found on the Georgia coast as well as the Miller ceramics from the Apalachee region of northwest Florida. There was a dramatic decrease in the number of these sites (one) compared to at least forty of the earlier Square Ground Lamar sites. European disruption through the introduction of disease and economic stress may have accounted for this decrease in site density. At 9CF17 in Coffee County, Altamaha-like jars with larger rim folds than their earlier Lamar counterparts occurred. The lower edges of the folded rims of jars were sometimes decorated with hollow reed or solid punctations, as well as with the more traditional finger pinches. Complicated stamping became bolder. A smoothed-over check-stamped ware, similar to Leon Check Stamped from mission sites in north Florida and Ocmulgee Check Stamped known from the Macon Plateau site, was also present. Some of these Altamaha sherds appear to have had charcoal included in their paste as a tempering agent. European trade items such as glass beads and copper were found with the Altamaha-like ceramics at 9CF17. Historic documents show that in 1685 a group of Yamassee from South Carolina made a raid on north Florida Mission Indians and stopped on their return at Tama to celebrate their success (Lawson 1987). Site 9CF17 would have been a likely spot for this celebration.

Creek Sites

Creek Indian components are recorded on 1 to 2 percent of the sites in the study area. Auchenehatchee is a small Creek site located in Telfair County at the confluence of Sugar Creek and the Little Ocmulgee River (Snow 1984). Five restorable vessels from here include an Ocmulgee Fields Incised bowl, an Ocmulgee Fields Incised plate, and three plain jars with ticked rims. Later Creek sites reveal the presence of Chattahoochee Brushed ceramics and English trade items. Two lead-glazed "dot ware" cups were found at site 9JD12 mixed with a restorable Mission Red Filmed vessel. Fragments of a Leon-Jefferson Complicated Stamped jar were also found at this site. Little else is known of these late Creek sites in this area at the present time.

2. The Lamar Ceramics of the Georgia Coast

Chad O. Braley

Introduction

The Lamar ceramic complex of the Georgia coast is a variant known as Irene. Its definition was based on Joseph Caldwell's excavation of the type site on Irene plantation adjacent to the lower Savannah River in Chatham County (Caldwell and McCann 1941). Geographically, Irene or related ceramics have been found from the Charleston, South Carolina, area south to St. Augustine, Florida (Anderson 1975). The core area, however, appears to be more restricted, bordered by the Savannah River on the north and the Altamaha River on the south.

Many of the data used in this paper were derived from excavations at a site on Harris Neck National Wildlife Refuge in McIntosh County, Georgia. The site, 9MC41, contained both prehistoric and historic Irene components (Braley, O'Steen, and Quitmyer 1986). The radiocarbon dates from two features indicate that the Irene ceramic complex developed during precontact times, and the dates thus provide important new information about a point that has been debated by several archaeologists. Some have believed that Irene, like other Lamar complexes in the Southeast, developed by about A.D. 1350 (Caldwell 1971; DePratter 1979; Pearson 1977), while others postulated that it developed after sixteenth-century European contact (Milanich 1977; Crook 1978a; Martinez 1975; Steinan 1984).

One reason for these differing interpretations is that coastal cultures both south and north of the Irene core area were manufacturing cord-marked ceramics well into the sixteenth century (Trinkley

1981; M. Smith et al. 1981; Crook 1978a). The cord-marked pottery resembles the type Savannah Cord Marked, a pre-Lamar type. This led to the conclusion that the Irene complex must have been introduced during the historic period. Outside the core area, however, the ceramic complexes lack the complicated stamped wares, which form a part of the assemblage of the Savannah culture of the north Georgia coast, the lower Savannah River, and the Georgia Piedmont. Although Savannah Cord Marked pottery is found outside the coastal Lamar culture area, the lack of nucleated settlements or aggregate villages (Crook 1978b) on the south Georgia coast suggests that a less complex sociopolitical system was in effect while chiefdoms were evolving along the estuaries between the Altamaha and Savannah rivers.

In addition to obtaining the first radiocarbon dates for the Irene complex, the zooarchaeological data from Harris Neck suggest that the site could have been occupied on a year-round basis. Stylistic differences between fifteenth- and seventeenth-century pottery attributes were noted and a preliminary vessel form analysis was conducted. Finally, assemblages from habitation sites and burial mounds in the area were compared.

The Site

Prior to the construction of a parking lot, nearly 1,280 square meters were excavated at site 9MC41. Although surface indications were restricted to a sparse scatter of shell fragments, over 500 features were exposed by the excavations. A partial aboriginal house pattern, daub processing pits, basin-shaped pits, smudge pits filled with charred corncobs, a human burial, and three large refuse-filled pits were excavated (Braley, O'Steen, and Quitmyer 1986).

Two radiocarbon dates were obtained from features containing Irene ceramics. These dates were A.D. 1430 ± 60 and A.D. 1400 ± 70 (uncorrected dates) (Beta 10841 and 10842). The Irene ceramics contained within these features were qualitatively and quantitatively different from aboriginal ceramics associated with Spanish artifacts from discrete midden accumulations. The European artifacts and a third radiocarbon date (A.D. 1650 ± 70—Beta 10840) establish a seventeenth-century date for the final aboriginal occupation at Harris Neck.

A total of 2,652 sherds from five areas within the site was obtained

(Table 3). Of note is the percentage of incised sherds (9.5 percent), which, excluding the presence of Spanish artifacts, indicates a late Irene affiliation. Joseph Caldwell recognized that the addition of incised wares marked the start of the Irene II phase. Fred Cook (1980) has provided additional data suggesting that the percentage increases through time. By the mid- to late sixteenth century, fine line incising had started to eclipse bold incised motifs, although the bold incising was retained until the seventeenth century. The trend from bold to fine line incising appears to be a common theme for many variants of Lamar ceramics in the Southeast. On the coast, the incised motifs begin as simple scroll-like elements composed of three or four boldly incised lines, typical of the early Irene assemblage recovered from the type site (Caldwell and McCann 1941; Waring 1968). The designs gradually become more complex and involve multiple lines by the late prehistoric period. Figures 8 and 9 show late prehistoric and postcontact Irene Incised sherds.

The rim treatment of jars also reflects a late prehistoric and

Table 3   Aboriginal Ceramics from Site 9MC41, All Proveniences

CERAMIC TYPES	BODY SHERDS	RIM SHERDS	TOTALS	PERCENT
Fiber-Tempered	11	3	14	0.50
Deptford Check Stamped	44	0	44	1.58
Savannah Check Stamped	0	1	1	0.05
Cord Marked	23	1	24	0.87
Complicated Stamped	1,291	77	1,368	48.67
Curvilinear Complicated Stamp	103	6	109	3.87
Rectilinear Complicated Stamp	13	0	13	0.47
Simple Stamped	8	0	8	0.28
Cross-Simple Stamped	33	0	33	1.17
Plain	310	27	337	11.98
Burnished Plain	49	0	49	1.74
Incised	229	39	268	9.53
Red Filmed	5	0	5	0.18
Unidentified small sherds	553	4	537	19.10
TOTALS	2,652	159	2,811	100.00

Figure 8. Irene Incised Sherds, Prehistoric (Courtesy of the U.S. Fish and Wildlife Service and Alabama State Museum of Natural History)

seventeenth-century occupation at site 9MC41. Absolutely no rims decorated with reed-punctated pellets, nodes, or rosettes—a trait of late Savannah (Moore 1897, 8, 40), early Irene (Caldwell and McCann 1941; Cook 1986), and early Pee Dee (DePratter and Judge 1986)—were present. Instead, the dominant rim treatment of jars from prehistoric features consisted of a cane-punctated strip or fillet applied below the rim, followed by a reed-punctated rim lacking an applied fillet, then by a segmented fillet scored with vertical lines. Cook (1986) has suggested that the segmented fillet developed early in the Irene sequence, with the reed-punctated rim treatments evolving during the latter part of the prehistoric period.

Instead of a cane-punctated fillet, the rim treatment of jars from midden deposits that also contained Spanish artifacts was dominated by a cane-punctated folded rim. The folded rim has parallels with late prehistoric and postcontact Lamar ceramics of the Georgia interior. Figure 10 shows prehistoric and postcontact jar rim treatments.

Figure 9. Irene Incised Sherds, Postcontact (Courtesy of the U.S. Fish and Wildlife Service and Alabama State Museum of Natural History)

Phase Designations

The evolutionary trends in the coastal Lamar assemblage, coupled with the first absolute dates from the Harris Neck site, suggest that refinements in terminology may be usefully implemented. A review of the literature shows there to be many interchangeable names in use. More than 30 years ago, Lewis Larson (1955) named the Pine Harbor complex to geographically separate the Irene material from the middle Georgia coast from the northern coast. This was done at a time when most of the Lamar-related cultures of the Southeast were suspected to date to the postcontact period (Griffin 1952). The distinction between Pine Harbor and Irene was based on the presence of the fine line incised wares (McIntosh Incised) found on the middle Georgia coast.

The fifteenth-century radiocarbon dates from site 9MC41 and the lack of early Irene ceramic attributes suggest that Larson's Pine Harbor complex is both geographically *and* temporally distinct from the Irene material from the north Georgia coast (Braley, O'Steen, and Quitmyer 1986, 138–40). Sixteenth-century ethnographic accounts indicate that the majority of the coastal population lived along a 60-kilometer stretch of coast from the mouth of the Alta-maha River north to Ossabaw Island (Jones 1978). Archaeological

Figure 10. Rim Treatment of Jars, Prehistoric and Postcontact (Courtesy of the U.S. Fish and Wildlife Service and Alabama State Museum of Natural History)

surveys around the mouth of the Savannah River indicate that late Irene sites are rare between Ossabaw Island and the sixteenth-century Spanish town of Santa Elena on the lower coast of South Carolina (Michie 1980; Braley 1982; Chester DePratter, personal communication). Similarly, the central Savannah Valley also appears to have been virtually abandoned after the Rembert phase of the early Lamar period, or by the early fifteenth century (Hally and Rudolph 1986).

It was during the fifteenth century that the Mississippian occupation along the upper Oconee River, a main tributary of the Altamaha, increased, especially during the Iron Horse and Dyar phases starting at about A.D. 1450. Possibly to allow direct lines of communication with the interior Oconee chiefdoms after this time, the coastal populations appear to have centered near the Altamaha River instead of the Savannah River. Based on the similarities between Dyar phase incised pottery from the Oconee Valley and the Irene Incised pottery from the prehistoric Harris Neck features, similar radiocarbon dates, and Caldwell's (1971) lead, it is proposed that Pine Harbor be elevated from a ceramic complex to a phase of the coastal Lamar culture. The Pine Harbor phase should be roughly contemporaneous with the Iron Horse and Dyar phases of the Oconee Valley. These date from about A.D. 1450–1580 (M. Smith 1981, 245; M. Williams 1988). Establishing Pine Harbor as a phase is not a radical departure from Larson's original concept, except to acknowledge the antiquity of the coastal Lamar culture and to suggest that somewhat parallel developments occurred almost simultaneously in the interior Oconee Valley and along the Georgia coast near the mouth of the Altamaha River.

If the addition of incising demarcates the Irene II phase from the Irene I phase (Caldwell 1971) and since it is now possible to distinguish early versus late incised motifs, then it stands to reason that further chronological subdivisions are now possible. Pipemaker's Creek, after the stream adjacent to the Irene mound site, is proposed as a phase name to distinguish assemblages containing early Irene incised wares from the subsequent Pine Harbor phase.

The postcontact phase designations also utilize conflicting terminology at present. Larson uses the term Sutherland Bluff, while Caldwell favored Altamaha I and II for the final sequence names. As demonstrated by the seventeenth-century wares at Harris Neck, wide folded cane-punctated rims were in vogue at this time on large jars, and fine line incising was common on carinated bowls and small jars. By the seventeenth century, complicated stamped designs became more sloppily applied, and the curvilinear filfot cross (Figure 11) was abandoned in favor of rectilinear designs. However, the complicated stamped wares resemble their prehistoric counterparts more than they do the San Marcos wares found in St. Augustine. The San Marcos cross-simple stamped motif, so common in post-1660 contexts in St. Augustine (H. Smith 1948; Otto and Lewis 1974), is rarely represented at site 9MC41.

Results of the Vessel Form Analysis

Eleven different shape categories were recognized for the Irene ceramic assemblage from the Harris Neck site and from vessels from a variety of other sites, notably, burial mounds (Figure 12). If only the vessel surface treatment is considered, the analysis confirms previous findings that there are no differences in the decoration of mound versus nonmound pottery and that vessels in mounds were originally utilitarian in function. However, significant differences in the distributions of vessel forms were noted between these

Figure 11. Irene Filfot Stamped Sherds (Courtesy of the U.S. Fish and Wildlife Service and Alabama State Museum of Natural History)

two contexts. The nonmound site assemblage (N77) is characterized by a high incidence of wide-mouthed, long-necked jars, whereas the mound ceramics (N39) show more diversity. Incidentally, the zooarchaeological remains suggest that quantities of seafood-based stews were prepared in the nonmound vessels.

Although both nonmound and mound assemblages are dominated by flaring-rimmed, long-necked jars, they are more common in a domestic context (46.5 percent versus 28.2 percent). Simple bowls are relatively common burial furniture but are rare in the Harris Neck assemblage (23 percent versus 7 percent). The inverse is true for carinated bowls, which form 23.9 percent of the Harris Neck collection but only 5.1 percent for mounds. Small restricted-necked jars occur at about the same percentage in both assemblages (16.9 percent at Harris Neck and 17.9 percent in mounds). Small carinated jars occur far more frequently in mounds than in domestic contexts (15.5 percent versus 1.4 percent). These vessels may represent a specialized mortuary ware. They are often intricately incised with curvilinear motifs and herringbone designs, and the only rim sherd of this style from Harris Neck is well burnished. Similar

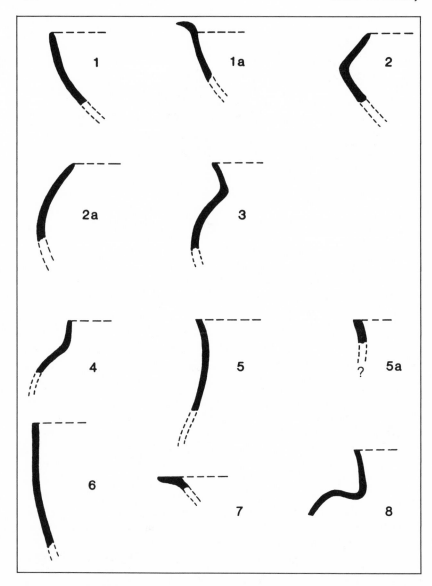

Figure 12. Coastal Lamar Vessel Shape Categories

forms have been found in burials in northwest Georgia (David Hally, personal communication) and in the Oconee Valley (Braley, Ledbetter, and Williams 1985).

Summary

In conclusion, the developmental sequence of the coastal Lamar pottery shows many similarities with the interior Mississippian ceramic complexes. Incised motifs became busier through time, and fine line incising became more popular. The rim treatment of large jars also shows some parallels with interior forms. Cane-punctated nodes are found on jars from early Irene sites, whereas a segmented or cane-punctated strip characterizes the rim treatment on late prehistoric jars. The wide rim fold evolved last. The changing attributes, combined with the first radiocarbon dates for coastal Lamar, make phase designations possible. Caldwell's Irene II phase can now be subdivided into early (Pipemaker's Creek) and late (Pine Harbor) phases based on the complexity of motifs and increasing frequency of incised wares.

The vessel form analysis has resulted in an inventory of vessel forms, which can be correlated with subsistence strategies, and has identified a sacred-secular distinction between mound and domestic assemblages. The coastal vessel data can also be compared with interior Lamar assemblages to test hypotheses regarding settlement systems, adaptation to different ecosystems, and other problems relating to the development of chiefdoms in the Southeast.

Acknowledgments

Many ideas presented in this paper are derived from the research of other archaeologists working with the Lamar cultures of the Georgia Piedmont and upper coastal plain. In particular, the ideas of Mark Williams, Gary Shapiro, David Hally, and David Anderson have been incorporated to some extent. Fred Cook's seriation of pottery attributes is also recognized. The U.S. Fish and Wildlife Service is also acknowledged for funding the excavations at Harris Neck National Wildlife Refuge.

3. Recent Investigations in the Core of the Coosa Province

James B. Langford, Jr., and Marvin T. Smith

Introduction

The purpose of this paper is to describe several aboriginal sites along the Coosawattee River in northwestern Georgia, which have yielded mid-sixteenth-century European artifacts and which may delineate the limits of the core of Coosa, a powerful chiefdom visited by Hernando de Soto in 1540. Research since 1963 in the Coosawattee River and Coosa River drainages has produced much information about the late Mississippian period in the area. More specifically, the Barnett phase (Hally 1970) has taken on increased significance as researchers have focused on the expeditions of De Soto (1540) and De Luna (1560). Members of these expeditions described the nature and boundaries of political territories and presented specific information about the life-styles of various aboriginal groups in the Southeast.

By combining archaeological research with Spanish accounts of the expeditions, it has been determined that the chiefdom of Coosa was a powerful political unit that stretched over a long and relatively narrow geographical area from eastern Tennessee to middle Alabama. It has been recently proposed that the capital of this unit was located at the Little Egypt site on the Coosawattee River at the junction of Talking Rock Creek (Hudson et al. 1985).

The De Luna chroniclers described the main town of Coosa as consisting of eight villages within 2 leagues (11 kilometers) of the main village. This paper discusses five sites believed to belong to the original group of eight villages (Figure 13). All five of the sites have yielded materials diagnostic of the Barnett phase. European materials typical of mid-sixteenth-century trade and military items have also been found by local people on four of the sites.

104

General Description of the Coosawattee River Valley

The Coosawattee River is approximately 80 kilometers long, with its headwaters in the mountains near Ellijay, Georgia, and its mouth about 9.6 kilometers northeast of Calhoun, Georgia, where the river joins with the Conasauga River to form the Oostanaula River. In the upper two-thirds of its route, the river follows a rocky and forested path, which changes abruptly when it breaks across an old fault line at the Cohutta Range. For the remaining third of the river's route, it meanders across a floodplain that varies in width from 0.8 to 3.2 kilometers. This discussion will focus exclusively on the portion of the river west of the Cohutta Range.

This downriver portion of the Coosawattee generally follows a northeast to southwest route, but the meandering path consists of frequent right-angle turns and occasional "backtrack" loops. For ease of discussion, we will refer to sites as being either on the north or south side of the river, although such a description may be mis-

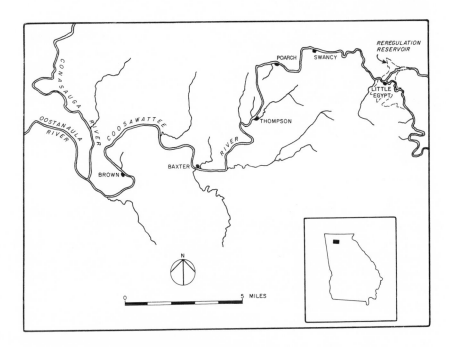

Figure 13. Coosawattee River Sites

leading as to the exact orientation of the site in relation to the river.

Most of the river valley is still in cultivation, although some areas are utilized as grazing land. Less than 5 percent of the alluvial valley is covered by timber, not including areas along the river and creek banks where cultivation is not possible.

The predominant soil types in the floodplain are Pope Fine Sandy Loam, Sequatchie Loam, and Whitwell Silt Loam. Significant annual flooding and associated soil movements occurred over the past 100 years up until the mid-1970s, at which time the completion of the Carters Dam complex greatly reduced the potential for flooding.

Prehistoric Context

Every major prehistoric horizon is represented in the valley, with no noticeable gaps in what appears to be a continuous occupation from at least middle Archaic through the late Mississippian periods. One significant late gap occurs between approximately A.D. 1600 and 1700.

The most significant prehistoric occupations that can be determined from surface collections and limited excavations date from the middle Woodland through late Mississippian periods. Components of Swift Creek, Woodstock, Etowah/Hiwassee Island, Wilbanks, and the Little Egypt (Hally 1979) and Barnett phases of Lamar are well represented in the alluvial plain of the Coosawattee. This paper will focus on the Barnett phase occupation of the valley.

Barnett Phase Sites

To date, five sites containing Barnett phase material have been found on the Coosawattee River between Carters Dam and the junction with the Conasauga River (Figure 13). The sites will be discussed individually, beginning at the mouth of the Coosawattee and moving upriver toward the main village of Coosa, probably located at the Little Egypt site at the junction of Talking Rock Creek and the Coosawattee River.

Brown Farm Site (9GO67)

Located in a large bend about 3 kilometers north of the mouth of the Coosawattee, this site is on the "north" side of the river. The site has been badly damaged by plow and water erosion and by untrained digging. Only small areas of occupational midden may remain intact. The landowner has recently halted all digging on the site.

The Brown Farm is the largest of the Barnett phase sites on the Coosawattee, excluding the Little Egypt site, and covers some 5.5 hectares. Surface collections, limited test excavations, and information from local informants indicate that the site is a single-component Barnett phase site. Discussions with local diggers indicate that the site yielded 200 to 300 burials. Associated burial furniture included Citico-style rattlesnake gorgets, slate spatulate celts, mask gorgets, shell beads, flint blades, and effigy pipes. Iron artifacts found in burials include spikes, a wedge, an oval-shaped piece (possibly a chain link), and a partial Spanish horseshoe. Burials of two or three individuals in the same pit were not uncommon, suggesting the possibility of European epidemic disease (M. Smith 1987). One unusual burial pit appeared to be covered with burned wooden boards, and the individual was extended with six trophy skulls arranged in rows on each side of the body.

House structures appear to be arranged in rows perpendicular to the river. Burials were said to be found immediately adjacent to houses, but not in house floors. Large numbers of burials, including multiple and mass burials, were located relatively near the river in an area approximately 15 meters by 40 meters.

While some local informants assert that a palisade existed at the site, aerial photographs and limited excavations in search of it do not support such a conclusion. If such a palisade existed, it probably was not accompanied by a ditch such as was found at the King site on the Coosa River (Garrow and Smith 1973; Hally 1975).

At least one hamlet site is known to be associated with the Brown Farm site. It is located approximately 1 kilometer downriver from the main village. Several burials at the hamlet were exposed by flooding in the early 1970s, but surface collections have yielded only very sparse ceramic and stone samples.

Baxter Site (9GO8)

The Baxter site is a multicomponent site that contains a large Hiwassee Island/Etowah component and a significant Barnett phase occupation. There is also a historic Cherokee component there. The Barnett phase occupation covers approximately 2 hectares. A mound is situated on the site and probably dates to the earliest Mississippian component. In the 1930s, the mound stood approximately 6 to 7 meters high but was bulldozed in the 1950s to allow for cultivation of the entire field. Subsequent plowing has reduced the mound to a height of 2 to 3 meters. It has not been possible to determine whether the mound was used during the Barnett phase.

Significant untrained digging over the past 20 years has concentrated on the mound and village area associated with the earlier components of the site. Barnett phase structures have also been damaged significantly. The Barnett phase area of the site appears to be situated between the mound and the river and extends over a rectangular area parallel to the river. The landowners recently stated that they would no longer permit such activity on the site.

The only known European artifact occurring in Barnett phase context was located in a burial that also contained two large flint blades, each approximately 25 centimeters long. The iron artifact was heavily corroded and has not been identified. It has been temporarily misplaced by the local collectors. Neither aerial photographs nor local diggers have established the presence of a palisade or associated ditch.

Thompson Site (9GO4)

The Thompson site is situated adjacent to a small island in the Coosawattee River approximately 5 kilometers upriver from the Baxter site. Occupation of the site appears to have been continuous from the Little Egypt phase through the Barnett phase. A Woodstock component also exists on a portion of the site.

The site covers approximately 2.43 hectares and includes a small mound in cultivation at the edge of the old river channel. The old channel is now dry, since the island was connected to the south bank of the river a few years ago by the landowner. The village area slopes away from the mound and riverbank. The mound and village have been in cultivation for many years, and much plow damage has been inflicted. Untrained diggers have also taken a heavy toll on the site since the 1950s. The landowner halted all digging on the property about 1980.

Information from local informants seems to indicate that burials extended in a northeast to southwest direction parallel to the old river channel and adjacent to the mound. One hundred to 200 burials were removed from this area, and many were multiple or mass burials. Numerous artifacts were recovered from the burials, including several Dallas strap-handled and effigy vessels. Frog, waterfowl, and human effigies appear to be the most common effigy types. Barnett phase artifacts recovered from the site include two or three iron awls or spikes, one of which was hafted into a piece of antler, and a ferrous metal object described as a belt buckle. These artifacts have not been examined and their location cannot be determined. No evidence has been detected of any palisade or associated earthworks.

Poarch Site (9GO1)

The Poarch site is one of the largest of the Barnett phase sites along the Coosawattee. The Barnett phase component covers some 3.28 hectares. The other major components appear to be Wilbanks and perhaps Little Egypt phases, but this area of the site is distinctly separated from the Barnett phase occupation. This latter occupation is relatively narrow and follows the river's edge for 370 meters. The site is 100 meters wide at the widest point.

Most of the site is covered by a thick layer (1 to 2 meters) of alluvium, which has protected much of it from plow erosion. Water erosion created some flood channels in the field until the mid-1970s, but the resultant water damage has not yet been determined. Untrained diggers worked extensively at the site during the 1970s and excavated 300 to 400 burials in the Barnett phase occupation area. Since that time, the property was sold, and the new landowner has halted digging on the property to preserve the site for academic research.

During the digging in the 1970s, several burials were recovered that contained European artifacts and indigenous artifacts diagnostic of the Barnett phase. Eight burials yielded several artifacts of

European manufacture. Because of their pertinence to the discussion of European contact, these burials are more completely described here. Burial 1 was an extended burial accompanied by 120 projectile points, three iron awls, and the brass tip of a crossbow bolt. Burial 2 was accompanied by three faceted chevron beads, a small Nueva Cadiz Plain bead, an unusual blown-glass bead, some copper and shell beads, and a small Dallas vessel. Burial 3 was a flexed burial in a circular pit. Grave accompaniments included a partial sword blade placed beneath the body and a large white flint triangular blade. Burial 4 was a flexed burial accompanied by a Clarksdale bell, a spatulate celt, and a discoidal stone. Burial 5 was a flexed burial with an iron ax blade near the pelvis. Burial 6 was a child burial covered by a rock and was accompanied by an iron wedge and a shell dipper. Burial 7 was an extended adult accompanied by a bent iron blade and a game stone. Burial 8 was an extended adult burial with an iron awl placed parallel to the body.

One additional burial contained a copper plate modified into a gorget. The plate was incised with human and animal figures, and it is currently being examined to determine its origin of manufacture. Results of early analysis indicate manufacture in Mexico, suggesting contact with the De Luna expedition of 1560. Local informants also report that one very large posthole, 1 meter in diameter and 2 meters deep below the occupation level, was excavated near the river in the western third of the site. Large posts of this type were a common feature of Creek villages, as reported in historic chronicles, and similar features were excavated at the King site (Hally 1975). No evidence of a palisade has been detected at the Poarch site. About 800 meters downstream, a small Barnett phase farmstead has been located but not investigated.

Swancy Site (9GO70)

The Swancy site is situated on the Coosawattee River 2.7 kilometers from the Poarch site and 4.8 kilometers from the Little Egypt site. A significant part of the site is wooded (approximately one-third), and its exact dimensions are unclear. An extrapolation of surface material found in the cultivated areas of the site, however, indicates that the site covered approximately 1.76 hectares.

Like the Poarch site, the Swancy site occupies an area directly alongside the riverbank and is relatively narrow in its extent, as compared to its width perpendicular to the river. The areas of the site in cultivation have suffered some plow and water erosional damage, but the wooded areas of the site could be relatively intact. Untrained diggers have worked extensively in the cultivated areas of the site. Approximately forty to fifty burials were uncovered prior to 1982 by one group before the landowner stopped all digging on the site.

Analysis of surface collections from the site indicates Woodstock and Barnett phase occupations; however, burial accompaniments indicative of the Barnett phase have been reported. One "four-cornered" Dallas vessel (Little Egypt phase?) and a Dallas incised strap-handled vessel were recovered from the site. No European artifacts are known to have been recovered from the Swancy site.

Little Egypt (9MU102), Potts' Tract (9MU105), Sixtoe (9MU100)

The Little Egypt site (Hally 1979; 1980), Potts' Tract site (Hally 1970), and Sixtoe site (Kelly et al. 1965) were extensively excavated as a part of the Carters Dam project conducted for the National Park Service by the University of Georgia. The results of this work will not be repeated here, but it should be noted that each of these sites produced European artifacts in controlled excavations. Recent interviews with local informants have documented the presence of Clarksdale bells at the Little Egypt site.

Regional Settlement Spacing

Straight-line distances between the known Barnett phase sites along the Coosawattee River are listed in Table 4.

The distances between the sites are relatively uniform when an allowance is made for topographic barriers such as river meanders and sharp valleys and ridges. In other words, travel time between the villages would be approximately equal, assuming that trails followed a line of least resistance.

There is a fairly uniform distribution of sites along the river when available alluvial land is considered. Only two hamlet-sized sites have been identified thus far between the larger sites, but it is likely that additional small occupations will be discovered as investiga-

Table 4   Distances between Barnett Phase Sites

Little Egypt to Swancy	4.8 kilometers
Swancy to Poarch	2.7 kilometers
Poarch to Thompson	3.9 kilometers
Thompson to Baxter	5.0 kilometers
Baxter to Brown	5.1 kilometers
Brown to mouth of Coosawattee	2.4 kilometers

tions in the valley continue. During the De Soto expedition of 1540, the Gentleman of Elvas described Coosa as follows: " . . . the country, thickly settled in numerous large towns, with fields between, extending from one to another, was pleasant, and had a rich soil with fair river margins" (Buckingham Smith 1968, 76). In 1560, members of a detachment of the De Luna expedition described the province: "There were seven little hamlets in its district, five of them smaller and two larger than Coza itself, which name prevailed for the fame it had enjoyed in antiquity" (Swanton 1922, 231). Both descriptions fit the archaeologically known settlement quite well.

The three central sites (Poarch, Thompson, and Baxter) all have very significant earlier components that collectively represent continuous Mississippian occupation from Woodstock through Barnett phases. While it is not certain that all these sites were contemporaneously occupied during the earlier Mississippian times, it appears very likely that all were occupied during the sixteenth century. It should be noted that no other Mississippian sites have been found between these three sites, suggesting that the distances between them represent some kind of optimum spacing for supporting the relevant populations and for accommodating interaction among the sites.

Discussion of Ceramics

Ceramic analysis (Table 5) of the collections from the five sites reveals similarities and differences among them. Beginning with the multicomponent sites, Baxter and Thompson, a distinct pattern of change over time is apparent.

The Baxter site exhibits apparently continuous occupation from Hiwassee Island/Etowah through Wilbanks, Little Egypt, and Barnett phases. The overwhelming presence of shell tempering in the sample (75 percent) suggests a longer or more extensive occupation of the site at the earlier time period. This interpretation is supported by analysis of the distribution of ceramics from untrained digger back-dirt piles, which indicates that the Barnett phase occupation of the site covered only approximately 25 percent of the area occupied by earlier inhabitants.

The Thompson site also appears to have two major components— Little Egypt and Barnett phases—which together represent a continuous occupation. It is impossible to confidently suggest that the population remained constant during these two phases. The ceramics, however, tend to indicate a rather fluid transition between the two phases.

Future excavations might give a better delineation between these two occupational phases, but until then it is somewhat difficult to compare the homogenous surface collection from the Thompson site to the better excavated data from Little Egypt (Hally 1979). However, if we combine Hally's data from the two phases and arrange the ceramic categories into a format similar to the one presented here, we find some striking similarities. Grit and shell tempering make up similar percentages of the samples, and Lamar Complicated Stamped also appears in a similar proportion at both sites (8.4 percent at Thompson versus 10 percent at Little Egypt). The width of Lamar folded rims at the Thompson site averaged 16.2 millimeters, while those at Little Egypt averaged 11.1 millimeters during the Little Egypt phase and 16.8 millimeters in the Barnett phase. Hally's data demonstrate the widening of rim folds over time, and data from these other five sites seem to confirm the trend.

The most obvious trend to emerge from comparing the Baxter and Thompson sites is the decline of shell tempering and the corresponding rise of grit tempering through time. Ceramics from the single-component sites (Brown, Poarch, and Swancy) indicate that the trend away from shell tempering becomes particularly pronounced in the Barnett phase. Dallas Incised vessels with strap handles appear as burial furniture at the three sites, but sherds in surface collections are relatively rare. Dallas filleted rims, punctated designs, salt pans, painted pottery, and other types apparently diminished significantly in importance or disappeared altogether from the Barnett phase ceramic assemblage. Water bottles and some effigy forms seem to have been present in the Barnett phase, but grit tempering seems to have increasingly replaced shell tempering in most

Table 5 Coosawattee Valley Ceramic Counts

	Brown		Baxter		Thompson		Poarch		Swancy		9Mu102 Barnett Ph.	L.E./Barn.
	#	%	#	%	#	%	#	%	#	%	%	%
Lamar Plain & Coarse Plain	324	60	118	10.6	1541	36	385	59	187	66.8	57.5	32
Lamar Comp. Stamped	77	14.3	49	4.4	352	8.2	70	10.7	28	10	9.7	10
Lamar Bold Incised	63	11.7	16	1.4	358	8.4	67	10.3	27	9.6	8.6	3.1
Lamar w/ features	2	-	-	-	31	1	-	-	-	-		
Lamar Folded Rims	29	5.4	12	1.1	68	1.6	29	4.5	11	3.9		
Fold Width - Avg.	(17.6 mm)		(16.1 mm)		(16.2 mm)		(17.2 mm)		(17.5 mm)		(16.8 mm)	(11.1 mm)
- Range	(13–22 mm)		(11–23 mm)		(10–32 mm)		(10–30 mm)		(13–20 mm)			(L.E. only)
Rim w/ Filleted Strip			1		1		2		2			
Etowah Stamped			44	4								
Wilbanks/Savannah Stamped			19	1.7	31	1	2					
Fabric Imp. (Grit)	2				2		3					
Cherokee Stamped			11	1								
Dallas Plain	67	12.4	683	61.5	1625	38	83	12.7	25	8.9	21.5	47.4
Dallas Incised/Punctated	1		40	3.6	102	2.4	3		2		1.8	1.6
Dallas w/ features	2		37	3.3	129	3	4					1
Hiwassee Island Stamped			60	5.4								
Dallas/H.I. Painted, Filmed			10	1	-	-	2		-	-		
Fabric Imp. & Salt Pans	1		10	1	22	.5	2		-	-		
Unidentified Stamped / Other												
Total	540		1,110		4,280		652		280			

* Lamar types may include some specimens which are tempered with a mixture of shell and medium to coarse grit.

** "Features" include effigies, Dallas filleted, Dallas modeled, strap handles, loop handles, and lugs.

*** Sample sizes for 9Mu102 are 1575 for Barnett Phase and 4875 for Barnett Phase and Little Egypt Phase combined.

vessel types. Even some effigy vessels were grit tempered, despite the fact that artistic rendering suffered.

In addition to the similarities about grit versus shell tempering, the single-component Brown, Poarch, and Swancy sites show almost identical proportions of Lamar Complicated Stamped, Lamar Bold Incised, and Lamar Plain and Lamar Coarse Plain. The average width of the rim folds is quite similar (17.2 millimeters versus 17.6 millimeters) and signifies a slightly wider fold than the Thompson and Baxter sites, which have some earlier Lamar occupations. In short, the Barnett phase material from the five sites appears identical in most respects. Certainly future research into incised and stamped motifs may yield more information about the differences between these villages, but additional research is just as likely to show even more subtle similarities among these villages. It is suggested that almost day-to-day interaction among the villages of the core of the Coosa province led to a homogenous ceramic tradition, and these similarities among the five sites can be seen in the ceramic data presented here (Table 5).

Summary, Conclusions, Future Research

The five sites described in this paper, combined with the Little Egypt site (Hally 1979, 1980), the Potts' Tract site (Hally 1970), and the Sixtoe site (Kelly et al. 1965), probably include most, if not all, of the eight towns of Coosa mentioned in the De Luna papers. Potts' Tract and Sixtoe Field may not be "town"-size sites; therefore, it is possible that one or two additional sites may be found in the vicinity later. To date, all of these eight known sites, with the exception of the Swancy site, have yielded evidence of European contact in the form of metal artifacts, brass bells, and/or glass beads. None of these sites shows evidence of seventeenth-century occupation, suggesting that the towns were rapidly abandoned shortly after the De Luna expedition. Elsewhere it has been suggested that European disease epidemics, suggested by the presence of mass and multiple burials at most of the sites, caused the Coosa inhabitants to flee the area and move south into Alabama (M. Smith 1984; 1987).

This cluster of towns has been badly damaged by untrained diggers over a period of years, but recent efforts at preservation have been effective for all sites. The degree of damage to the sites is unknown but appears to be extensive—particularly to burials. Yet there is still much information that needs to be collected. Controlled surface collections would help provide information about the distributions of the various components on several of the sites. Limited test excavations might determine the presence or absence of palisades on the sites. It is quite possible that large excavations could still produce excellent data on the sites. Most of the untrained digging activity seems to have been concentrated near the river, although several of the sites are quite extensive. Larger ceramic collections are necessary to study the degree of internal variability in a large political unit. Thanks to the work of David Hally (1979; 1980), we now know much of the everyday domestic activity carried out in Coosa towns. Now is the time to step back and look at larger questions of the interrelationships of several towns within a complex chiefdom.

4. Two Late Lamar Sites near Ray's Corner, Oconee County, Georgia

Daniel T. Elliott

A brief examination of several upland locations in central Oconee County, Georgia, in 1980 produced some interesting archaeological information. Two upland Lamar sites are discussed, but the discussion will attempt to transcend a typical site report and focus on the implications of these two sites on the mechanics of Lamar society.

The piedmont portion of the Oconee Valley is thought to contain the province of Ocute, described in the mid-sixteenth century by the chroniclers of the De Soto expedition (Smith and Kowalewski 1980). A greatly refined cultural sequence based on stratigraphic excavations at several mound sites (Smith 1981; Williams 1984) is emerging for the late prehistoric and protohistoric periods in this area. A great deal of Lamar research was conducted as part of the Wallace Reservoir excavations. These include work by Wood and Lee (1973), DePratter (1976), Lee (1977), M. Smith (1981; 1983; 1984), Williams (1983), Shapiro (1983; 1984), Rudolph (1983), and Smith, Hally, and Shapiro (1981). Following on the heels of the Wallace Reservoir research, other studies of other portions of the Oconee Valley were conducted (Elliott 1981; Ledbetter and O'Steen 1986; Williams 1984; Smith and Kowalewski 1980). These studies have allowed the tentative identification of the province of Ocute from the archaeological and historical record.

As noted by Fish and Hally (1983, 7) in their overview of the Wallace Reservoir Project, "one cultural phenomenon of enduring interest to Southeastern archaeologists is the consolidation of population resulting in the appearance of large village and ceremonial centers in late prehistoric times." An important question guiding subsequent surveys in the region was (and continues to be): Where, geographically, does the tremendous expansion of Lamar sites wit-

117

nessed within the Wallace Reservoir end? One survey area, the Ray's
Corner tract, was selected as part of that attempt to define the
northern limits of the expansion into present-day Oconee County
(Figure 14). A Lamar occupation was readily identified within this
area and thus moved the known limit of Lamar settlement within
the overall Oconee River drainage further to the north than previously known in 1980.

Oconee County is bounded on the west by the Apalachee River
and on the east by the Oconee River, with no major rivers in between. The slope map of Georgia (U.S. Geological Survey 1973)
shows that a large portion of central Oconee County has slopes
of less than 3 degrees and an even larger area with slopes under
8 degrees. Site surveys in the Wallace Reservoir area to the southeast had shown that such gentle slopes often had abundant Lamar
occupational debris. Previous archaeological assumptions have
characterized the uplands of the piedmont as merely used for temporary hunting camps and specialized task sites by the Lamar period
Indians, but the abundance of Lamar sites in the Oconee Valley
documented by recent surveys implies that these upland areas may
well have been used for more sedentary tasks. Although these soils
were not as fertile as the river floodplains, which are replenished
annually by silt-laden floodwaters, the upland piedmont slopes may
have been rich enough for prehistoric agriculture on a modest scale.
With the apparent increase in population in the Oconee Valley during the late prehistoric period, the advantages of cultivating the
upland ridges may have outweighed the disadvantages of overcrowd-
ing the bottomlands. The availability of water in the uplands was
not a problem in the Georgia Piedmont, since springs and small
drainages are in close proximity to many upland settings. Navigable
watercourses suitable for canoe transport are more restricted, however.

The sampling techniques in this reconnaissance were not highly
structured but consisted of selecting survey areas with adequate
ground exposure in a geomorphological area that had fairly level
terrain, and, yet, which were several kilometers from a large creek
or river. Visual inspection throughout Oconee County quickly
showed that there were many plowed fields that would meet these
criteria. The short-term goal was part of an ongoing exploratory
survey in the region at large. A fairly level upland area situated
at considerable distance from the Oconee River was selected near
Ray's Corner, north of Watkinsville, Georgia. The area included a

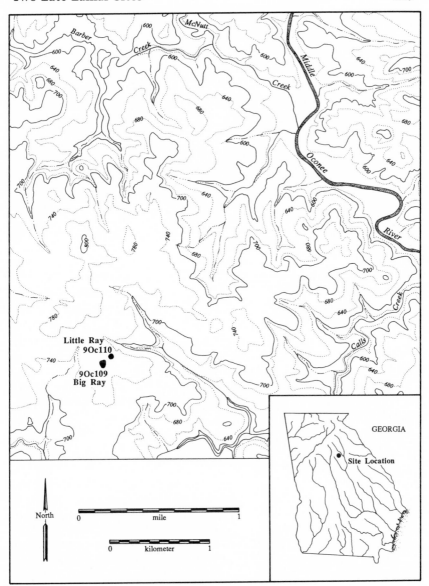

Figure 14. Ray's Corner Location

large plowed field at an elevation of 760 feet above sea level (U.S. Geological Survey Athens West 7.5 minute topographic quad).

Two Lamar sites, located approximately 100 meters apart, were found; soils on each site were Cecil Sandy Loam—a familiar soil type to late prehistoric researchers in the Wallace Reservoir area. Several springheads were within 200 meters of each site and may have served as an attraction to this location. Surface remains of these two sites, referred to here as Big Ray (9OC109) and Little Ray (9OC110), were examined, and a controlled sample surface collection of approximately 20 percent of each site was made. Big Ray measured 90 meters by 110 meters and covered approximately 9,900 square meters, while Little Ray measured 50 meters by 50 meters and covered only 2,500 square meters.

Both sites contained a scatter of Lamar ceramics as well as lithics that could not be directly linked with the Lamar occupation. Surface material at Big Ray was more dense than Little Ray—the density of ceramics at Big Ray was 0.72 sherds per square meter, while the density at Little Ray was 0.52 sherds per square meter. Both sites contained small fragments of unidentified marine shells (possibly weathered bead fragments), deer bones, turtle bones, and unidentified bird bones. Both sites contained a variety of ceramic forms, including jars, cazuela bowls, and tobacco pipes. Taken together, all these suggest that the use of both locations was more than temporary. The ceramics from both sites appear to date to the late prehistoric period, probably between A.D. 1575 and 1630, based on similarity to dated assemblages to the south (M. Smith 1981; Williams 1983). Big Ray probably dates to the early Bell phase, while Little Ray dates somewhere between the Dyar or early Bell phase. The two sites may have been contemporaneous occupations or may represent a slight relocation of one household during a single generation. Both sites are badly disturbed by many years of cultivation, and the present site size is probably larger than the original site dimensions. I believe that Little Ray represents the remains of a single house that was occupied for a short duration, while Big Ray may contain the remains of multiple structures but still may be the residue of a single extended household. Survey of the surrounding cultivated fields in a radius of 250 meters around the two sites failed to yield additional Lamar remains. No subsurface investigations were attempted on either site.

The ceramic assemblage at Big Ray (1,519 specimens) included 192 Lamar Incised sherds (or 12.6 percent of the assemblage), 34

Lamar folded pinched rims, 14 stamped sherds (less than 1 percent of the sample), one corncob-impressed sherd, four tobacco pipe sherds, and 1,274 plain or weathered sherds (83.8 percent of the sample). A breakdown of the Lamar Incised wares revealed a predominance of fine incised (108 sherds, or 41.7 percent of the incised wares) and a minor amount of bold incised (4 sherds, or 2 percent of the sample). No folded punctated rims, characteristic of the earlier Duvall phase, were recovered. Similarly, no crosshatched incised sherds of the type Morgan Incised (attributable to the Duvall and Iron Horse phases) were found on either Big or Little Ray. Vessel forms at Big Ray included jars and cazuela bowls, suggesting use for cooking and storage (Figure 15). The presence of burned bone also suggests that cooking was conducted on-site. A minimum estimate of twenty-nine distinct vessels and four tobacco pipes was made from the ceramic collection at Big Ray.

The ceramics at Little Ray (263 specimens) included 23 Lamar Incised sherds (or 8.7 percent of the collection), 10 folded pinched rims, 1 punctated body sherd, 2 stamped sherds, 1 tobacco pipe fragment, and 226 Lamar Plain or weathered sherds (85.9 percent of the collection). As with Big Ray, no folded punctated rims sherds characteristic of earlier Lamar phases were found. A breakdown by incised line width of the wares at Little Ray revealed a predominance of medium incised (thirteen sherds, or 56.5 percent) followed by slightly lower amounts of fine incised (nine sherds, or 39.1 percent). No bold incised sherds were recovered on Little Ray. Both cazuela bowls and jars were present on Little Ray, indicating use for cooking and storage. A minimum estimate of seven vessels and one tobacco pipe was made from the collection at Little Ray.

Other surveys in Oconee County (Ledbetter and O'Steen 1986) have demonstrated a settlement peak during the Dyar or early Bell phases. This is somewhat later than the peak of settlement seen farther south in the Wallace Reservoir area. Following De Soto's tour of southeastern North America, the political system of the Oconee Valley underwent a series of changes. The Wallace data indicate that settlement may have increased in the area at approximately the same time as De Soto's journey. By the Bell phase, the mound centers in the Oconee Valley had been abandoned. This may have been due to a collapse in the political structure. This collapse may have been accompanied by a general shake-up of religious concepts, as their religious faith was put to the test by the effects of European contact (Williams 1982). In the Wallace Reservoir area,

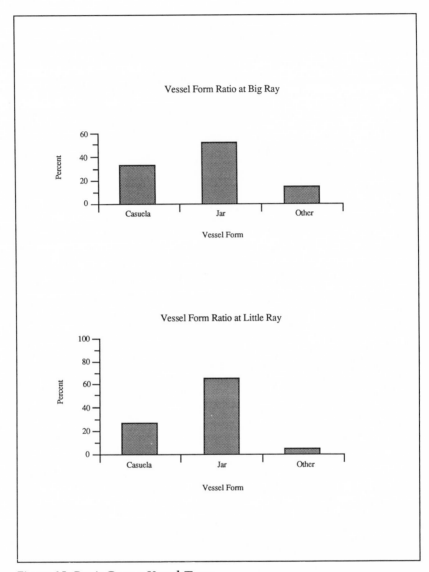

Figure 15. Ray's Corner Vessel Types

there were many small dispersed upland sites dating throughout the phases of the Lamar period. These data suggest that the use of the uplands in the form of scattered settlements had developed prior to European contact. By the Bell phase, however, peoples formerly settled in large villages may have dispersed into the uplands once the importance of the mound centers ceased. Groups may have subsisted in small extended family units. Bell phase villages are uncommon in the Oconee Valley, although some are known to exist (Williams 1983); small upland sites are much more common for this period.

The end of the sixteenth century was a period of increased contact between Europeans and Indians in Georgia (M. Smith 1984). Along with the spread of trade materials came diseases, and the dispersal to the uplands may have helped protect the late Lamar people from becoming extinct due to these diseases. One would normally expect that the waves of epidemic diseases that swept through North America would have resulted in fewer aboriginal settlements, but in the Oconee Valley, the opposite appears to be true. By the late sixteenth century, numerous contacts had been made between the Spaniards based at the missions on the coast and the Indians of the Georgia Piedmont. The extent of this contact and the degree of acculturation that accompanied it is not yet defined beyond the recognition of scattered trade beads and peach pits of piedmont sites. Firearms were not yet a trade commodity. The English deerskin trade had not yet blossomed, and the Spanish may not have significantly affected the general subsistence strategy of the Oconee Valley Indians. Contact with the coast is demonstrated at Big Ray by the presence of several pieces of marine shell, although no European trade material was found there. Further research on the interaction between the coast and the piedmont during the Lamar period is necessary to better define these relationships.

Population density north of the Wallace Reservoir area also was apparently quite high during the Dyar and Bell phases. For the same period, population continued to be high in the Wallace Reservoir area. The population expansion toward the north during this time may have resulted from the weakened political strength of neighboring chiefdoms. The former political grandeur of Mississippian Ocute society was only a faded memory.

Big and Little Ray were house sites located on a ridgetop over 3 kilometers from the Oconee River. Judging from ongoing surveys, these two sites are certainly not unique to the region, although the site type has received little attention in the Georgia literature. The two sites were probably permanently settled, although more activity occurred at Big Ray. Big Ray probably had more than one structure, while Little Ray may have had only a single structure. Consumption of wild animal foods is documented at both sites, but it is quite likely that farming also was conducted in the vicinity. The two sites may have been situated near a major upland trail (possibly paralleling present-day U.S. Highway 441). Both sites were probably occupied between A.D. 1575 and 1630 and show no evidence of having been utilized during earlier Lamar phases. In the absence of excavation data from Big Ray, Little Ray, and other upland sites, a more detailed interpretation of this site type must remain incomplete.

At Ray's Corner, life went on much as it had before European contact. People lived in houses, ate wild foods, smoked nicotine, and broke pots much as they had before. These sites probably represent single-family farmsteads—Cecil Sandy Loam is well suited for cropland. These small groups of late Lamar folk grew crops in the small creek floodplains and fertile ridge slopes, admired the view from their ridgetop homes, and drank their clear springwater. The selection of the upland site locality could make use of several springheads and broad areas of gently sloping ridgetops. The two sites at Ray's Corner are examples of what may be a widespread pattern in the Oconee Valley. However, the upland sites are probably not of a homogenous character. Springhead ridgetop sites may have functioned differently from sites situated on the toe slopes of ridges above narrow creek floodplains. These two examples of upland late Lamar sites possess much information, even though their contents have been virtually homogenized by historic land use. Such sites should not be simply disregarded as destroyed cultural resources—they are not. Descriptions of other such sites are essential to our understanding of the Lamar settlement machine in the Southeast. Explication of the late prehistoric settlement in this region may prove to solve many puzzles about the effects of European contact on the decline of prehistoric societies.

5. Dallas Phase Architecture and Sociopolitical Structure

Richard R. Polhemus

Introduction

The architectural or structural aspects of a society reflect both the technological level and the sociopolitical structure of that society. This paper will summarize several aspects of ongoing research concerning the Dallas culture in the east Tennessee Valley. Technological aspects of Mississippian architecture are dealt with elsewhere (Polhemus 1985a). The Dallas culture is now frequently characterized as a combination of ceramic, mortuary, subsistence, and architectural traits (Polhemus 1985b) displaying many of the characteristics of a chiefdom level of sociopolitical organization. There is an underlying assumption that Mississippian societies were organized at a chiefdom level or at least had some form of ranked sociopolitical hierarchy (Peebles 1974; Depratter 1983).

Goldstein (1976), Hatch (1974; 1976), Peebles (1978), and Steponaitis (1978) have examined various aspects of chiefdom-level societies from an archaeological standpoint. The archaeological correlates of a chiefdom should include: (1) clear evidence of ascribed ranking, (2) a hierarchy of settlement types and sizes, (3) settlement location allowing a high degree of subsistence sufficiency, (4) evidence of centralized power or organized productive activities that extend beyond the basic household unit, and (5) a correlation between those elements of a cultural system's environment that are less predictable and evidence of society-wide organizational activity to deal with them (Peebles and Kus 1977).

The rigidity or formality of this sociopolitical structure obviously varied through time and space, adding to the difficulty of identifying

125

the archaeological correlates of such structures at any one site. Hudson (1976, 203) has stressed that "not all chiefdoms comprised comparable numbers of people, nor were they equally centralized. Chiefdoms may have small populations or large, and their chiefs may be relatively weak or strong." This variability in the size and complexity of chiefdoms should be carefully considered when attempting to apply the concept to the archaeological record (Goldstein 1976). Not all archaeologically defined chiefdoms should be expected to display the magnitude of centers such as Etowah (Larson 1971a) or Moundville (Peebles 1978). Architectural or structural aspects of ranked societies may be expected to differ in degree or relative complexity rather than in kind.

Data concerning not only individual structures but also structure content and discernible site structure have been examined for this study. Although the primary emphasis was concentrated upon the Toqua site (40MR6) and other Dallas sites on the Little Tennessee River, data from throughout the Dallas culture area on file at the Frank H. McClung Museum, University of Tennessee, were included. The architectural or "built" environment of a society includes not only the individual sheltering structures but also the spaces between them. Site structure, like individual structure units, reflects the spatial needs of the society responsible for its construction and therefore grades into the greater realm of settlement patterning. Several aspects of structures and the built environment are discussed with respect to such patterning.

Structure Types

Two basic structure types are represented at all adequately excavated Dallas sites. The first, consisting of a square structure of rigid single-set-post construction possessing an interior square pattern of main roof supports, served as the primary building within each settlement unit. The second, consisting of a smaller, more open, rectangular structure of rigid single-set-post construction, served as a secondary building within each settlement unit. These two structure forms occur together in a range of sociopolitical contexts within Dallas society and differ in size, proportion, interior elaboration, and content in relation to the position occupied within the sociopolitical context. At the most basic level, the paired primary and secondary structures, in conjunction with other facilities, make up the minimal settlement unit described below. At the highest level, such paired primary and secondary structures functioned as public buildings of great size and interior elaboration.

Dallas primary structures consistently display evidence of partitioning and the differential use of space. Such structures, usually possessing four main roof supports, were divided into an open "public" area and a subdivided "private" area. The public area was made up of the central portion of the structure, centering on the prepared clay central hearth and bounded by the main roof supports, and served a variety of purposes, such as access, food preparation, and other activities requiring heat and/or light. The private area was made up of that portion of the structure situated between the main roof supports and the exterior wall and was frequently divided by partitions into sections serving different purposes. The central portion along each wall, flanked by main roof supports, served as a bed or bench for individuals occupying the structure. The corners of the structure served a storage function. Food supplies and other materials were most frequently stored in the northwest and southeast corners. Food preparation activities were concentrated on the side of the hearth toward the entryway. Residues from food processing, food consumption, and manufacturing activities were allowed to accumulate within the structure, and only the public area in the vicinity of the central hearth was kept relatively free of debris. Public buildings of the primary form were better maintained than village domestic structures and were kept relatively clean.

The secondary structure making up each minimal settlement unit consisted of a rectangular open or semiopen building situated near the entrance to each primary structure. This structure form is characterized by its relatively small size and the presence of large postholes, surface fired areas, and burials placed beneath the floor. Structural debris from a burned example identified at the Toqua site included cane, wood fragments, and maize cobs bearing kernels. The combination of archaeological attributes, coupled with ethnohistoric data, suggests that such structures served both as food processing and food storage facilities. Secondary structures associated with primary buildings were considerably larger than domestic examples and assumed the function of a sheltered pavilion in front of the primary structure.

The Minimal Settlement Unit

The archaeological correlate of the household, the minimal settlement unit (MSU), is made up of those tangible elements required to maintain a discrete social group within its environment. Archaeologically, the MSU is represented by a primary structure, a secondary structure, and an outdoor activity area with associated processing facilities (Figure 16). At some reasonable distance, a sufficient cultivatable support area is situated. Two classes of material culture may be associated with the MSU: (1) basic subsistence and maintenance materials with refuse resulting from activities performed in every household and (2) items linked to activities and roles extending beyond a particular household.

The spatial patterning of the burials frequently found within Dallas structures, when viewed in the light of ethnohistoric references to burial practices, provides evidence of mortuary structure within domestic dwellings and perhaps within public buildings as well. The domestic model, for those individuals not removed due to status or other social or political ties, may be stated in the following manner: those individuals who die at home will be interred within the structure beneath or near the bed or "cabin" occupied in life. The spatial patterning of burials by age, sex, and associations for Toqua village structures containing eighteen or more individuals was examined.

The structures displayed a circular to rectangular pattern of burials, of all ages and both sexes, situated along the walls of each structure (Figure 17). Burials tended to be concentrated toward the center of each wall between the main roof supports. Adults tended to be situated near the center of the north, west, and south walls of each structure. Females were more frequently found along the north and south walls, and when present within the structure, adult males tended to be found along the west wall. Subadults were concentrated toward the front edge of the beds or benches along all four sides of each structure. Burial associations with subadults were more common and of greater variety within the west half of each structure. Examination of such structure groups and of articulated multiple burials may provide additional data concerning the size and makeup of the social unit occupying the household or MSU. Minimal settlement units may represent matrilocal, matrilineal residence units. The pairing of primary and secondary structure types

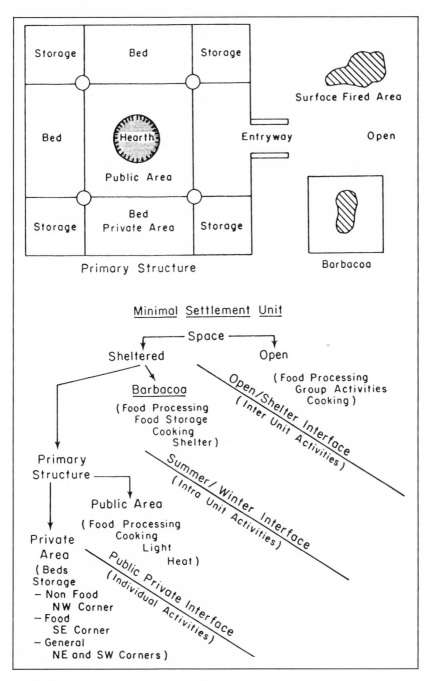

Figure 16. Dallas Minimal Settlement Unit

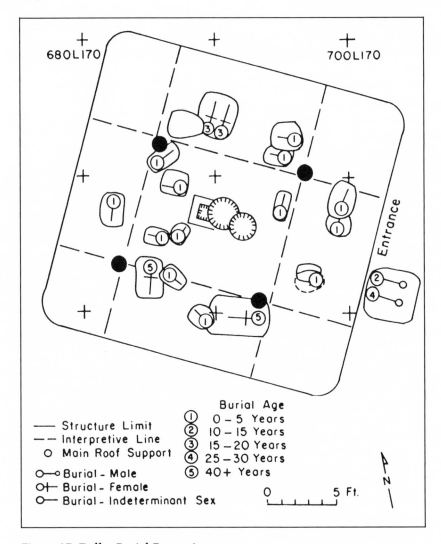

Figure 17. Dallas Burial Patterning

illustrated by the Dallas MSU likely represents an earlier stage of
the winter house/summer house pattern encountered in both historic Cherokee and historic Creek towns during the eighteenth century.

Public Buildings

Dallas public buildings were much like domestic structures and differed more in size, relative proportions, and interior elaboration than in overall form or technology. Each public primary structure at the Toqua site had its associated secondary structure, although the secondary structure was considerably larger in proportion to domestic examples and assumed the function of a sheltered pavilion in front of the primary structure upon each mound summit surface. Public buildings possessed a greater percentage (31 to 40 percent) of public or central floor space than did domestic structures in the village areas (14 to 32 percent) or high status domestic structures on the summit of Mound A (25 to 33 percent). One of each pair of primary structures on the summit of Mound A was identified as a high-status dwelling and the other as a building serving a primarily public function. The former closely resembled—in size, content, and use of floor space—the largest village structures near the plaza. The latter, even when nearly of the same size, were distinguished by the greater percentage of public floor space and interior elaboration. Interior elaboration took the form of modeled clay rims on prepared clay hearths; clay rather than perishable materials utilized in the construction of beds, benches, partitions, and pilasters; painted or otherwise decorated interior construction; and features allowing greater seating capacity than other structures. Public buildings were frequently linked to both the paired high-status dwelling and to the open pavilion in front of each structure by wall trench entryways. Both of the primary structures upon each mound summit were usually enclosed by a clay embankment. The interior of the roof structure in both public and domestic primary structures was plastered with clay in an attempt to fireproof the flammable thatched-roof structure.

Burials and structure contents confirm the differentiation between high-status domestic structures and public buildings on the summit of Mound A at the Toqua site. The few burials recovered from mound domestic structure contexts display an age and sex profile resembling village structure contexts, in contrast to burial populations from public building contexts, such as Structure 87 (Figure 18). These display an older male-dominated age and sex profile. Burials recovered from the central summit area of Mound B at the Toqua site display an even older male-dominated age and sex profile, in addition to a distinctly different array of burial associations.

Symbolic Use of Space

The symbolic use or allotment of space, particularly within structures or functions connected with public or religious activities, was a common feature among groups encountered by European observers in the interior southeastern United States (Swanton 1931 and 1946; Howard 1968; Hudson 1976; Waring 1968). Specified seating patterns based upon rank, title, status, and kinship are evident in both town house and square ground use. Historic Creek square ground form and the terminology used for elements making up the square ground are analogous to the elements making up the town house (Swanton 1931) and, indeed, serve similar functions. If one were to enclose and roof the Creek square ground, one would duplicate, on a larger scale, the traditional form of a town house and, on a still more reduced scale, the traditional form of a primary dwelling or domestic structure. The prerogative of certain Creek towns to embower or lightly roof the square ground (Swanton 1946) may, in fact, reflect earlier status differentiation between towns or other social entities. The facilities centered on each side are referred to as "beds" or "cabins" and are provided with partitions or other physical elements controlling the use of space in each case. The corners between adjoining beds serve storage functions in the case of square grounds (Swanton 1931), as well as within domestic structures. The focal point of social interaction in each case is the central hearth or fire, and the space encompassed by the beds is equally accessible to all participants. The town house is frequently accompanied by a more open structure or summer pavilion for warm season use. The town house complex and the still larger square ground complex in actuality mirror the traditional domestic household or MSU. Certain symbolic aspects in the use of space may have differed only in degree rather than kind for all three. Patterning and the symbolic use of space, therefore, may be reflected in the form of the domestic unit.

The orientation and placement of structures, substructure mounds, and other elements of site structure may also reflect the symbolic order of the occupants or, at the least, may reflect the degree of planning or social control exerted within the resident cultural system. Figure 19 illustrates selected elements of site structure compared to structure and burial orientation. The placement and orientation of structures through time at the Toqua site indicate a level of planning and social control not previously recognized for

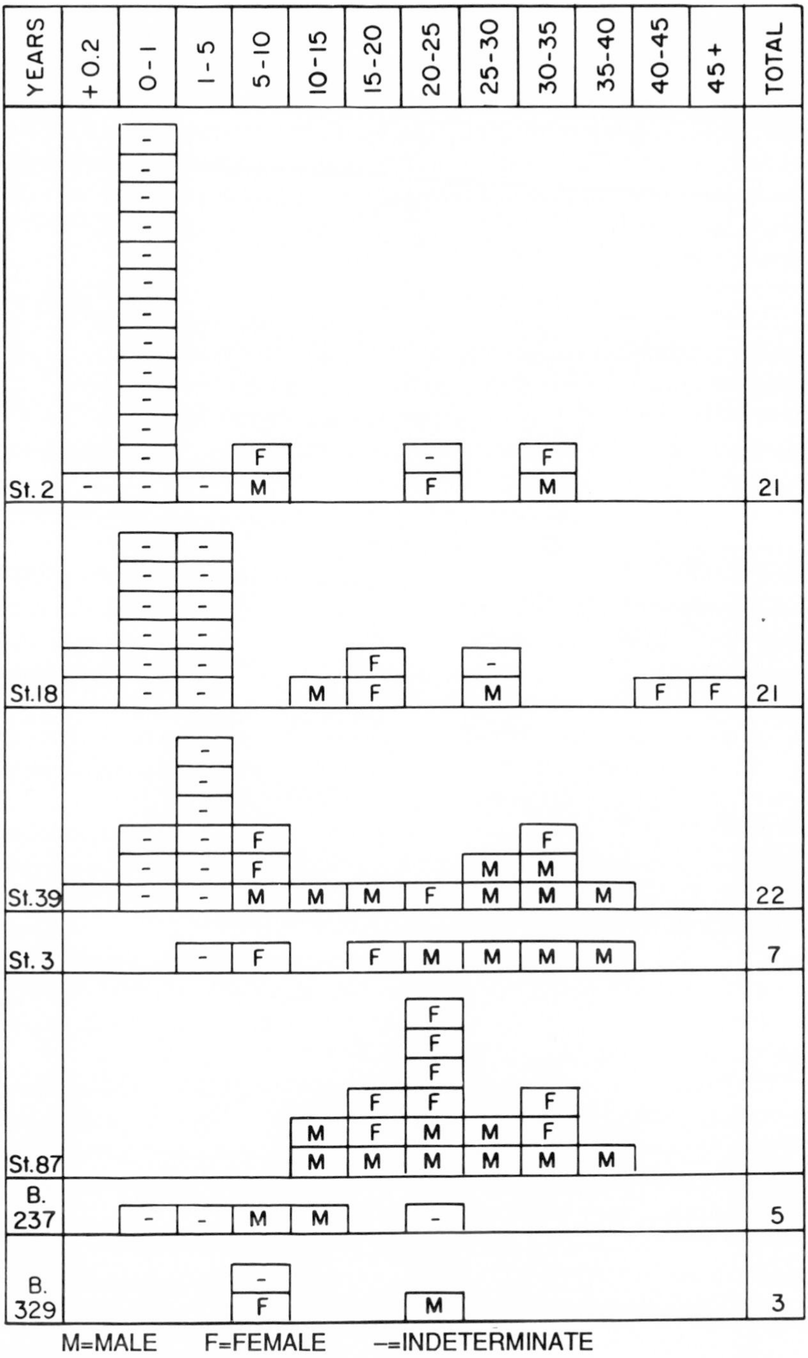

Figure 18 — Dallas Burial Age-Sex Profiles (cell contents read top-to-bottom within each age column):

Burial	+0.2	0–1	1–5	5–10	10–15	15–20	20–25	25–30	30–35	35–40	40–45	45+	TOTAL
St. 2	–	– (×13)	–	F, M			–, F		F, M				21
St. 18	–	– (×7)	– (×6)	M	F, F		–, M				F	F	21
St. 39	–	– (×3)	– (×6)	F, F, M	M	M	M, F	F, M, M	M				22
St. 3			–	F		F	M	M	M	M			7
St. 87					M, M	M, M, F	F, F, F, F, F, M	M, M	M, M, F	M, F	M		
B. 237		–	–	M	M	–							5
B. 329			–, F				M						3

M=MALE   F=FEMALE   −=INDETERMINATE

Figure 18. Dallas Burial Age-Sex Profiles

the Dallas culture. The recognition of this patterning (which includes a site axis linked to the winter solstice—a pattern known only for the Toqua site at the present time) does not suggest that other Dallas sites do not possess similar patterning. More likely, those questions have not been asked of the existing data, or else those sites have been insufficiently investigated.

Settlement Patterning

The settlement patterning of the Dallas culture is, as yet, not fully understood. However, much has been compiled toward that end, and at least tentative statements may be made concerning the elements of the built environment making up the Dallas settlement system. The Dallas system may be viewed as a succession of five interrelated levels of sociopolitical complexity (Figure 20). The basic unit upon which the succession is constructed is the household (Level I), identified with the archaeological correlate previously described as the MSU. Aggregates of two or more such MSUs, fronting on a common open activity area or courtyard, make up the next unit of sociopolitical complexity (Level II). Some processing facilities, such as stone-filled pits or earthen ovens, as well as the outdoor activity area, may be utilized by groups representing more extended kin or lineage units. Not all primary structures are the same size. This may indicate variation in household size or relative status within such extended units. During the Dallas phase, MSUs (Level I) and household aggregates (Level II) are rarely encountered as isolated or dispersed cultural entities.

Villages or towns (Level III) are made up of 8 or 10 to perhaps as many as 100 Level II household aggregates. Towns possess a tangible spatial sociopolitical structure encompassing public elements, such as one or more public buildings on a plaza, a surrounding residential zone, and, frequently, a defensive perimeter such as a palisade. Public building locations, given sufficient time and population, frequently became raised platforms or substructure mounds supporting public buildings. In addition to site size, a rough measure of sociopolitical importance frequently utilized in the development of Mississippian settlement hierarchies is the size, number, and form of the mounds at a particular site. Such an approach has served reasonably well, in spite of problems of contemporaneity and rela-

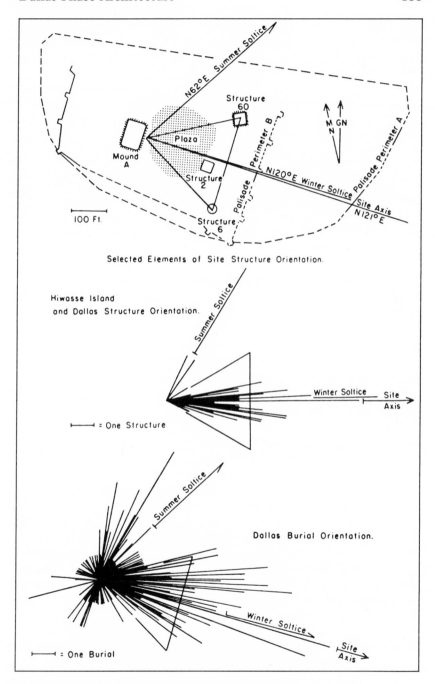

Figure 19. Dallas Structure and Burial Orientation

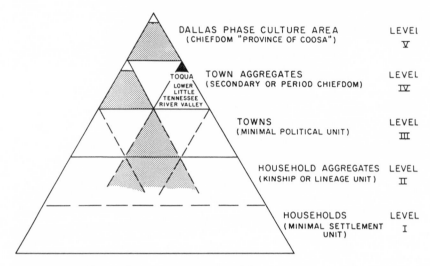

Figure 20. Dallas Culture Settlement Model

tive use or disuse on sites occupied over a span of 400 years or more.

The great majority of Dallas sites possess a single substructure mound bearing a single primary structure upon its summit. A small number of Dallas sites possess more than one substructure mound. The summit of the larger mound on such multiple-mound sites frequently has a pair of primary structures upon it, sometimes on different elevations. Although not formally differentiated in this settlement system model, sites having mounds bearing more than one primary structure likely represent a higher level of sociopolitical organization. The Toqua site (Figure 21), possessing the characteristics of this higher level of organization, represents a relatively large Level III town made up of perhaps forty Level II units. The town is the basic unit in the Dallas spatial settlement hierarchy, rather than farmsteads, as has been proposed for other Mississippian settlement systems (Bruce Smith 1978). The Toqua site appears to have dominated the lower Little Tennessee Valley from the middle of the thirteenth century to the early part of the sixteenth century, when the Citico site (40MR7), situated upstream, superseded it.

Town aggregates (Level IV) have yet to be precisely defined archaeologically but may be compared to a district or geographical subarea comprised of towns demonstrating a closer linkage to each other than to other Dallas phase sites. Such districts may be indicated by the spatial clustering of sites, localized ceramic traits, or other minor variations in material culture. Level IV units as well as Level III units experience fluctuations in size, population, and political power as a result of interaction with neighboring districts and outside groups. Town aggregates may represent secondary political alliances or minor chiefdoms.

The Dallas culture area, comprising much of the Ridge and Valley physiographic province in east Tennessee and extending south and west into portions of Georgia and Alabama, makes up the largest unit (Level V) in the Dallas settlement model. This unit encompasses all those Level IV groups of districts possessing the material culture assemblage identified as Dallas. The Dallas culture area may be viewed as a sociopolitical mosaic made up of Level IV districts in a state of flux. Political ties and dominance shifted through time. During the mid-sixteenth century, most, if not all, of the Dallas culture area was affiliated with, or subject to, Coosa, a powerful

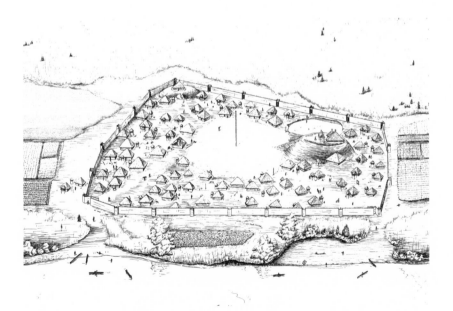

Figure 21. Toqua (Artist's Reconstruction)

chiefdom encountered by the De Soto and De Luna expeditions.

Dallas settlement patterning is characterized by compact towns, frequently situated at relatively close intervals and distributed along the major alluvial bottomland systems within the Ridge and Valley province. Few isolated MSUs or Level II household aggregates appear to exist outside of compact Level III towns. The majority of Dallas towns possess a single substructure mound bearing a single primary structure upon its summit. Only a few towns, including Toqua and Hiwassee Island, possess more than one primary structure on a mound summit or more than one mound. This differentiation may serve to identify local or district centers.

The Toqua site appears to be contemporaneous with the Citico site (40MR7), the Talassee site (40BT8), and the Chilhowee site (40BT7) upstream from it, and the Bussell Island site (40LD17) downstream from it on the Little Tennessee River. The Dallas portion of the Tomotley site (40MR5a), situated a mile downstream from Toqua, appears to have been established late in the sixteenth century near the end of the Mississippian occupation of Toqua. During the sixteenth century, the Citico site (40MR7), probably the "Satapo" visited by Juan Pardo in 1568 (Hudson et al. 1985), appears to have been the more important of the two towns, based upon the greater frequency of Spanish materials and late Dallas ceramic types at Citico.

The architectural summary and the Dallas settlement system pattern model discussed above have been constructed from all available data from previously investigated Dallas sites, as well as from the extensive investigation of the Toqua site. However, these projections should be considered as working entities rather than end products and could be subject to change in response to additional data.

6. A Study of Lamar Ecology on the Western Edge of the Southern Piedmont

C. Roger Nance

The tendency for Mississippian sites to be located on ecotones is widely recognized, and Lamar sites are no exception. In the western Lamar region, prehistoric and protohistoric sites occur on the boundary of two physiographic provinces—the Ridge and Valley and the Piedmont in the southern Appalachians. Included in this list are well-documented sites such as Little Egypt, Potts' Tract, and Etowah in northwest Georgia. In east-central Alabama, the Rodgers-CETA site is another example. This paper deals with the prehistoric ecology of the Rodgers-CETA Lamar village site.

Prehistoric relationships between the Lamar culture and its environment are reconstructed to some extent through reference to four kinds of information: studies of the modern environment; historic references about the nineteenth-century environment; plant and animal remains recovered during archaeological research at the site; and ethnohistoric literature on Native American cultures in the Eastern Woodlands. The focus here is on two questions. First, what advantages accrued to Lamar people by settling on the floodplain of a major stream at the point where it leaves Piedmont and enters the Ridge and Valley province to the west? Second, what role did forest fires play in the prehistoric ecology? Since the southern Piedmont environment was probably maintained through forest fires, the importance of accidental or deliberate burning to Lamar subsistence must be examined.

Talladega County is in east-central Alabama and in the drainage system of the Coosa River. The climate for the entire state of Alabama is characterized as humid and subtropical (Lineback and Traylor 1973, 12). The mean daily temperature in Talladega County is 62 degrees Fahrenheit, and the average length of the growing season is between 200 and 210 days (Gallup 1980, 10). Annual rainfall

139

averages about 21.3 centimeters (Lineback and Traylor 1973, 13).

Talladega Creek flows west to southwest out of the Piedmont hills and crosses Talladega County to join the Coosa River at the county's western edge. The Rodgers-CETA site is situated on the south bank of Talladega Creek on an alluvial soil described as Toccoa Loam of the Toccoa series. In Talladega County, "most of the [Toccoa Loam] acreage has been cleared and is used mainly for corn, soybeans, cotton, and hay" (Cotton et al. 1974, 44).

At its location on the Talladega Creek floodplain, the Rodgers-CETA site is on an ecotone at the eastern edge of the Ridge and Valley province and only about 200 meters west of the Piedmont boundary (Figure 22). The Piedmont front is marked by the appearance of steep hills, with the range producing the highest elevations in Alabama; today this region is almost entirely in forest. The topography in the Ridge and Valley area is more variable, with broad valleys and lower, less steeply inclined hills and ridges. Farmlands presently alternate with forests west of the Piedmont.

There is also a major shift in vegetation at the Piedmont boundary. Harper (1943, 106–13) defines the Coosa Valley forest type to the west, where deciduous trees generally make up 60 percent of the forest cover. The remainder is pine and cedar. Along the western portion of the Piedmont, however, the Blue Ridge forest type (Harper 1943, 114–19) consists predominantly of pine, with longleaf pine (*Pinus palustris*) as the most common species.

The location of the Rodgers-CETA site on the floodplain of a major tributary is typical of Mississippian sites in the Southeast, and this general tendency has been attributed to the presence of easily tilled soils and the importance of horticulture to Mississippian communities (Bruce Smith 1978). Why a major Lamar village would have been located as far upstream as possible on Talladega Creek is not so clear. In the Piedmont, the creek is confined to a narrow valley where the floodplain is discontinuous to nonexistent. West of the site, a relatively broad floodplain contains easily tilled soils along most of the stream's course to the Coosa River. The question, then, is: What resources in the Piedmont drew Lamar populations to the eastern end of the Talladega Creek floodplain?

This question led the author to a meeting with ecological zoologists in the Department of Zoology-Entomology, Auburn University (Keith Causey, James Dobie, and Dan Speake), and with H. D. Kelly, a biologist with the U.S. Department of Agriculture Soil Conservation Service, also at Auburn, Alabama. The following discussion

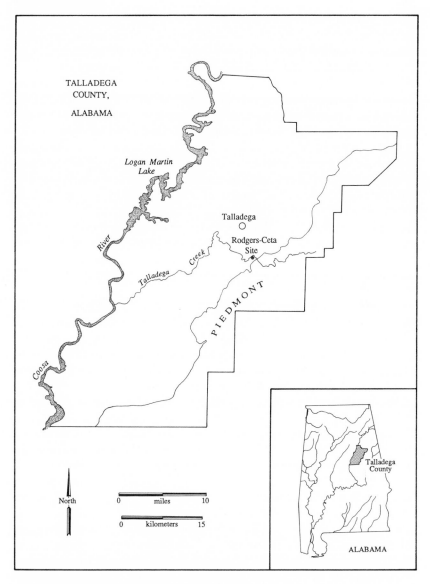

Figure 22. Location of Rodgers-CETA Site

is based on their ideas and suggestions. An initial assumption was that agriculture would not have been practiced in the immediately adjacent Piedmont, where the soils are shallow and unsuitable, so the focus there was on wild plant and animal resources.

One factor that might have enhanced the immediate site environment for human occupants is the presence of ponds on the nearby floodplain (James Dobie, personal communication). Given the marked reduction in stream gradient at the Piedmont escarpment, periodic flooding might have been relatively frequent on the floodplain just to the west, thus creating and maintaining these ponds. These would have attracted turtles and small mammals (James Dobie, personal communication) and supported fish as well (H. D. Kelly, personal communication)—all available for human consumption. Inspection of detailed soil maps for Talladega County (Cotton et al. 1974) reveals three perennial ponds, each 100 to 150 meters in length—all within 450 meters of the site. Only one other perennial pond was identified on these maps to the west of the site locality along Talladega Creek.

Within the Piedmont, there is some evidence that the vegetational differences between the Blue Ridge and Coosa Valley forest types, as defined by Harper (1943), are long-standing. Mohr (1901, 59–61) described open longleaf pine forest in the Piedmont, and many of his observations date well back into the nineteenth century. In his recent study of the Coosa Valley, Waselkov (1980, 207) studied four 800-meter-by-8-kilometer transects across the valley and reconstructed early forest composition by using 1820–1842 survey records and plotting identified witness trees. While his survey was limited to small areas no more than 4 kilometers from the Coosa River, Waselkov did find a sharp break in forest type between the floodplain and upland terraces of the Coosa. On the former, he found mainly hardwoods; on the terraces, pine percentages varied between 60 and 95 percent. His data suggest that pine was more common across the Ridge and Valley province in the early nineteenth century than more recently. If so, this would follow the general historical trend noted by Mobley and Balmer (1981, 17) of hardwoods tending to replace pine in the Southeast. Taken together, an early hardwood forest is suggested for the Talladega Creek floodplain and longleaf and shortleaf pine forest for the adjacent Piedmont. Hardwoods most likely occurred in the Piedmont as well, mostly at higher elevations and in valley bottoms (Mohr 1901, 59).

An important feature of these pine forests is that they are maintained through periodic burning. Harper (1943, 34) estimates that the burning of longleaf pine forests was as frequent as five years in every ten. He also wrote (1943, 34) that longleaf pines are probably the most resistant to fire of any pine. This burning kills underbrush and seedling trees. It also maintains an open forest habitat and benefits important game species, particularly bobwhite (quail) and wild turkey. Burning promotes the growth of food plants (Harper 1943; Landers 1981; Hurst 1981) and prevents their being crowded out by grass, shrubbery, and pine straw (Harper 1943, 38). Deer populations also may benefit from burning in pine forests through the production of new growth with high protein content (Stransky and Harlow 1981, 136).

Kormareck (1981) details the history of controlled burning for wildlife management in the South. He describes the transmission of local knowledge from southern Indians to early European settlers and the perpetuation of burning techniques into the twentieth century on private hunting plantations, primarily to produce quail. The U.S. Forest Service became convinced of the value of prescribed burning between 1940 and 1960. Between 1977 and 1980, the Forest Service burned an average of 3,094,000 acres a year in the South, with about one-third of the acreage burned specifically for wildlife management purposes (Kormareck 1981, Table 1). Prescribed burning is used to improve conditions for deer, quail, and turkey (Mobley and Balmer 1981, 16).

Cotton et al. (1974, 3) wrote in reference to Talladega County that the Piedmont forest is famous for its wild game, particularly white-tailed deer, wild turkey, squirrel, and raccoon. Putting this together with the above discussion of fire as an important element in maintaining longleaf pine forests, it may be possible to conceptualize activity in the prehistoric Piedmont. Lamar people may have practiced controlled burning in the Piedmont hills and not relied entirely on fires set by lightning. Moisture, time of year, and the amount of accumulated brush determine the severity of any one fire. This in turn produces either harmful or positive effects on the various animal species in the environment (Wood 1981). Recent studies indicate that deliberate burnings at timed intervals would have better produced the desired results than by reliance on random lightning fires alone.

In fact, Cronin (1983, 49, 51, 57) has nicely documented Indian forest burning in New England in order to promote hunting. In a study of colonial New England ecology, he concludes that the Indians in southern New England altered their environment in other ways than cutting trees for firewood and burning areas to clear land for agriculture. Extensive tracts of forest were burned over by the Indians as often as twice a year. Cronin (1983, 51) wrote: "Selective Indian burning thus promoted the mosaic quality of New England ecosystems, creating forest in many different states of ecological succession . . . [and thus] . . . ideal habitats for a host of wildlife species."

The Piedmont–Ridge and Valley ecotone in the vicinity of Talladega Creek probably supported large populations of deer, quail, and turkey. These species may have moved back and forth between several environments, feeding on seeds, berries, and young shoots in the Piedmont during the spring and summer and on hard mast (acorns and hickory nuts) on the Talladega Creek floodplain in the late summer and fall (Keith Causey and Dan Speake, personal communication).

Human communities with a capacity for horticulture and an otherwise diversified economy based on hunting, fishing, and wild plant food gathering would have found the Rodgers-CETA site an ideal habitat. Deer, quail, and turkey were likely important resources. Wild plant foods would have been abundant near the site, including acorns and hickory nuts on the floodplain and blackberries, blueberries, and pine seeds in the adjacent Piedmont. Small mammals and turtles would have been trapped and hunted at nearby ponds, and good horticultural land was on the site proper.

The potential of fishing remains to be discussed. While Talladega Creek is a large stream, studies by the Alabama Department of Conservation indicate a relatively low density of fish in it today, compared to other nearby streams and the Coosa River itself. Netted and weighed samples of fish from Talladega Creek indicate an average of less than 18 kilograms of fish per acre of water surface, compared to 27 and 31 kilograms per acre for two other streams in Talladega County and compared to about 36 kilograms per acre for the Coosa River prior to dam construction (H. D. Kelly, personal communication). Due to local bedrock mineralogy, Talladega Creek is more acidic than nearby streams, and this reduces mineral content and the potential for fish growth (H. D. Kelly, personal communication). Fishing may never have been important at the site locality on a year-round basis, but sucker runs in the early spring could have provided a major source of food. Four sucker species are found in the Coosa River and migrate in large numbers up its tributaries to spawn. The river red-horse (*Moxostoma carinatum*) is the largest and was probably the most important species to the Indians (Herbert Bochung, personal communication).

The above reconstruction is supported to some extent by faunal and floral remains from the site—all recovered from Lamar levels. Brian Hesse and Susan Henson (n.d.) analyzed 3,208 animal bones and bone fragments from the site. Of 765 identifiable specimens, 50 percent were deer, 3 percent were bear, 10 percent were small mammal (including beaver, squirrel, raccoon, and carnivore), 12 percent were bird (including turkey), and 25 percent were turtle. Hesse and Henson compared faunal remains from two sequential Lamar components and found no significant changes in the proportions of bones by species. When deer bones were compared by component, Hesse and Henson found "the deer carcass equally represented in the two periods." They concluded that "the picture is thus of a stable deer focused economy" (Hesse and Henson n.d.).

While these data do indicate that most of the meat was derived from deer hunting, small mammal bones, abundant turtle remains, and a few fish, frog, and snake bones also point to the importance of smaller game—the kinds of resources that would be available along Talladega Creek and at the two large ponds mentioned above.

The plant remains from Rodgers-CETA were studied by Eddie Morgan, and these point both to economic diversity and to a variety of microenvironments near the site. Corn is well represented as the single important cultigen, but nineteen wild taxa were also identified in the charred seed remains. Morgan (n.d.) summarized these plants and their habitats as follows:

These native plants inhabit micro-environments [today] ranging from the wet creek margin to drier slopes and ridge tops. Open and disturbed areas support a variety of plants which readily spread into such environments. Hickory (mockernut, pignut) is one of the dominant trees in lowland and upland woods, and seven species of grape (Vitis rotundifolia), fox grape (Vitis labrusca), frost grape (Vitis vulpina), possum grape (Vitis baileyana), summer grape (Vitis aestivalis), pigeon grape (Vitis cinerea), and riverside grape (Vitis riparia) occur along the creek bank, in moist lowland woods, and in drier upland woods. Water parsnip grows in wet creek margins, and many species in the sedge, aster, legume, and grass families are the most common flora in open areas. Corn fields and clearings around houses would provide ideal habitats for weedy plants such as amaranths, chenopods, pokeweed, knotweed, chickweed, carpit weed, sour grass, fescue, panic grass, goose grass, and maypop. Blackberries which grow in open areas would likely spread into areas around houses and fields also.

The open pine forest of the frequently burned Piedmont, along with the heavily wooded valley floor and areas cleared by Lamar people for their settlements and agriculture, would have provided this varied environment. Economic stability is indicated not only by the faunal remains but also by the distribution of plant species through the two-component Lamar sequence.

Summary

In summary, the importance of ecotone habitats in Lamar prehistory has been emphasized both by Larson (1971b, 24–25) for Etowah and by Hally (1979, 10–11) for Little Egypt. At the Rodgers-CETA site in east-central Alabama, 200 to 300 years of successful Lamar occupation depended on the varied resources afforded by the surrounding floodplain and Piedmont environments. Economic diversity is strongly indicated by the floral and faunal remains excavated from the site, and so is economic stability. In other words, a strategy of maintaining resource diversity was apparently perpetuated throughout the Lamar sequence. Finally, ethnohistorical data, at least from New England, and the modern longleaf pine forest of the Alabama Piedmont both suggest that forest fires, either accidentally set or resulting from prehistoric forest management, played an important role in Lamar ecology at this locality.

7. Bottomlands and Rapids
A Mississippian Adaptive Niche in the Georgia Piedmont

Gary Shapiro

Introduction

Environmentally based models of Mississippian settlement have been widely used by archaeologists in recent years. Most archaeologists would agree that difficulties arise when such models are applied over increasingly larger geographic areas. But rather than discounting the applicability of general environmental models, researchers will find there is much to be gained by investigating reasons for deviations from the model. Here I will examine the applicability of Bruce Smith's (1978) model of the "Mississippian adaptive niche" to the Oconee Valley, a region of intensive Mississippian occupation in the Georgia Piedmont. Smith's model cannot be applied directly to this study area, but when two sources of variation are considered, his model provides a good basis for understanding the use and function of several sites in the Oconee Valley. These two sources of variation are, first, regional political structure and, second, environmental differences between the Mississippi Valley (where the model was formulated) and the Georgia Piedmont.

In its most simplified form, Bruce Smith's environmental model can be summarized by recognizing the Indians' need to balance access to two major subsistence resources. These are favored horticultural soils and aquatic resources. To a large extent, these two resources are important because of the seasonal nature of southeastern Indian subsistence.

The economic cycle in the Southeast consisted of a cold season, during which deer was most important, and a warm season, during which crops were grown. To some extent, southeastern Indians were tied to their horticultural fields in the summer months, and it is during this time that deer are most difficult to locate and capture.

147

Aquatic resources, however, are one form of animal protein available in predictable locations during the summer.

In the Mississippi Valley, it was possible for people to locate their settlements adjacent to both kinds of resources. The best horticultural soils there were found on the fossil levees of broad river floodplains. The levees were often adjacent to oxbow lakes, which contained aquatic resources that became even more accessible as the water level dropped through the summer.

Oconee Valley Settlement

I will show that these two resources are not so juxtaposed in the Georgia Piedmont, but first I need to explain the broader context of Mississippian settlement in the Oconee Valley. Afterward, consideration of the first source of variation from Smith's model—variation due to regional political structure—can begin.

The existence of a single Mississippian polity in the Oconee River drainage was first suggested by Marvin Smith and Stephen Kowalewski (1980). They recognized that four village sites, each with more than a single mound, were located equidistant relative to one another (Figure 23). They also noted that the Shoulderbone site, which had the greatest number of mounds, was centrally located relative to the remaining three. This patterned, evenly spaced distribution of multiple-mound Lamar sites suggested that village location was determined to some extent by political or social factors. This seems even more apparent when the distribution of floodplain soils, usually thought to have been the most powerful environmental determinant of Mississippian site location, is taken into account. Among the four sites, a tremendous disparity exists in the amount of floodplain soils within 10- and 20-kilometer radii of each. In some cases the difference is fifteenfold (Table 6).

Surprisingly, the Shoulderbone site, which was thought to have been the regional capital, is located in a portion of the Oconee Valley with the smallest amount of floodplain soils. Recent work by the LAMAR Institute has enabled a refinement of Smith and Kowalewski's original hypothesis (Williams and Shapiro 1987). With improved chronological data, it is now possible to observe dynamic changes in the configuration of the valley's mound sites over a span of five centuries. These new data add further evidence for social, political, and demographic influences on site location in the valley.

Oconee Valley Resource Distribution

At the broad regional scale, there is good evidence for these extraenvironmental determinants of settlement location, but at a more site-specific scale, environmental factors can also be seen to play an important role. Let's examine the distribution of favored horticultural soils and aquatic resources in the Oconee Valley and then consider the specific use and function of three sites.

The distribution of broad river floodplains in the Piedmont differs from that found in the Mississippi Valley and other Coastal Plain rivers. This reflects certain characteristics of Piedmont geomorphology. Piedmont river floodplains can best be described as segmented. Rivers meander within relatively broad floodplains until they flow over a "nick point," which is an area of more resistant substrata. Nick points in the Piedmont usually occur where the river flows over granitic outcrops. In such areas, the river valley is narrow, and its channel broadens to occupy most of the valley. The channel is shallow, rocky, and filled with rapids, and there is very little bottomland. Shoals may continue for 5 kilometers before the river valley again broadens. Each segment of broad river floodplain that is pinched off at shoals is called a "Boudin valley" (Woodruff and Parizek 1956). The significance of Boudin valley geomorphology is that there may be a great disparity in the amount of bottomland found at different locations along a given

Table 6 Oconee Valley Floodplain Soils

	SHOULDER-BONE	LITTLE RIVER	SCULL SHOALS	SHIN-HOLSER
0–10 km	5.0	11.7	12.5	85.1
Area percent	1.6	3.7	4.0	27.1
10–20 km	4.7	24.4	39.0	111.7
Area percent	0.5	2.6	4.1	11.8
0–20 km	9.7	36.1	51.5	196.8
Area percent	0.8	2.9	4.1	15.7

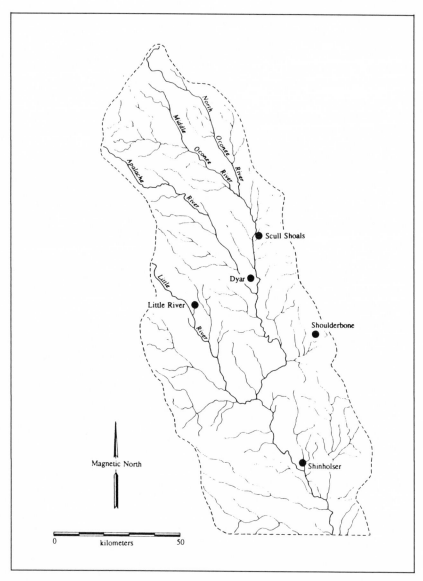

Figure 23. Oconee Valley Mound Sites

river. Unlike the Mississippi Valley, the Piedmont shows a segmented distribution of broad floodplains, with only small pockets
of bottomlands at the shoals.

Another important difference between Piedmont and Coastal
Plain rivers is the absence of true oxbows in the Piedmont. Although backwater aquatic resources may have occasionally been
available, true oxbow lakes are not found in the Piedmont. The
best place to gather aquatic resources in the Piedmont was likely
at the shoals.

Shoals, like oxbows, are reliable locations for gathering aquatic
resources during the summer months. Several characteristics ren-
der them so. In part, the high productivity at shoals is due to a
juxtaposition of microenvironments that are suitable for species
of both slow- and fast-water habitat preference. At shoals, rapid
channels alternate with relatively still pools that lie immediately
upstream. Bottom characteristics include both rocky and sandy
bottoms, and the relatively still pools collect detritus—a major
food source for bottom-feeding fish such as suckers and some cat-
fish (Nelson and Scott 1962).

The turbulence at shoals enhances the stability of water with
respect to dissolved gases (Gameson 1957). This characteristic,
combined with the greater light penetration to the shallow bottoms of broad shoals, accounts for the abundance of attached
algae and moss in swift water (Hynes 1970, 42, 79). These provide
habitat for a variety of larval insects, which attract the more car-
nivorous species of fish, such as bass, bluegills, and sunfish (Peterson 1956). Yet another factor that contributes to the abundance of
fish at shoals is that the large boulders provide resting stations for
fish in rapid water (Hynes 1970, 309). In studies of fish territoriality, it has been demonstrated that where there are many large
stones or artificial barriers, more fish amicably occupy the same
area (Kalleburg 1958).

Like the distribution of broad floodplains, the distribution of
major shoals is determined by underlying geologic structure. In
many areas of the Piedmont, these two kinds of features have
complementary distributions and may be separated by considerable distance. The significance of Piedmont stream morphology
for understanding Mississippian settlement is that two important
warm season resources, the favored horticultural soils of bottomlands and the abundant aquatic resources of the shoals, are often
geographically separate. Gaining access to both kinds of resources

in the Georgia Piedmont requires some variation from the kind of settlement pattern found in the Mississippi Valley, where it is possible to settle adjacent to both.

Bruce Smith describes an idealized Mississippian settlement system as composed of numerous small farmsteads or hamlets. These would be dispersed to occupy the linear bands of favored horticultural soil adjacent to oxbow lakes. These numerous farmsteads would be integrated through their affiliation with a larger village or mound center.

Given these general Mississippian settlement characteristics and given the complementary distribution of favored horticultural soils and aquatic resources in the Georgia Piedmont, several kinds of Mississippian sites can be expected in the Oconee Valley. First, I would expect to find larger, permanently occupied mound and village sites in the upper portions of Boudin valleys and adjacent to the larger tracts of bottomland. Second, I would expect to find numerous small sites at the shoals. Most of these would be aquatic resource extractive sites that were periodically visited by people whose more permanent home was located away from shoals. A third kind of site would be small homesteads located adjacent to the few small pockets of bottomland at the shoals. A description of three such sites follows. The sites were located and excavated by the University of Georgia as part of the Wallace Reservoir Project.

Three Sites

The Dyar site (9GE5) consists of a large platform mound and an associated village of approximately 2.5 hectares (M. Smith 1981). This site, which was part of the first Mississippian village to be established in the Oconee Valley, is located in the largest expanse of river bottomland in the 35-kilometer length of the valley surveyed during the Wallace Reservoir Project (Figure 24). The segment of floodplain contiguous with the Dyar site is more than 7 kilometers long and, in places, over 1.5 kilometers wide. Let's contrast the setting of the Dyar site with that of the numerous small contemporaneous sites located 25 kilometers downstream.

Figure 25 shows a few of the sites at two of the major shoals on the Oconee River. Note the limited amount of bottomland in this portion of the valley. In contrast to the Dyar site, where 57 percent of the area within a 1-kilometer radius was occupied by floodplain soils, only 9 percent of the soils within 1 kilometer of site 9GE175 are bottomlands.

Ogeltree and site 9GE175 are two sites of interest here. The Ogeltree site (9GE153) is located on one of the small pockets of bottomland adjacent to the shoals (Smith, Hally, and Shapiro 1981). This site, covering an area of only 1,600 square meters, showed evidence of a single structure, two hearths, and three burials. While similar in shape to those of the Dyar village, the Ogeltree structure was not as substantial as those from the Dyar site. Its wall posts were smaller, its hearth was irregular in shape, and its floor was not carefully prepared.

A second shoals site, 9GE175, is located among a cluster of boulders adjacent to a low fall in the river channel (Shapiro 1981). The site is extremely small, about 60 square meters in size, and yet midden deposits extended to more than a meter in depth. Unlike the Ogeltree site, 9GE175 showed no evidence of posts, pits, burials, or hearths.

General site characteristics of Dyar, Ogeltree, and 9GE175 suggest that each was an example of three kinds of sites expected, given the complementary distribution of bottomland and aquatic resources in the Piedmont. The Dyar site, located in a large tract of bottomland, was a permanently occupied village. The Ogeltree site, located on a small pocket of bottomland adjacent to shoals, was a small farmstead. Site 9GE175, located adjacent to a low fall at the river's edge, was a seasonally reoccupied camp where aquatic resources were intensively exploited. Detailed comparisons of faunal remains (Table 7) and ceramic vessel forms support these site-function identifications.

Figure 26 shows the relative frequency of bone fragments from aquatic versus terrestrial fauna at each site. The Dyar and Ogeltree sites both show a greater frequency of terrestrial species. By contrast, terrestrial species are poorly represented at site 9GE175. These data are from units screened through 1/4-inch mesh, a method that results in an underrepresentation of aquatic resources. Portions of each site were water-screened through 1/16-inch mesh window screen, but larger sample sizes needed for these intersite comparisons were only available for 1/4-inch screened data (see Shapiro 1983 for a detailed discussion of the faunal analysis).

The faunal data were regrouped to examine another aspect of

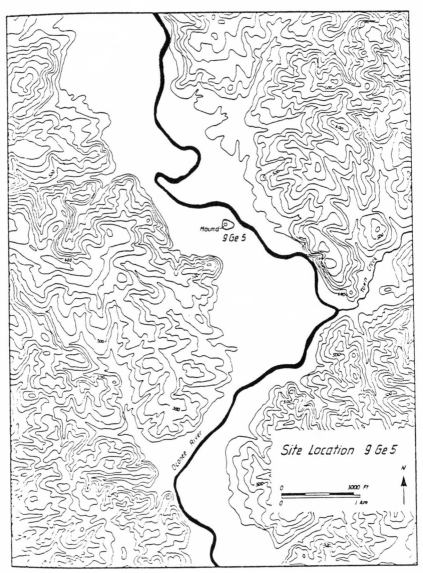

Figure 24. Dyar Site Location

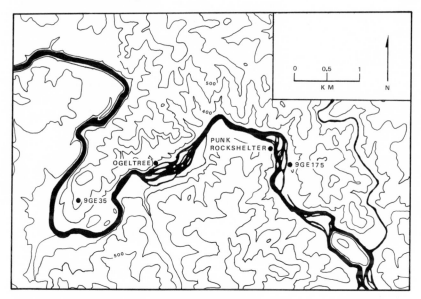

Figure 25. Oconee Valley, Sites near Shoals

site use—site seasonality. Figure 27 shows the relative frequencies of faunal remains from cold versus warm season species. As expected, the permanently occupied Dyar site showed the most balanced representation. In contrast, both site 9GE175 and the Ogeltree site showed a greater representation of warm season species. The apparent warm season occupation of the Ogeltree site was unexpected, because small Mississippian farmsteads known elsewhere appear to have been year-round occupations. Analysis of ceramic vessel forms provided further evidence for the semipermanent nature of site use at Ogeltree.

I have identified several categories of vessel shape in Oconee Valley ceramic assemblages (Shapiro 1984). Among these, cazuelas and jars are two forms for which vessel use can be interpreted with some confidence (Figure 28). Jars are used for storage or for temporary containment. These are relatively tall vessels with a constriction below the rim. Both these characteristics limit access to vessel contents. Jars always have rounded bottoms, a feature that suggests they were not moved around as frequently as the flat-bottomed cazuelas. Jars have flared rims that facilitate pouring

Table 7 Oconee Valley Faunal Remains

	DYAR SITE				OGELTREE SITE				SITE 9GE175			
	#	%	MNI	%MNI	#	%	MNI	%MNI	#	%	MNI	%MNI
BOWFIN (*Amia calva*)	7	O.84	1	2.44	22	1.13	1	1.30	4	0.64	1	1.79
GARFISH (*Lepisosteus* sp.)	2	0.24	1	2.44	30	1.54	7	9.09	72	11.59	13	23.21
CATFISH (*Ictalurus* sp.)	40	4.78	6	14.63	11	0.57	1	1.30	40	6.44	6	10.71
SUCKERS (Catostomidae)	23	2.75	3	7.32	2	0.10	1	1.30	8	1.29	3	5.36
SUNFISHES (*Lepomis* sp.)	7	0.84	3	7.32	9	0.46	2	2.60	19	3.06	4	7.14
BASS (*Micropterus* sp.)	9	1.08	3	7.32								
TOTAL ID FISH	88	10.51	17	41.46	74	3.81	12	15.58	143	23.03	27	48.21
FROG (*Rana* sp.)	3	0.36	1	2.44		0.00		0.00	2	0.32	1	1.79
SNAPPING TURTLE (*Chelydra serpentina*)	1	0.12	1	2.44					7	1.13	1	1.79
MUD/MUSK TURTLES (Kinosternidae)	17	2.03			36	1.85			141	22.71		
MUD TURTLE (*Kinosternon* sp.)	35	4.18	1	2.44	32	1.65	6	7.79				
MUSK TURTLE (*Sternotherus* sp.)	24	2.87	2	4.88	190	9.78	5	6.49	84	13.53	5	16.07
AQUATIC TURTLES (Emydidae)	6	0.72			117	6.02			6	0.97		
COOTER (*Chrysemys* sp.)	7	0.84	1	2.44					20	3.22	2	3.57
BOX TURTLE (*Terrapene carolina*)	57	6.81	2	4.86	1078	55.51	35	45.45	145	23.35	7	12.50
SOFT-SHELLED TURTLE (*Trionyx ferox*)	5	0.60	1	2.44	117	6.02	3	3.90	4	0.64	1	1.79
TOTAL ID TURTLE	152	18.16	8	19.51	1570	80.84	49	63.64	407	65.54	20	35.71
NONVENOMOUS SNAKES (Colubridae)	15	1.79	1	2.44	14	0.72			45	7.41	1	1.79

Table 7 *continued*

	DYAR SITE				OGELTREE SITE				SITE 9GE175			
	#	%	MNI	%MNI	#	%	MNI	%MNI	#	%	MNI	%MNI
PROBABLE MUD SNAKE (*Farancia* sp.)	1	0.12	1	2.44	1	0.05	1	1.30				
VENOMOUS SNAKES (Crotalidae)					12	0.62	1	1.30	6	0.97	1	1.79
TOTAL ID SNAKE	16	1.91	2	4.88	27	1.39	2	2.60	52	8.37	2	3.57
TURKEY (*Meleagris gallopavo*)	45	5.38	2	4.88								
MOURNING DOVE (*Zenaidura macroura*)	1	0.12	1	2.44								
TOTAL ID BIRD	46	5.50	3	7.32	0	0.00	0	0.00	0	0.00	0	0.00
OPOSSUM (*Didelphis virginianus*)					1	0.05	1	1.30	2	0.32	1	1.79
RABBIT (*Sylvilagus* sp.)	27	3.23	2	4.88	2	0.10	1	1.30	1	0.16	1	1.79
EASTERN CHIPMUNK (*Tamias striatus*)	3	0.36	1	2.44								
GRAY SQUIRREL (*Sciurus carolinensis*)	17	2.03	1	2.44	7	0.36	1	1.30				
BEAVER (*Castor canadensis*)					7	0.36	1	1.30	8	1.29	1	1.79
MUSKRAT (*Ondatra zibethica*)					2	0.10	1	1.30	1	0.16	1	1.79
STRIPED SKUNK (*Mephitis mephitis*)					1	0.05	1	1.30				
BOBCAT (*Lynx rufus*)					12	0.62	1	1.30				
RACCOON (*Procyon lotor*)	7	0.84	1	2.44	1	0.05	1	1.30				
WOLF OR DOG (*Canis* sp.)									1	0.16	1	1.79
DEER (*Odocoileus virginianus*)	478	57.11	5	12.20	238	12.26	6	7.79	4	0.64	1	1.79
TOTAL ID MAMMAL	532	63.56	10	24.39	271	13.95	14	18.18	17	2.74	6	10.71
TOTAL ID BONE	837	100	41	100	1942	100	77	100	621	100	56	100

Table 7 Oconee Valley Faunal Remains, *continued*

	DYAR SITE #	%	OGELTREE SITE #	%	SITE 9GE175 #	%
UNID FISH	245		67		157	
UNID TURTLE	348		3101		294	
UNID SNAKE	5		14		12	
UNID BIRD	115		8			
UNID MAMMAL	1087		777		25	
UNID SMALL MAMMAL	32		5			
UNID LARGE MAMMAL	156		86		2	
TOTAL UNID MAMMAL	1275		868		2	
UNID BONE FRAGMENTS	4755		430		85	
	#	%	#	%	#	%
TOTAL (UNID + ID) FISH	333	11.79	141	2.35	300	27.62
TOTAL AMPHIBIAN	3	0.11		0.00	2	0.18
TOTAL TURTLE	500	17.70	4671	77.85	701	64.55
TOTAL SNAKE	21	0.74	41	0.68	64	5.89
TOTAL BIRD	161	5.70	8	0.13		0.00
TOTAL MAMMAL	1807	63.96	1139	18.98	19	1.75
TOTAL BONE IDENT. TO CLASS	2825	100.00	6000	100.00	1086	100.00

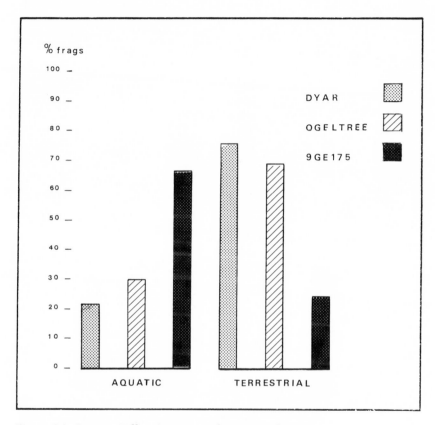

Figure 26. Oconee Valley Aquatic and Terrestrial Fauna

and allow the fastening of a flexible cover. Unlike cazuelas, which are cooking vessels, large jars, with a rim diameter greater than 30 centimeters, show little evidence of exterior sooting.

Because these vessels are related to storage, the relative abundance and size of jars at each site should provide evidence for site permanence. The relative frequencies of vessel shapes at each site supported hypotheses concerning storage and, by inference, the permanence of each site's occupation. Jars made up 28 percent of the total vessel assemblage from the permanent Dyar village, 15 percent at the seasonally occupied Ogeltree farmstead, and 12 percent at the aquatic resource extractive site, 9GE175.

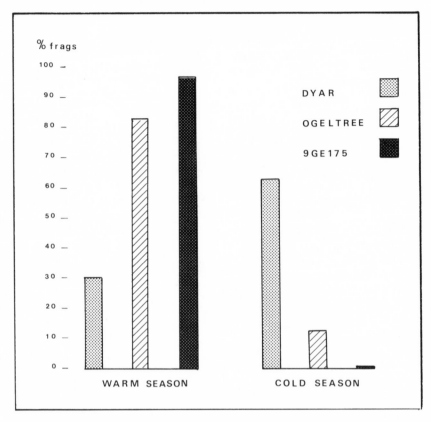

Figure 27. Oconee Valley Cold versus Warm Season Fauna

The relative sizes of jars from each site tell a similar story.
Size-frequency histograms in Figure 29 show that only at the Dyar
site were there storage jars with rim diameters greater than 30
centimeters.

Detailed analyses of site plan, faunal remains, and ceramic vessels support the identification of the Dyar site as a permanently
occupied village, site 9GE175 as a seasonally reoccupied encampment where aquatic resources were intensively exploited, and the
Ogeltree site as a small farmstead occupied during the warm season. These sites occur where they are expected. The Dyar site is
in a broad expanse of floodplain, the Ogeltree site at one of the

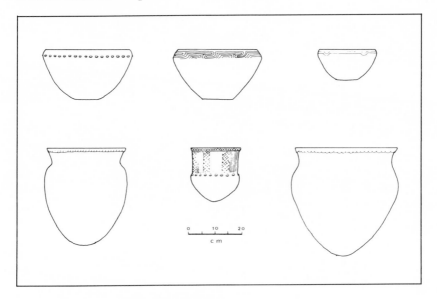

Figure 28. Oconee Valley Vessel Forms

few small pockets of bottomland adjacent to shoals, and site
9GE175 adjacent to a low fall, also at the shoals.

Summary

At a larger scale of analysis, there is evidence for social and political determinants of site location in the Oconee Valley. At a
site-specific scale, however, the influence of environmental variables can be easily seen. When environmental differences between
the Mississippi Valley and the Georgia Piedmont are taken into
account, Bruce Smith's general model of Mississippian settlement
provides a useful framework for understanding the use and function of specific sites. The major point of this study is simple.
Rather than discount the applicability of environmental models
to environmentally different regions, it is more interesting to try
to understand the reasons for deviation from the model. If regional variations are taken into account, general environmental

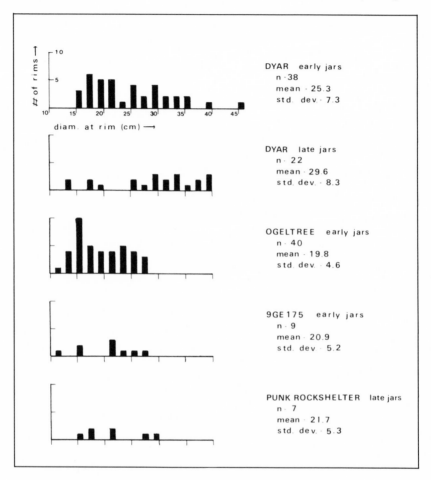

Figure 29. Oconee Valley Jar Size Frequencies

models can provide useful insights, or at least good hypotheses, about the use and function of different kinds of sites within a single settlement system.

8. Paired Towns

Mark Williams and Gary Shapiro

Problem

The summer 1985 excavations at the Scull Shoals site (9GE4) generated an interesting question with both chronological and cultural implications (Williams 1988). Scull Shoals is on the east bank of the Oconee River in Greene County, Georgia, and is the most northerly of the mound centers suggested by Marvin Smith and Stephen Kowalewski (1980) as forming the "Oconee Province." Research was first undertaken there in 1983 and consisted of mapping, determining site size and location, and test excavating in the village (Williams 1984). The site chronology was crudely determined, but extensive early nineteenth-century plowing and flooding damage to the village made this difficult.

The 1985 excavations there were designed, among other things, to more accurately determine the internal site chronology. This was accomplished by excavations in the two mounds. Mound B, a 3-meter-high platform, had a large pothole in its northern edge that provided a convenient way to acquire a profile of half the mound. Sherds were recovered from most of the levels. The most useful excavation in terms of site chronology was a 2-meter excavation square placed on the northeast edge of the 11-meter-high Mound A. This yielded stratified deposits to a depth of over 3 meters.

We could not fit the resulting Scull Shoals ceramic sequence into the existing Oconee Valley chronology Smith developed at the Dyar site, only 16 kilometers to the south (M. Smith 1981), without modification. After refining the valley chronology, it became clear that neither Scull Shoals nor the Dyar site showed clear evidence of occupation during all phases. This was totally unexpected. The general sequence at the two centers is as follows: the Dyar site has a heavy occupation during the late Etowah Stillhouse phase (A.D. 1100–1225), but the Scull Shoals site does not. The later Savannah period Scull Shoals phase (1225–1350) is represented by a heavy occupation at the Scull Shoals site. The bulk of Mound B there appears to have been made during that period. The Dyar site was apparently not occupied during this time period. During the early Lamar Duvall phase (1350–1450), the Dyar site was intensively used, and the Scull Shoals site appears to have been either abandoned or only lightly occupied. Finally, both sites were occupied during the Iron Horse phase (1450–1540) and Dyar phase (1540–1590) of the Lamar period.

In short, these two nearby sites (16 kilometers) appear to have been alternately occupied from the late Etowah period through the early Lamar period, a span of about 250 years. Why were these sites repeatedly abandoned and reoccupied in turn?

Paired Sites

In a brief examination of the archaeological record for Georgia, it appears that there are a number of what might be called "paired" mound centers. These are mound sites that are in the range of only 8 to 16 kilometers apart. Included in this category are Neisler and Hartley-Posey on the Flint River at the fall line; Lamar and Stubbs on the Ocmulgee at the fall line; Tugalo and Chauga on the upper Savannah; Park and Avery on the Chattahoochee; Hollywood and Silver Bluff on the Savannah; Beaverdam and Rembert also on the Savannah; Red Lake and Lawton also on the Savannah; and Rood's Landing and Singer on the Chattahoochee (Figure 30). There are probably many other such pairs of mound sites in the Southeast.

Traditional understanding of such close sites is that they represent nearby and probably allied towns within a single small chiefdom. This may explain some of these paired sites, but perhaps not all. Stated in the form of a hypothesis, the occupation at some adjacent Mississippian mound centers may be alternating rather than cocontinuous. This form of alternating settlement, as illustrated by the Dyar and Scull Shoals sites, may be quite common in much of the late prehistoric Southeast.

Potential Explanations

There are surely a number of possible reasons for such a pattern.
These can be divided into those that have an obvious cultural material explanation and those that do not. Material explanations include the local exhaustion of some important resource, with atten-
dant movement of the town. Potential critical resources include
firewood, agricultural soil quality, and wild food resources. Other
potential explanations include military conquest and the social consequences of chiefly succession. The rest of this paper will examine
these potential explanations in greater depth.

Soil Exhaustion

The question of soil exhaustion must be dealt with depending
on whether or not the agricultural soil around a given site was in
the river floodplain or in the uplands. Most, but not all, of the
mound sites listed above are in or adjacent to large areas of floodplain. Given the high natural fertility of these soils and the high
rate of nutrient renewal through flooding, the likelihood of total
exhaustion seems low. In historic times, these soils have been used
in some cases for well over 100 years and still produced large crops.

The use of nonfloodplain soils is another matter entirely. Although there has been doubt in the past that these were used at
all by Southeast Indians, it is becoming increasingly clear, particularly in the Oconee Valley, that upland soils were used in some
cases for agriculture. Upland soils are slow to renew themselves,
and some form of shifting cultivation would have been essential.

Wood Exhaustion

There has been an implied, but unstated, assumption for years
in the East that, because of the very nature of the eastern "Woodlands," wood could not have been a limiting resource for Indian
groups. While this must be true on a large scale, it may well be
untrue on the local level.

One of the best-stated examples of this is presented by Heidenreich with reference to the Huron. He first estimates the wood in

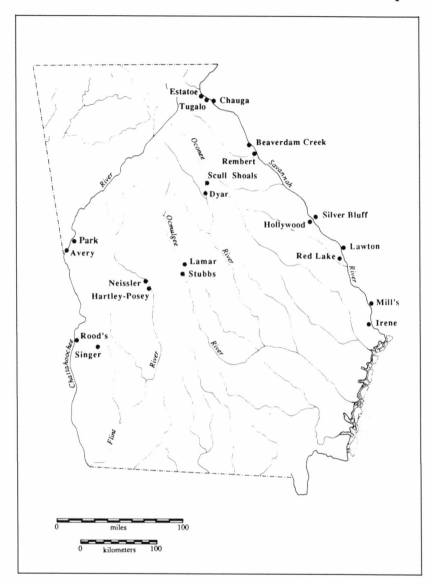

Figure 30. Paired Mound Sites in Georgia

the form of trees that would be required to construct a Huron village and the area needed for fields (Heidenreich 1971, 152–53, 174). He then discusses the patterns of firewood gathering (women gathering limbs and sticks of woods that do not smoke heavily when burned) and observes: "With gradual land clearing and yearly burning, one could reason that by eight to twelve years good firewood had to be obtained from areas beyond the cleared fields. Since all the firewood was carried to the village on the backs of the women, this could have become quite a troublesome job once the forested areas were more than a mile from the village" (125).

He concludes that this decreasing availability of firewood led, along with soil exhaustion, to a movement of Huron villages every 8 to 12 years (216). He further adds that the location of the new town must not be in a climax forest situation but in a secondary one of 30 to 60 years of age (63). This is because trees of the proper sizes for constructing houses and stockades would be available in sufficient quantity only in secondary forests near the new town. Finally, since women are the gatherers of the firewood, Heidenreich points out that as the distance they had to go to procure firewood increased, so would the difficulty of adequately protecting them from kidnap by roving bands of enemy Indians (215).

There are clear environmental differences between the Huron area in southeastern Canada and the Lamar area in the southeastern United States. There is more hardwood in the Southeast, and the winters are significantly milder. This of course leads to less need for winter heating wood. Also, the houses of the Huron used much more wood in their construction than did those of the Southeast. All this implies that wood was perhaps not as critical a resource among the Indians of the Southeast compared to the Huron farther to the north. This does not imply that wood was never a limiting resource in the Southeast. In fact, there is some historic evidence to the contrary.

In 1657, the chief of the Apalachee town of Bacuqua met with Spanish officials in order to request that a mission be placed at his town. At the same time he wanted to move the location of the town because:

> this village, where they are settled, is ancient, and as its environs
> are cleared out, with the results that it does not produce the fruit
> that are sown and does not have firewood, and, that, in view of the

fact that it does not have a church or principal lodge or house-of-importance, as do the other villages, he grants them permission to move and settle half a league distant from this place in order to have sufficient lands (Hann 1986, 90–91).

This reference makes it clear that the Apalachee towns normally moved from time to time and that the lack of firewood was one of the important reasons for such a move.

Swanton does not list many references to movement of towns or to details of firewood use. There is, however, a relevant account from John Smith on the Powhatan. In discussing some small communities of different sizes, John Smith says that "neare their habitations is little small wood, or old trees on the ground, by reason of their burning of them for fire. So that a man may gallop a horse amongst these woods any waie . . . " (Swanton 1946, 630). This implies that, while the small trees and fallen limbs are gone, there is still a "woods" present, probably of large trees—likely the large hardwoods such as oaks and hickories.

There is much logic in not girdling and killing these large trees. These trees are constant producers of nuts and firewood while they are alive. We know both historically and archaeologically that nuts, particularly hickory nuts, were important sources of food and fuel for Mississippian agricultural societies. To kill all of the large hardwood trees in the vicinity of a town would be shortsighted and inefficient.

John R. White (1983) has recently presented an analysis of wood depletion resulting from the use of blast furnaces in the nineteenth-century United States. His model shows increasing distance to usable wood as concentric circles of ever-greater diameter away from the center point. A model of this sort can be applied to the situation for Indian towns also. To more explicitly examine the need for wood in late Mississippian towns, particularly in the Georgia Piedmont, we have developed a model for wood use and implemented it in the form of a spreadsheet-style computer program.

For those not familiar with such a program, a spreadsheet program is one designed as a large empty table with rows and columns. Individual cells in the table can have data (numbers), text (labels), or mathematical formulas entered into them. Cells with formulas can calculate and display the results of a formula, such as the sum of two other cells divided by yet another cell's numeric value. The calculated and displayed value in the cell with the formula may then be used as data for calculations in other cells, with their own formulas if desired. Spreadsheets can be used to build a model that automatically recalculates many values upon varying a single variable of interest and ultimately allows an examination of the effect of that variable on various outcomes.

Our model includes as variables: (1) estimates of wood necessary to build individual houses and (2) palisades, (3) the yearly maintenance percentage for these, (4) the fuel needed for cooking and (5) heating, (6) the quantity of wood used for tools and utensils, (7) the number of appropriate trees available per unit area, (8) the rate of regrowth of trees in areas already stripped of wood, (9) the population of the town, and (10) the time the town was occupied. The result of the model is an estimate of the distance people would have had to go for usable wood. We have run this program using several sets of assumptions, and accordingly, the results are varied, but some things are fairly clear.

First, the quantity of wood used is far more dependent upon the use of wood for cooking and heating than for construction, perhaps by more than a factor of ten. Abrams (1986) has recently determined that this is also the case around the Maya center of Copán in Honduras. Second, and more importantly, this analysis shows that after two or three generations, the distance necessary to obtain wood may grow to 1.5 kilometers or more. The energy necessary to obtain fuel could likely reach the point of diminishing return, and pressure could mount to move the village, as it did for the Huron and the Apalachee town of Bacuqua. Interestingly, it would take a fallow period of only about two generations (perhaps 50 to 75 years) to renew the forests around an abandoned town and thus make its reoccupation possible. As Heidenreich (1971, 215–16) pointed out, the secondary forest developed around an abandoned village would make it attractive for resettlement because of the new availability of logs of the proper size for construction. He also points out that if an entire town burned for whatever reason, and particularly if it had been there for a while, it would be difficult to rebuild it in the same location because of the lack of appropriate building materials. This would almost certainly result in the movement of the town.

Animal Depletion

The potential exhaustion of animals used for food does not seem to be a major reason for moving a town a distance of only 8 to 16 kilometers. This is true even though the most important of these animals, the deer, has a limited individual home range. Deer also have tremendous reproductive potential. The Indians are known routinely to have gone long distances on deer hunts, undoubtedly farther than 16 kilometers. Other animals were less important sources of meat, and while they were perhaps more prone to localized depletion, it seems unlikely, for example, that a town would have to move for lack of opossum close at hand.

Fish are basically a constantly renewable resource at the level of environmental disturbance of which these societies were capable. Short-term decreases in fish populations adjacent to sites may have occurred, particularly if poisoning or fish weirs were used, but this does not appear to have been a likely source of pressure for moving a town. Likewise, shellfish might have been overexploited, but it does not appear likely that these were important as food sources in the Georgia Piedmont until the late prehistoric period anyway (Rudolph 1983).

Although it represents the opposite of exhaustion, Heidenreich (1971, 214–15) suggests another possible cause for the movement of Huron villages based upon a single group of animals—rats and mice. Of the Huron, he states: "After six to ten years of continuous occupation the villages must have accumulated a substantial population of mice. Except for their dogs, the Huron had no way of ridding themselves of these rodents. In some Central American countries rodents and other pests have been cited as causes for land abandonment and there is reason to suppose that the situation in Huronia was no different." Mississippian towns, with their stored corn and openly discarded food remains, must have had many such pests, not to mention infestations of insects for which the region is famous today. To paraphrase Heidenreich, there is no reason to suppose that the situation in the Southeast was any different from that in Central America.

Wild Plant Depletion

Wild plants used for food included many kinds of nuts, herbs, greens, and berries. Complete exhaustion of these resources seems unlikely, and even if they were, the lack of these would not seem to have been sufficient reason for moving an entire town. In all this, however, it must be admitted that we presently do not have adequate data to weigh the relative importance of wild plants or their potential for local depletion.

Military Conquest

This is intended to include within-valley military conquest of one town by another nearby town (approximately 16 kilometers or less). The conquered town might have been abandoned and then later, after a hiatus of unknown length, been reoccupied. Such a situation must have occurred in the Southeast at one time or another when two chiefdom centers were, for whatever historical reasons, this close together. To postulate this as a widespread and recurrent process, however, is less than satisfying.

Chiefly Succession

Another possible explanation for the pattern involves the concept of chiefly succession. Historical accounts make it clear that chiefly power within a region did not always reside at the same town. There is much evidence to this effect in the De Soto narratives, even from the Oconee Valley. As Garcilaso de la Vega relates, when De Soto's army was in central Georgia at the town of the powerful chief Cofa (Ocute in the other accounts), the expedition left "for a province called Cofaqui which belonged to the Cacique Cofa's elder brother, a man who was richer and more powerful than his kinsman" (Varner and Varner 1962, 273). The original Spanish words make it clear that Cofaqui was actually a sibling of the chief of Cofa (Ocute).

We learn from the account of Ranjel that " . . . chief Cofaqui was an old man, with a full beard, and his nephew ruled for him . . . " (Bourne 1904, 91). While on the road from Cofa (Ocute) to Cofaqui, Cofa "commanded an Indian nobleman to go in advance and inform his brother Cofaqui that the Spaniards were coming to his land and that since they deserved favorable treatment, he begged his brother to accept them peacefully and serve them as he himself had done" (Varner and Varner 1962, 274). De Soto and his army stayed a few days at Cofaqui before heading east for Cofitachequi. They were accompanied by many Indians from the province of Cofaqui, who were led by the war chief Patofa, a younger man from another town who was apparently subject to Cofaqui.

Clearly, when De Soto's army arrived in this province, chiefly power was in transition. The chief, Cofaqui, was an old man, and it was not clear to the De Soto chroniclers who the next chief in the valley would be. The question is: How could the transfer of chiefly power lead to the abandonment or near-abandonment of a mound site?

A chief who has recently acquired or inherited regional power must decide whether to rule from his own village where he was viceroy or to rule from the old regional head town. There would be many pluses and minuses to either decision. If we assume that he did decide to move to the old capital, perhaps because it was historically the sacred home of his original lineage, there are several possible outcomes for the town he leaves behind. These depend upon the percentage of the town's population represented by the chief, his wives, children, and retainers. If they were only a small part of it and thus most of the people stayed behind, there would be little archaeological record of the town's population decrease. If, on the other hand, the chief and his retinue made up a large part of the population, then the size of the town would have dropped significantly. The town might even appear to have been abandoned.

Now we have the key to understanding how chiefly succession may account for the pattern of paired mound sites. Contrary to the conventional wisdom, late prehistoric mound sites may have been populated by only a select subset of the region's population. Rather than containing a cross section of society, perhaps mound sites were occupied only by the chief and his retinue.

This is not so farfetched. In African chiefdoms in Cameroon and Senegal, the chief's compound consisted of the chief's abode, those of his wives—one per wife—and slaves quarters. All of this was usually surrounded by a wall and, depending upon the number of wives he had, could be of considerable size. Indeed, in many cases, Cameroon chiefdom "towns" consisted exclusively of the chief's compound. The common people lived in small huts arranged throughout the countryside (Brain 1972; Kofele-Kale 1981; Ritzenthaler 1966; Reyher 1952). Given the relatively small size of mound centers in much of the Lamar area, it is possible that some of them were not "towns" as we have come to think of them. This apparently was the case for the eighteenth-century Natchez (Neitzel 1965, 67).

These African chiefdoms appear to have had many similarities to those that were in Georgia at the time of De Soto. They, however, were reasonably intact until even the middle of this century and should form an important analogue for the study of Lamar chiefdoms in the future.

Conclusions

The movement of Indian towns is no surprise to those who have studied the maps of the eighteenth-century Southeast. There are many cases of entire towns moving, and the map makers of the historic period were constantly confused by the movements of named towns. The Cherokee town of Estatoe had at least three locations between 1690 and 1760, for example. This pattern was not likely one that originated in the turbulent historic Southeast but may well have developed out of earlier patterns.

The delimiting of alternating occupations at adjacent sites is difficult at best, but we should look for it with fine stratigraphic excavations, particularly on the dumps on the northeast edges of mounds (Williams and Shapiro 1985). We believe archaeologists should assume that there *are* differences between the ceramic sequences at nearby mound sites until proven otherwise. If this is true, there is an important chronological implication to note. A ceramic chronology developed at only one of the mound centers in a valley or area will be incomplete because it is filled with gaps. Excavations must be done at all of the major sites in an area and the results then collated to develop a complete regional chronology. This has proved to be the case in the Oconee Valley.

Even though we have gone to great lengths to posit a relationship between chiefly succession and the apparent abandonment of paired mound sites, we see no reason to exclude the role of material considerations in the relocation of towns. Surely a new chief, in deciding whether or not to move his court, would seriously weigh the material consequences of his decision. Among these material considerations, we are most impressed by the importance of firewood as a local limiting resource. Firewood exhaustion is likely far more important than has been traditionally thought. Finally, as we continue to learn more about the Indians who once ruled the Southeast, we must truly accept that their societies were highly dynamic, and we must leave behind the old notions of the Indians at peace with their world.

9. The Rise, Transformation, and Fall of Apalachee
A Case Study of Political Change in a Chiefly Society

John F. Scarry

Introduction

When the first European explorers entered the southeastern United States in the early sixteenth century, they encountered a flourishing native population. Accounts of expeditions to the southeast (for example, the reports of the Narváez and De Soto expeditions—Bandelier 1964; Buckingham Smith 1968; Varner and Varner 1962) speak of kings and princesses, caciques and micos. They describe mounds with temples, symbols of office, and elaborate costumes worn by important personages. They talk of chiefs, warriors, and farmers. And they mention agricultural fields and battlefields. It is clear from these accounts that the aboriginal societies of the Southeast were politically complex, militarily powerful, and materially wealthy.

At contact, there were many distinct and independent societies in the Southeast. The early historical accounts suggest that most southeastern societies (at least those north of peninsular Florida) shared significant cultural features and were, in many respects, quite similar to each other. Archaeological research has reinforced this picture of cultural similarity during the early historic period and traced it back into the late prehistoric period. Over wide areas of the Southeast, native peoples constructed pyramidal earthen mounds, decorated their pottery with similar motifs, shared iconographic forms, and exchanged the work of individual craftsmen. These commonalities have led archaeologists to group the late societies of the Southeast together as the Mississippian societies.

The criteria used to identify a Mississippian society have changed dramatically over the years as our research interests and theoretical sophistication have changed. Current definitions stress political or-

175

ganization and subsistence economy as key characteristics. For example, Peebles and Kus (1977) define Mississippian societies as those late prehistoric and early historic aboriginal societies possessing agricultural subsistence economies and hierarchical decision-making organizations. Definitions by Griffin (1984) and Bruce Smith (1984b) echo this emphasis. In this paper, I focus on Mississippian political organization; for political hierarchies are among the most intriguing features of the Mississippian societies.

The Mississippian societies were chiefdoms—societies where access to political power was limited. Political positions were few in number. While not everyone could gain political office, there were still fewer positions than people qualified to fill them. The individuals with access to political power and offices formed elite classes that were clearly distinct from the bulk of the populations. From both archaeological and ethnohistorical data, it is clear that the elite classes had privileges and commanded resources denied other members of the societies.

On scales of organizational complexity, chiefdoms hold an intermediate position, lying between band societies and complex states and empires. Many would assign them to an intermediate evolutionary position as well. In fact, Robert Carneiro (1981) has argued that chiefdoms are necessary precursors of pristine states and that we cannot hope to understand the origins of states until we understand the evolution of chiefdoms. Regardless of one's opinion of the role of chiefdoms in the origins of the state, it is obvious that such societies as the Mississippian polities of the Southeast can tell us much about the evolution of social and political complexity, about the operation of hierarchical societies, and, ultimately, about the processes that produced our own society.

Expectations of Change in Complex Chiefdoms

In this paper, I consider one model of change in chiefly societies and its implications for explaining the archaeological and ethnohistorical record of the Apalachee, a Mississippian society of northwest Florida. The model I examine was proposed by Henry Wright (1984). Using a combination of processual and structural terms, Wright presents a definition of chiefdoms and a discussion of the evolution of complex chiefdoms that addresses both their origins and their later evolutionary trajectories.

Wright's definition differs somewhat from the better-known definitions of Fried (1967) and Service (1962). Like Fried and Service, Wright considers chiefdoms to be societies where few individuals have access to political power. He further specifies, however, that these few form a segment of society that is distinct from the rest of the populace but that is not internally specialized. That is, there are formal political positions, but those positions are generalized, not functionally variable and specialized. There are chiefs, but not bureaucrats, legislators, judges, or presidents.

Following Earle (1978) and Steponaitis (1978, 419–21), Wright makes a distinction between simple and complex chiefdoms. In simple chiefdoms, leaders come from a local hereditary elite, and there is generally only one political level above the local community. In complex chiefdoms, political control is exercised by individuals drawn from an elite class that crosscuts local communities. Within this class, individuals compete for offices, but they stand together in opposition to the masses. Complex chiefdoms have at least two political levels above the local community.

If the productive system supporting a simple chiefdom can sustain that society, Wright suggests, intermarriages and disputes among the ranking families will both multiply and disperse claimants to office. Nobles will compete for offices to which they have a legal claim but no local connection. Each family within the chiefly class will have widespread marriage ties with other elite, forming alliance networks that are unlike those of commoners. The elite will be more closely linked to each other than they will be to their subjects.

In competition for offices, the elite will seek to raise their relative status by emphasizing "geographically distant prestige links or temporally distant divine links" (Wright 1984, 50). To demonstrate these connections, they might use exotic sumptuary goods derived from far-flung exchange networks, for, as Tilley (1982) points out, ideological forms of manipulation are among the strongest forms of legitimation of the social order. For successful office seekers, the claims to cosmic power these links supposedly support would serve to bolster authority. As competition among the elite inflates claims to power, the gulf between the chiefly class and commoners will increase. Over time, there will be less need for the elite to return value for the goods they receive from commoners. Systems of reciprocity and redistribution will be transformed into tribute mobilization. Once a flow to tribute is initiated, it will increase the power and authority of the chief, allow him to become more than first among equals, and make other officeholders permanent political and ritual subordinates.

The tenure of a successful chief will be marked by an upward flow of consumables and status-related craft goods. These he will keep for his own use, distribute to his subordinates, or exchange for exotica (over which he can maintain some monopoly) from the rulers of other systems. To maintain his authority over the lesser elite, the chief must control the distribution of those goods that establish or verify authority, thus making potential rivals dependent on him. Any diminution of the distribution of such items will, of course, produce resentment among subchiefs and lesser elite. Confronted with shortages, successful chiefs will reorganize production or increase their income by seizing productive capacity from their neighbors. Unsuccessful chiefs face secession, rebellion, or assassination by nobles with rival claims to chiefly office. Whatever the specifics, people are killed, political relations break down, and the building process starts anew.

If Wright's model is accurate, complex chiefdoms will show a characteristic pattern of political centralization and decentralization through time. There will be brief periods of breakdown every generation or so: successional disputes, minor rebellions, and small wars. Region-wide rebellions, civil wars, and the replacement of one chiefly line by another will occur less frequently, maybe after long and successful dynasties during which chiefly families have multiplied and segmented. These major breakdowns should be evident in the destruction or abandonment of great centers or by changes in traditional chiefly symbolism.

In the following pages, I take a brief look at some archaeological and ethnohistorical data on the Apalachee and their ancestors and see how these data can be informed by Wright's model. At the outset, I want to stress that this is not a test of that model. To evaluate Wright's construct, we would need more and better data than I bring to bear in this paper.

The Apalachee Data: Centralization and Decentralization

The Apalachee polity of northern Florida was among the richest and most powerful of the aboriginal societies encountered by the

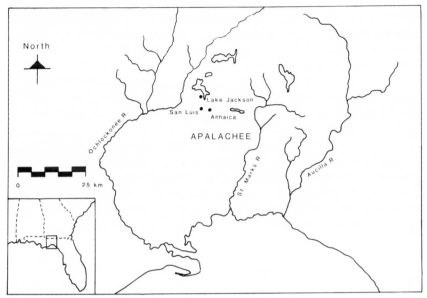

Figure 31. Northern Florida Ethnic Areas

early European explorers of the Southeast (Figure 31). Ethnohistorical accounts indicate that the Apalachee possessed a hierarchical
political organization with hereditary offices and clear status differences between the high-ranking elite and the bulk of the population
(Varner and Varner 1962; Hann 1987a). The Apalachee polity was
clearly a complex chiefdom during the sixteenth and seventeenth
centuries. Archaeological evidence suggests that the Apalachee's
ancestors were part of a major southeastern polity for hundreds of
years before contact and that, like their sixteenth-century descendants, they were organized as a complex chiefdom (Jones 1982;
Payne 1981 and 1982; Scarry 1984, 379–99, and 1987; Scarry and
Payne 1986).

For our purposes, the story of the Apalachee begins about A.D.
1100 with the emergence of the Lake Jackson phase (Scarry 1987).
It ends in 1704 when the Apalachee and their Spanish masters fled
the province following the raids of James Moore and his Creek allies
(Boyd 1951; Bushnell 1979; Covington 1972; Jones 1972). Between
these dates, we can distinguish three sequential manifestations of
Apalachee society: the Lake Jackson phase, the Velda phase, and

the San Luis phase (Scarry 1984, 379–99). Two of the presently defined phases, the Lake Jackson and Velda, were independent chiefdoms; the other, the San Luis phase, was a subordinate polity controlled by the Spaniards.

Current research on protohistoric and historic period Apalachee sites promises to refine this tripartite chronology. Significant sites now being studied include: the Martin site, a portion of Anhaica Apalachee (the sixteenth-century capital of Apalachee) containing the 1539–40 winter encampment of the De Soto expedition (Calvin Jones and Charles Ewen 1987); the Patale site, an Apalachee mission dating to the period 1633–47 (Jones et al. 1987); and the San Luis site, the late seventeenth-century capital of Apalachee province (Shapiro 1987). Analyses of the material cultures from these well-dated contexts should allow us to subdivide the Velda and San Luis phases.

The Lake Jackson phase is the first recognizable Apalachee system. I believe that it existed from the twelfth century into the fifteenth century. For much of its existence it was a complex chiefdom. Two lines of evidence, drawn from settlement pattern and mortuary data, lead to this view of Lake Jackson phase political structure.

The Lake Jackson phase had a well-developed settlement hierarchy with at least four classes of settlement (Payne 1981 and 1982; Scarry 1984, 383–84; Scarry and Payne 1986). At the bottom of the hierarchy were small farmsteads with one or more family dwellings. Above the farmsteads were hamlets with several dwellings and a larger structure that may have served some civic function. Above the hamlets were minor centers, each possessing a pyramidal mound. These were undoubtedly the seats of lesser elite—subordinate chiefs controlling a portion of the Lake Jackson phase polity. At the top of the hierarchy stood the paramount center, Lake Jackson. This site possessed seven mounds and was larger and more complex than the subordinate centers.

Mortuary data from Lake Jackson phase contexts are limited, but those that do exist reflect a social hierarchy consistent with a chiefly organization. At the Winewood site (Jones and Penman 1973), several individuals were found buried in refuse-filled pits thought to lie near a late Lake Jackson phase farmstead. These individuals were either unaccompanied by grave goods or were found with utilitarian ceramics. At the Borrow Pit site, a hamlet, several burials were found inside a large structure thought to be a council house (Calvin

Jones, personal communication, 1987). At the paramount center, Lake Jackson, elite burials were excavated from a small pyramidal mound (Jones 1982). These burials were spatially segregated and had burial programs that differed qualitatively and quantitatively from those of lower-ranking individuals.

The elite burials from Mound 3 at Lake Jackson were accompanied by grave goods that provide valuable clues about how the Lake Jackson phase society operated. The goods included copper and greenstone celts, shell and pearl beads, engraved shell gorgets, and repoussé copper plates and ornaments—specialized craft items, symbols of office, and parts of uniforms. They were clearly sumptuary goods, intended to identify the chiefs, remind others of the (presumably divine?) source of their power, and reinforce the distinctions between chief and subject. Many were manufactured outside the Lake Jackson chiefdom or were made from nonlocal raw materials; they suggest that the rulers of the Lake Jackson chiefdom participated in a prestige economy (sensu Frankenstein and Rowlands 1978) that included the elite of other systems.

The burials from Mound 3 also provide information about changes in the Lake Jackson chiefdom. Several chronological trends are evident in the distribution of grave goods (Table 8). First, it appears that the absolute amount of copper accompanying burials increased through time. Later burials contained more copper objects than the earlier burials. Unfortunately, we do not have a measure of the mass of copper accompanying any of the burials. Second, later burials contain items—copper celts, engraved shell gorgets, and copper headdress elements—not found in earlier burials. Lastly, celts and copper plates, which were found throughout the mound, were found in separate burials in the earlier mound stages and together in later burials.

In general, I would argue that the Mound 3 data are consistent with a picture of increasingly centralized political authority during the Lake Jackson phase. The increase in the number of copper artifacts and perhaps in the amount of copper accompanying the burials might indicate that the chief's ability to acquire and retain exotic sumptuary goods increased through time. It might also indicate inflation, as competition among members of the elite class caused chiefs to need more and more exotica to support their claims to office. If celts and copper plates mark two different offices, a suggestion not inconsistent with findings at other Mississippian centers (e.g., Moundville [Peebles 1978] and Spiro [Brown 1971]), their later

Table 8 Apalachee Grave Goods Distribution

Mound Stage	Burial	Age	Sex	Beads	Copper Plate	Copper Ornaments	Shell Gorget	Celts	
								Stone	Copper
1 or	K1	A	M	X	X	X			X
post 1	K2	A	?	X	X	X	X		X
	K3	?	?	?		?			?
	K4	A	?	X	X		X		X
	K5	A	?	?			X		
	K6	A	?	?					X
	1	M-O	M	X	X			X	X
	3	Y	F	X					X
	4		?	?					X
2	10	M	M	X	X	?			
3	K9	Y	F	X		X		?	
4-7	16	O	F	X	X				
	5	M	M					X	
8	13	A	M	X	X				
	14	C	?	X					
	11	M-O	M	X					
9	15	M	F						
	7	M	M	X	X				
10	2	M	M	X				X	
11	6	A	M	X					
?	17	?	?						
	18	Y	?						

*Coding for skeletal ages: O - Older adult 45 years old; M - Middle-aged adult 30-45 years old; Y - Young adult 20-30 years old; C - child.

association might indicate the consolidation of offices in a single individual. If so, it would suggest that chiefly authority increased.

The transition from the Lake Jackson phase to the Velda phase is marked by dramatic changes in the archaeological record, although there are clear indications of cultural continuity. The capital of the system shifted from the Lake Jackson site to historic Anhaica (the Martin site and its environs) some 5 miles to the southeast. The major mound centers were abandoned (or at least the Lake Jackson and Velda centers were). We have no evidence that new mound construction was undertaken at Anhaica. New pottery types appeared and earlier types disappeared (see Scarry 1985). Vessel forms changed. Nevertheless, there are clear indications of continuity in both ceramics and in settlement location.

This transition can be viewed as an example of the major breakdowns described in Wright's model. The abandonment of the mound centers and the apparent absence of new mound construction indicate that there was a significant change in the allocation of the surplus labor controlled by the chiefs. The end of mound burial for the high elite points to significant changes in the symbolic expression of social rank and political position. It is also possible, since several major centers involved in the Southeastern Ceremonial Complex exchange system appear to have collapsed at roughly this time, that many of the Southeastern Ceremonial Complex items so prominent in Mound 3 were no longer used as high-status markers. If true, this would imply significant changes in political symbolism or the abandonment or collapse of the networks that supplied the status markers of the earlier rulers. Changes in the ceramic assemblage also suggest a shift in external alliances and exchange networks. All these events point to the replacement of one ruling faction by another.

Despite the social disruptions undoubtedly associated with this dramatic change, the Apalachee polity did not completely disintegrate. The Velda phase was a complex chiefdom when Europeans first entered the region and was among the richest and most powerful societies in the Southeast. In fact, the chroniclers of the De Soto expedition used the Apalachee as a standard of comparison even after they reached the lower Mississippi Valley (see, for instance, Elvas's description of Nilco in Buckingham Smith [1968, 136]).

We do not know what impact the Narváez and De Soto expeditions had on the Apalachee. The Apalachee acquitted themselves well militarily, but we know that one important consequence of European contact was the introduction of diseases into native populations (M. Smith 1984). If the Apalachee were decimated by disease in the sixteenth century (and it would be surprising if they were not, given the five-month stay of the De Soto expedition at Anhaica); the authority of the chiefs would have been severely weakened.

The Apalachee's attitude toward the Spaniards changed markedly during the sixteenth and seventeenth centuries. In the sixteenth century, the Narváez and De Soto expeditions met strong military resistance. But at the beginning of the seventeenth century, some Velda phase chiefs requested that missionaries be sent to the province and some even traveled to St. Augustine to pledge allegiance to the Spanish king (Hann 1987b). The Spaniards did not come immediately because they said the chiefs could not control their people.

The Apalachee's behavior toward the Spaniards was controlled by the nature of political relations within the chiefdom and the political strategies of the various elite (see Paynter 1981). During periods of strong central leadership, lesser elite would have employed or been forced to employ dependency strategies, sending surpluses to their superiors in exchange for support from the center. During times of decentralization or weakened central leadership, they could have pursued development strategies retaining surpluses to strengthen their own positions vis-à-vis the paramount and their peers. I suggest that the early seventeenth century was a time of political decentralization and weakened central authority, when the elite competed for political superiority. The Spaniards were invited to bolster the claims of one elite faction (just such a thing happened to the Jesuit missionaries to the Calusa of south Florida [Marotti 1985, 273–74]). Of course, the Spaniards did much more than serve an Apalachee political faction.

In 1633, Spanish missionaries entered the Apalachee territory and established the first of the Apalachee missions (Hann 1987b). This marked the end of the independent Velda phase chiefdom. Although the missionized Apalachee were no longer an independent society, the descriptions contained in Spanish documents can shed considerable light on earlier Apalachee society.

Seventeenth-century documents indicate that chiefly office was inherited, with chiefs being succeeded by their sister's eldest son (Bushnell 1979, 2). Records suggest that at least some of the functions and privileges of the elite were retained, including the privilege of collecting tribute for themselves (Bushnell 1978, 3). The Leturiondo *visita* of 1678 describes disputes over succession and the usurpation of power and office (Hann 1985). Some documents also hint at competition for supremacy between two great families who, between them, controlled many chiefly offices (Hann 1987a). During the Lake Jackson phase and during the Velda phase at the time of Narváez and De Soto, the capital of the Apalachee was toward the western end of their territory—at Lake Jackson and later at Anhaica. During the seventeenth century, the Spaniards established San Luis, the capital of Apalachee province near but apparently not at Anhaica. By the end of the seventeenth century, however, the principal chief of the Apalachee came from Ivitachuco, at the eastern end of the province (Boyd 1951, 24–26; Bushnell 1979). Not surprisingly, an earlier chief of Ivitachuco was among the faction who asked the Spaniards to come to Apalachee. Late in the seventeenth century, much of the power of the chief of San Luis had been assumed by his captain (Hann 1987a). All these points imply the existence and operation of processes of political interaction and reproduction that could generate the larger patterns seen in the history and prehistory of the Apalachee chiefdom.

Conclusions

The Apalachee data are stimulating but, unfortunately, not conclusive. They suggest that Wright's model has considerable merit as a description of the emergence and operation of complex chiefdoms. But they do not prove his model.

I hope that this preliminary examination of the Apalachee data will encourage archaeologists in the Southeast to examine the Mississippian societies in much greater detail, to refine our pictures of their history, and to use new theoretical frameworks to inform our data. We must not simply classify the Mississippian societies as chiefdoms and assume that this is sufficient to understand them. Instead, we must recognize that they were different, that they were not static, and that they each had their own specific history. As they passed through time, as chief replaced chief, the Mississippian societies evolved—not necessarily in any particular direction, but they did change.

I believe we should pursue this avenue of study and ask how and why the Mississippian societies changed through time, not in general but in the specific (see Shennan 1986)—not focusing exclusively on external or internal structural variables. In this manner, we can address the how and the why of change, both process and mechanism. Then, perhaps, someday we will be able to use Mississippian data to provide answers to a question proposed by Marshall Sahlins (1981, 8): "How does the reproduction of a structure become its transformation?"

10. Stability and Change in Chiefdom-Level Societies
An Examination of Mississippian Political Evolution on the South Atlantic Slope

David G. Anderson

Introduction

In this paper, I propose to examine factors influencing the stability of chiefly societies. The focus for this research will be the Mississippian societies of the South Atlantic Slope, specifically those within the Savannah River Basin. A major premise of this research is that broad geographic and theoretical perspectives are essential if we are to understand the political and social histories of individual chiefdoms. It is argued that the evolution of Mississippian societies must be examined, at least in part, from a regional perspective, using knowledge drawn from general anthropological and ecological theory.

Problem Definition: Cycling in Chiefly Societies

Subsumed under the analysis of political evolution is the question of why some societies appear to cycle (i.e., expand, collapse, and reconstitute), while others take off to higher levels of sociopolitical complexity. Why, for example, do some groups (such as the tribal or chiefdom-level societies observed in New Guinea, portions of lowland South and Central America in Venezuela, Colombia, and Panama, and in central Africa) appear to have stayed at approximately the same level for hundreds or thousands of years, while in other areas more complex societies emerged fairly quickly? Why, furthermore, should large, complex, and seemingly successful chiefdom-level societies fall apart or disappear entirely?

Among Mississippian researchers in the southeastern United

States there is considerable interest in chiefly cycling, since it may help us understand why major centers such as Cahokia, Moundville, or Etowah were abandoned. Williams's (1982) Vacant Quarter hypothesis—that the central Mississippi Valley was largely depopulated after around A.D. 1400—is perhaps the most dramatic prehistoric case in the Eastern Woodlands warranting explanation. This problem is not, however, restricted to a few unusual or enigmatic cases. Upon close examination, the Mississippian archaeological record from across the Southeast is replete with evidence for cycling behavior. In every area that has been carefully examined, evidence for the emergence, expansion, collapse, and reemergence or replacement of local chiefly societies has been found. In some areas, towns and centers were occupied for extended periods, up to several centuries, while in other areas chiefly polities appear to have lasted for little more than a generation or two (e.g., Bruce Smith 1978; Chapman 1980; DePratter 1983, 204–11; Morse and Morse 1983; Steponaitis 1983; Williams and Shapiro 1987 and this volume; Hally 1987). Even within seemingly stable chiefly societies, there is evidence for a kind of cycling behavior in the form of periodic rebuilding episodes at ceremonial centers, particularly the replacement of buildings and the addition of new mounds or mound stages. Exactly what is represented by these examples of cycling behavior, which range from regional depopulations to localized renewal ceremonies, is only partially understood at present. Even less well understood are the reasons why these changes occurred.

To understand these aspects of the southeastern archaeological record and chiefly societies in general, we need to try to learn what it is about Mississippian societies that translates into greater or lesser social stability. Once developed, such knowledge should prove useful to the development of larger theories of sociocultural evolution. Before proceeding, however, a discussion of theoretical approaches to the study of chiefly political evolution is in order.

Chiefly Evolutionary Trajectories and the Importance of Legitimizing Ideologies

A number of definitions of what is meant by a "chiefdom" have appeared in the literature, most of which emphasize the nature of leadership and organizational structures (e.g., Service 1962, 133–34; Fried 1967, 110–53; Earle 1977; Peebles and Kus 1977; Wright 1984;

Feinman and Neitzel 1984; Drennan and Uribe 1987). While something of a truism, sociopolitical stability in any society ultimately depends on the permanence of these organizational structures. In chiefly societies there is, following Wright (1984, 42–43):

> . . . one generalized kind of political control. . . . Simple chiefdoms are those in which such control is exercised by figures drawn from an ascribed elite subgroup; these chiefdoms characteristically have only one level of control above the level of the local community. . . . Complex chiefdoms characteristically cycle between one and two levels of control hierarchy above the level of the local community . . . such sociopolitical entities [are characterized by] a chiefly class or nobility, members of which control generalized, polity wide decision making.

This appears to be a useful definition and one that incorporates evolutionary cycling as a basic characteristic of complex chiefdoms. According to Carneiro (1981, 37–38), the emergence of chiefdom level societies represents: "the first transcending of local autonomy in human history. With chiefdoms, multi-community political units emerged for the first time. . . . The emergence of chiefdoms was a qualitative step. Everything that followed, including the rise of states and empires, was, in a sense, merely quantitative." To Carneiro, the emergence of chiefdoms thus represents the emergence of multicommunity political units, while to Wright, it represents the development of hereditary social inequality—the emergence of classes of people having unequal access to resources. How this development occurred is a critical question in the evolution of society (Flannery 1972, 402). This transition, furthermore, can only be examined in pristine chiefly societies. The formation of secondary chiefdoms, typically brought about through the existence and/or encroachment of other chiefdoms or more complex systems, comes about as a reactionary process and thus may follow a different trajectory than that of pristine chiefdoms (Sanders and Price 1968, 132; Webster 1975, 467; Carneiro 1981, 66).

The emergence of pristine chiefdoms has been the subject of considerable analysis and speculation. A number of causal mechanisms have been advanced, including warfare, competition among elites, and arguments based on resource control and redistribution (e.g., Sahlins 1958; Service 1962, 134–43; Fried 1967, 191–223; Flannery 1972, 402–18; Carneiro 1981, 54–65; Wright 1984, 41–51). While precise explanations remain elusive, one thing is likely: however pristine chiefdoms emerged, they probably did so fairly gradually. The development of chiefly elites is unlikely to have occurred instantaneously but, instead, probably took a fair amount of time, on the order of several generations. Suggested mechanisms for this emergence might be the increasing control by specific individuals of access to strategic resources (e.g., Fried 1967, 186; Helms 1979) and/or prestige items useful for status enhancement and alliance formation (e.g., Shennan 1982; Braun and Plog 1982, 507; Wright 1984, 69; Bender 1985, 58–59). It has been suggested that a critical aspect of this process in many of these societies was the development of an ideology of power or chiefly sanctity (Wright 1984, 69; Bender 1985, 59). The strength of this rationalizing idiom, or appeal to sacred authority capable of legitimizing social inequality and its acceptance by all segments of a population, should thus determine, to some extent, the degree of societal stability.

In all probability, the emergence of resource control, alliance and exchange networks, and supporting ideologies occurred slowly and were in place in some form well before the appearance of chiefly organizational and control structures. This is evident in the archaeological record of the Eastern Woodlands of North America where the existence of exchange networks precedes the emergence of recognizable chiefdoms by millennia (Griffin 1967; Winters 1968; Webb 1977). Braun and Plog (1982) have suggested that such exchange and alliance networks emerged in tribal societies as risk minimization strategies. The emergence of these networks, they argue, was directly linked to the emergence of sanctifying ideologies as an essential underpinning of chiefly authority structures (see also Wright 1984). In this view, successful practitioners of strategies that led to long-term enhancement of group living conditions might be accorded a measure of sanctity. Wright (1984, 69) has suggested that "continued competition for alliance and offices among local ranking groups would weld such groups into a region-wide chiefly or noble class . . . such a process of competition should generate an ideology of chiefly sanctity." It is this possible pattern of gradual emergence that particularly distinguishes pristine from secondary chiefly polities. One result is the development of entrenched ideological mechanisms for the maintenance of chiefly power; such mechanisms may be absent or less effective in secondary chiefdoms.

Once a chiefdom (primary or secondary) has formed in an area, it should tend to grow. There are both biological and social reasons for this, including a need to disperse potential chiefly contenders and because growth may be an effective mechanism for maintaining the prerogatives of chiefly lineages. Chiefly elites, with greater access to resources (including, presumably, food), may have enjoyed a high level of reproductive success. That is, given better than average nutrition, children of elites probably enjoyed a higher survival rate than the children of commoners. These children, innocuous while young, would grow up to be contenders for power. Dispersing these possible rivals by imposing them as chiefly administrators/elites over conquered groups or through advantageous marital alliances would be one way to remove their influence. The need to quell potential instability caused by elite population growth in the absence of culturally mediated leveling mechanisms appears, in fact, to be a primary cause of expansion in chiefdom-level societies. Parenthetically, successful chiefly decision making would have also probably translated into greater relative reproductive success for all members of society and not just the elite, thus further prompting societal expansion.

Population increase was also probably a mechanism by which the prestige and prerogatives of elites were maintained. Large populations at chiefly centers undoubtedly served as a highly visible indicator of elite power. Such populations also provided a large, readily available source of labor for public works, tribute, craft goods production, and defensive support. Keeping chiefly rivals close at hand and under direct supervision might be an effective alternative method of heading off potential rebellion to that of dispersal. Population nucleation, including the incorporation of other groups and the co-opting of potential rivals, may thus also occur with chiefdom development.

The initial appearance of a chiefly society in a region is likely to trigger the rapid emergence of other such polities. As Carneiro (1981, 66) has noted:

Once chiefdoms begin to form in a region, the process proceeds rapidly. The military advantage that size alone confers on a society means that even a minimal chiefdom will have a significant edge over its neighbors if they are still independent villages. As a result, it will not be long before autonomous villages as such will cease to exist. Either they will be defeated by and incorporated into one of the existing chiefdoms or they will join forces with other such villages in a defensive alliance, which will itself tend to become a chiefdom.

Carneiro further suggests that the nature of chiefly warfare and the incorporation of defeated enemies may be linked to structural elaboration. That is, a change in organization, specifically the development of intermediate leadership positions, may be necessary if entire chiefdoms rather than isolated villages are to be absorbed. Effective reorganization would lead to continued structural elaboration and would result in increasingly complex chiefdoms or state formation. Alternatively, the collapse of chiefly polities may be due to overextension and a failure to effectively reorganize. The ethnohistoric record from the Southeast suggests that complex chiefdoms in the area were fragile and particularly vulnerable to internal dissension.

It can also be argued that the stability of chiefly societies, at least in part, is related to the effectiveness of the mechanisms by which the elite maintain their positions of authority. The stability of these societies, furthermore, should be directly related to the nature of their emergence and subsequent development, particularly as this relates to the establishment of chiefly elites. Significant differences should be evident in the evolutionary trajectories, social hierarchies, and legitimizing ideologies of these differing kinds of political formations. The relatively rapid emergence of secondary chiefly societies, for example, means there is little time for a rationalizing idiom—an ideology of chiefly sanctity—to develop. Chiefly authority may thus be more likely to reside in coercive or cooperative measures. That is, political authority in secondary chiefdoms, at least initially, may have to be maintained through overt use of force, probably to a greater extent than in primary or "sacred" chiefdoms, or it may have to rest on cooperative agreements between participating constituents. As such, these structures are likely to be fragile and short-lived, unless they manage to survive until a legitimizing ideology can be set in place. Finally, leadership positions in secondary chiefdoms may be less likely initially to be hereditary, since prowess in warfare or decision making, rather than membership in a sanctified elite, was probably the most important criterion for social advancement.

The effectiveness of ideological mechanisms for maintaining authority structures may also be related to the size and time depth of chiefly societies in a region. The relationship and importance of "sacred" (i.e., consensual, ideologically based) as opposed to "secular" (i.e., coercive authority, use of force) mechanisms for maintaining power in chiefly societies need to be explored. This relationship appears to be scale dependent. Following arguments developed by Sahlins (1958, 11–12), appeal to sacred authority as a means of maintaining power appears to be associated with fairly simple chiefdoms such as his Types IIb or III societies (i.e., Tikopia, Marquesas, Pukapuka, Ontong Java). Authority in more complex chiefdoms such as Sahlins's Types I or IIa societies (e.g., Hawaii, Tonga, Samoa, Mangareva), in contrast, appears increasingly based on secular power—the use of force—regardless of the underlying ideological framework.

Recognizing the ideological and secular bases of chiefly authority archaeologically is an important task. Following Sahlins, it is suggested that in the first chiefly societies in a region (or in fairly simple chiefly societies at any time), appeals to sacred authority as a means of justifying elite prerogatives will be more important than the use of force or the imposition of secular authority. The opposite pattern is suggested in more complex chiefly societies or in regions where chiefdoms have been in place for some time. In the southeastern United States, a decline in the sacred/ideological spheres (at least in their domination by elites) is suggested over the course of the Mississippian period. The highly developed mound building, mortuary ceremonialism, and iconography of the Southeastern Ceremonial Complex, for example, peaks around the twelfth through fourteenth centuries and declines thereafter throughout the region. Knight (1986, 682–83) has argued that this reflects a communalization of symbolism formerly co-opted by elites. An alternate complementary interpretation advanced here is that it also reflects a basic change in the nature and operation of control or authority structures within these societies.

In this view, it is hypothesized that a major shift in the procedures by which southeastern Mississippian societies maintained their elite authority structures took place over the interval from around A.D. 900–1400. This change was from societies where elite power was based, at least in part, on appeals to sacred authority, to societies where secular authority was increasingly dominant. This shift is manifested in a decline in major mound building efforts and a marked decline in the complexity of elite interments. Mound construction in most areas of the Southeast after around A.D. 1350 in no way equals the efforts undertaken before this time. At sites such as Etowah, Moundville, and Cahokia, for example, major construction activity had largely ceased by this time. While mound construction continued in many areas, the effort put into it is markedly diminished.

This diminution does not appear to be linked to a decline in the size or strength of Mississippian societies in the region. At the time of the De Soto entrada, for example, there is little doubt that complex, geographically extensive, and powerful chiefdoms were present in the Southeast (Hudson, Smith, and DePratter 1984; Hudson et al. 1985). These societies were probably equal in scale to anything that had come before them. In these presumably more secular chiefdoms, however, the material correlates of dominant ideological structures—massive mound constructions and elaborate interment rituals—no longer appear to be a prominent focus of social energy. This is not to suggest that social ritual disappeared; far from it. Religion continued to play a major role in Mississippian life. The decreased emphasis on the use of ideology in the legitimization of elite authority, however, suggests that such a role was no longer of critical importance. The emergence of secular chiefdoms over the region, if this interpretation is valid, may be due to a greater incidence of warfare (possibly brought about by increasing regional populations) and a concomitant growth in pressure on available resources. Greater social effort may have had to have been directed to food protection and defense, leaving less time and energy for ideological activity. Furthermore, given the establishment of coercive authority structures, there may have been less need for sanctifying ideologies underpinning elite rule.

The developmental trajectories of chiefly societies–their emergence, expansion, decline, and collapse—thus warrants careful attention and can be useful to the development of broader anthropological theory. If the emergence and spread of Mississippian culture in the southeastern United States reflects a combination of primary and secondary chiefdom formation, the differing attributes and evolutionary trajectories of these kinds of sociopolitical entities will need to be better understood to permit their recognition archaeologically. In particular, the relationships between a polity's time depth and geographic scale and its control and ideological structures would appear a fruitful area for future southeastern Mississippian research.

Several characteristics have been postulated as differentiating pristine from secondary chiefly societies: (1) slow versus rapid development; (2) stable versus less stable authority structures; (3) well-established genealogically sanctioned authority structures, as opposed to weakly sanctioned cooperative or coercive authority structures; and (4) hereditary elites and a restricted system of social advancement, as opposed to a more open social system where authority was probably based to a fair degree on personal ability. To the extent that the presence of primary and secondary chiefdoms can be identified in the archaeological record, the viability of these characteristics should be examined. Coupled with this research should be an examination of the nature and strength of ideological structures over time to see if changes in the ideological sphere can be linked to the size and stability of local Mississippian polities.

In the South Appalachian area, concerns such as these have puzzled researchers for almost half a century. Was warfare, for example, an important factor in the emergence of complex chiefly societies locally (cf., Carneiro 1981)? The origin of Macon Plateau, one of the earliest Mississippian cultures in the region, and its effects on other groups has attracted considerable attention and appears related to this question (e.g., Willey et al. 1956; Bruce Smith 1984a). Archaeologists are still uncertain about the temporal range and cultural affinities of Macon Plateau, although it bears so little relationship to presumed local antecedents that it may well reflect population movement into the area (Williams 1986). If it is an example of an intrusion or migration, could this have triggered a wave of secondary chiefdom formation over the surrounding region? In this view, the appearance of fortifications at other local early Mississippian sites such as Woodstock Fort, although over 185 kilometers away to the northwest, may reflect a defensive reaction and social reorganization by indigenous groups in response to the appearance of powerful neighbors (Sanders and Price 1968, 132; Webster 1975, 46; Carneiro 1981, 66).

The rise of the complex chiefdom centered at Etowah in northwest Georgia in the eleventh and twelfth centuries may have had a similar effect. Some of the earliest Mississippian ceramics in the Oconee and Savannah valleys, well to the east of Etowah, are characterized by Etowah design motifs and suggest possible trade, colonization, conquest, imposition of outside elites, or tributary relationships. Minimally, they indicate interaction and influence occurred over considerable distances, although the precise mechanisms remain to be determined. The time-transgressive spread of Mississip-

pian over the South Appalachian–South Atlantic Slope area, with
centers in west Georgia appearing some 200 years earlier than those
in central South Carolina (Ferguson 1971; Ferguson and Green 1984;
Anderson, Hally, and Rudolph 1986; DePratter and Judge 1986), appears to reflect a gradual spread of the generalized Mississippian
adaptation over the region—a spread that may be characterized by
both primary and secondary chiefdom development. These possibil-
ities need to be seriously explored.

Chiefly Veneration and the Stability of Southeastern Chiefdoms

Iconographic representations and the veneration of chiefly ancestors can be best interpreted as devices to legitimize and reinforce
the ideology of sacred chiefly power that permeated and gave structure to early southeastern Mississippian life. Brown (1976, 126;
1985) and Knight (1986) have defined three roughly similar foci of
this socially defining sacred power: (1) the temple/mortuary-based
ancestor cults; (2) the chiefly elites with a warrior cult subsumed
or co-opted under this sphere; and (3) communal earth or fertility
cults. The first two spheres were the domain of the elite and functioned to reinforce their prestige and status. The third, in contrast,
encompassed all sectors of society. The stability of elite authority
structures, and hence of individual Mississippian polities, it is argued, was directly related to the strength or importance attached
to these ideological structures.

The cult surrounding the veneration of chiefly/elite ancestors appears to have been the central focus of the Mississippian ideological
sphere. Major sites throughout the Southeast are characterized by
the presence of temple/mortuary complexes where the bodies of
the elite were maintained in honored status in shrines that were
often physically, and hence symbolically, elevated above and maintained apart from the surrounding populace. Objects of wealth,
sumptuary devices, weapons, statuary, fetishes, and sacred relics—
what Brown (1985, 106) has called "condensed symbols of sacred
ancestral power"—were held within these temple-shrines, in addition to the remains of the noble dead. An extended description of
one such shrine, the temple of Talomeco, where the sacred wealth
and chiefly elite of Cofitachequi were placed, was recorded in Garcilaso de la Vega's account of the De Soto entrada (Varner and Varner

1962, 315–25). This location may well be that of the Adamson mound group near Camden, South Carolina (DePratter, Hudson, and Smith 1983).

Ties to ancestral territories and to the actual bodies of ancestors, rather than to ceremonial facilities such as mounds and earthworks, appears to have been a particularly important aspect of Mississippian ideology (Brown 1985, 104; Knight 1986). There is convincing ethnohistoric evidence that these shrines were the ideological centers of individual polities. Desecration of a rival society's temple, specifically its ancestral burials, was considered the ultimate insult and a primary goal in warfare (Varner and Varner 1962, 292–93, 438–39, 493; Anderson 1987). Permanent site abandonment might follow such desecration; the attached dishonor might have been such as to preclude any reuse, regardless of the extent of the facilities in place (DePratter 1983, 63). This behavior may help to explain why major Mississippian centers, once abandoned, were not invariably reoccupied. In this view, newly ascendant Mississippian polities were ideologically bound to remain centered about their places of origin. Relocation to previously dominant centers where elaborate ceremonial facilities were already in place does not appear to have invariably or even typically occurred. The central town of the sixteenth-century province of Coosa, apparently at the Little Egypt site (Hudson et al. 1985, 732), for example, was characterized by only small mounds. This suggests that, unless there was a general decline in mound building at this time, the chiefdom was just emerging and perhaps had a fairly shallow time depth. Its physical appearance, with mounds less than 4 meters high, was certainly far less imposing than the nearby Etowah site, which was characterized by mounds up to 18 meters high. By the early sixteenth century, however, Etowah had lost its former regional preeminence and was a tributary town to Coosa (Hudson et al. 1985). Occupying former centers of power, even those with impressive physical facilities, does not, therefore, appear to have been a prerequisite for claiming or maintaining leadership in some southeastern chiefly societies.

The iconography of the elite chiefs and powerful warriors was expressed by three themes according to Brown (1985): the chiefly litter, the chunky player, and the falcon warrior. There are a number of archaeological traces of this iconography that can tell us something of the nature and strength of local legitimizing ideologies. Emblems of office—badges of chiefly power or elite status—included the columella pendant and a heart-shaped apron. Specific emblems may have been linked to the elite of particular polities. The distribution in time and space of the distinctive entwined rattlesnake design known as the Citico-style gorget, for example, appears to be coextensive with the polity of Coosa (Hudson et al. 1985, Figure 7). But in this case, the emblem occurs almost exclusively with young women and appears to reflect an age grade (Hatch 1975, 133). Chiefly litters, described in De Soto's encounter with the caciques of Coosa, Cofitachequi, and other southeastern polities, were found in Mound 72 at Cahokia and are sometimes depicted or suggested on gorget and pottery motifs (DePratter 1983, 189–96). Chunky players are also sometimes depicted on gorgets, and chunky stones are a fairly common item on southeastern Mississippian sites. The game is thought to have been a mechanism for integrating the population through the play of individuals or teams, just as during the historic period.

The third major symbol of the chiefly elite was the falcon impersonator, perhaps the single most distinctive of all Mississippian symbols. The falcon impersonator is typically shown brandishing a club in one hand and carrying a severed head or head-shaped rattle in the other. Perhaps the most famous representation of the falcon impersonator is on one of the copper plates from Etowah; one of the elite burials from that site appears to have been similarly costumed (Larson 1971a). The falcon impersonator is thought to have been the primary symbol of a major military cult dominated by the elite but, in all probability, co-opting especially brave or talented commoners. Another probable military cult symbol, the monolithic ax, is assumed to have been a nonfunctional high-status item. In Mississippian society, warriors stood midway between the chiefly elite and commoners. Brown (1985, 140) suggests that the ubiquity of warrior symbols indicates that warfare was quite common and that it probably served as a mechanism for mediating social tension by providing commoners a means for increasing their personal status (see also Gibson 1974). Peaceful conditions, interestingly, may have thus been undesirable for purely social reasons.

The third major sector of Mississippian iconography encompassed earth/fertility beliefs (Brown 1985, 123–29). These were closely linked to maize agriculture, the success of which was, of course, of great importance to local Mississippian societies. Earth/fertility iconography and beliefs were identified, to some extent, with the position of the chief, although all sectors of society appear to have shared in them (Waring 1968; Brown 1985; Knight 1986). Fertility

cults, iconography, and ancestor worship thus combined to symbol-
ize and legitimize the positions and aspirations of the participants
in major sectors of southeastern Mississippian societies. The di-
verse symbolism, furthermore, served to accentuate and simultaneously mediate tensions in these same nonegalitarian societies.
Chiefly stability unquestionably depended on the success with
which these social tensions were mediated. Challenges to chiefly
authority reflected challenges to sacred authority. Extended crop
or hunting failures, defeats in warfare, or disastrous weather, while
potentially destabilizing in and of itself, would have additionally
led to a weakening of chiefly authority by posing direct questions
about the sacred position and intermediary role of the elite. In Mississippian societies where chiefly sanctity was strongly accepted,
perturbations would probably have to be severe before challenges
to leadership or changes in organization would be likely. Where legitimizing ideologies were weakly developed, as in emerging or
secondary chiefdoms, however, such stresses might have brought
about rapid social collapse or reorganization.

Mechanisms of Chiefly Succession and the Stability of Southeastern Chiefdoms

Mechanisms by which chiefly societies deal with succession or
changes in leadership are of critical importance to the long-term
stability of these societies. Where rules of succession are poorly
defined or subject to challenge, the death of a paramount may trigger
widespread social upheaval until a successor can consolidate his
grasp on authority. Competition between rival factions among
elites is widely recognized as a primary factor contributing to the
instability of these kinds of political systems (Sahlins 1958, 176–96;
Goldman 1970; Helms 1979, 24; Wright 1984). Ethnographic accounts from chiefly societies are filled with accounts of rebellion,
treachery, and warfare directed toward obtaining chiefly authority.
In such circumstances, the power of the chief often depends on the
skill by which he maintains control of and subordinates potential
rivals. How southeastern Mississippian societies dealt with problems of chiefly succession remains incompletely explored, although
it is possible to draw inferences from both the ethnohistoric and
the archaeological record.

A traditional method of exploring chiefly succession in southeastern Mississippian societies has been to examine the incidence of construction stages and burials in temple mounds. This usually proceeds by assuming that successive mound stages reflect social renewal behavior, most probably associated with the death of a chief and the elevation of his replacement. As such, mound stage construction may be interpreted as a demonstration of the power and sanctity of both the deceased and his replacement (Waring 1968, 58–62, 66). Such an interpretation is supported by ethnohistoric accounts (DePratter 1983, 179) and from the archaeological record itself (Schnell, Knight, and Schnell 1981, 126–45; Hally 1987). If one divides the number of mound stages by the length of time it is assumed to have been in use, stage construction every 15 to 25 years or so is indicated at a number of sites. This, coincidentally or otherwise, is about the duration of a generation and may indicate the average tenure of a local paramount (DePratter 1983, 179–80).

Knight (1986, 678) has argued that mound building was a product of communal/fertility cults reflecting "a purely expressive act . . . a mortuary rite for the mound itself rather than for any individual . . . the symbolism of the earthen platform is that of an icon representative of earth, manipulated by periodic burial as a temporary means of achieving purification in the context of a communal rite of intensification." While this is undoubtedly a correct interpretation, it can be argued that an additional purpose of mound building was the sanctification of the elite—the linking of successors with predecessors—through the rebuilding of suprastructural ancestral temples and places of residence. The comparatively infrequent occurrence of mound stage construction, on the order of once a generation or so at some sites, suggests that this activity is unlikely to have been a regular or periodic intensification rite. Instead, at least some mound construction, it is argued, reflects successional events, specifically the replacement of chiefly elites. This activity served to legitimize the power of the former chief and demonstrate that of his successor. As the strength or necessity for legitimizing ideologies declined over the course of the Mississippian period, if the argument about the rise of increasingly power-based authority structures is correct, this would explain the diminished role of mound building in later Mississippian times.

Rules of succession probably played a major role in determining how long power was maintained at particular centers. From ethnohistoric and ethnographic accounts, it appears that chiefly succession was matrilineal in most southeastern Mississippian polities

(Hudson 1976, 185–95; DePratter 1983, 100–10). That is, succession passed from a chief to his sister's son. Postmarital residence was typically matrilocal, however. This would indicate that heirs to the succession would have stayed within individual communities, at least until marriage (Figure 32). Given postmarital residence rules, however, upon reaching maturity, chiefly heirs might be required to marry outside the local community, unless rules granting exceptions were in play. This appears to have been the case. Ethnohistoric accounts indicate that polygyny and the out-marriage of high-status females were common among elites in complex Mississippian chiefdoms (Hudson 1976, 199; DePratter 1983). Both polygyny and elite marriage were apparently critical to alliance development and provided a foundation for the maintenance of chiefly power. These practices would have dramatically reduced the possibility of chiefly succession continuing within a given community, however. That is, matrilocal postmarital residence rules, coupled with the out-marriage of elite females, specifically the sisters of chiefs, would mean that the heirs to chiefly succession would be raised in or relocate to other communities. Thus, matrilineal succession was a structurally ingrained, potentially destabilizing characteristic of southeastern Mississippian society.

Matrilineal succession coupled with elite female out-marriage could thus result in the relocation of chiefly centers on the maturity of the heir, unless effective mechanisms for keeping the heir at the former paramounts' center or relocating him there were ingrained in the system. The presence of ceremonial facilities, notably, temple/mortuary complexes requiring the presence of the chief at the central town, would be one method of ensuring such a relocation. It is suggested that the maintenance of temple/mortuary complexes would ideologically predispose a southeastern elite who was succeeding to the chiefdomship to relocate to near this ancestral temple/mortuary complex (Blake 1986). Where succession was interrupted, specifically when a rival seized power, this same ideological predisposition could prompt the relocation of the center to the community where the new chief's ancestral temple/mortuary complex was located. Chiefly elites, alternatively or additionally, might have been exempt from matrilocal postmarital residence rules. Given the incidence of polygyny, this appears probable at least in some groups.

Williams and Shapiro (1987; this volume) have noted that several Mississippian centers in central Georgia were characterized by alter-

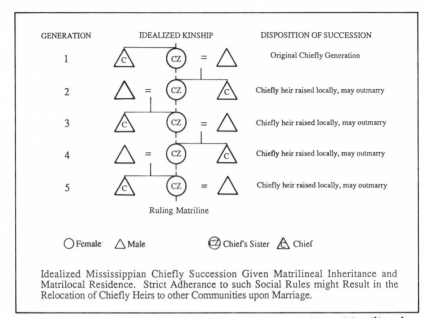

GENERATION   IDEALIZED KINSHIP   DISPOSITION OF SUCCESSION

1   Original Chiefly Generation

2   Chiefly heir raised locally, may outmarry

3   Chiefly heir raised locally, may outmarry

4   Chiefly heir raised locally, may outmarry

5   Chiefly heir raised locally, may outmarry

Ruling Matriline

○ Female   △ Male   Ⓩ Chief's Sister   △ Chief

Idealized Mississippian Chiefly Succession Given Matrilineal Inheritance and Matrilocal Residence. Strict Adherence to such Social Rules might Result in the Relocation of Chiefly Heirs to other Communities upon Marriage.

Figure 32. Idealized Mississippian Chiefly Succession, Given Matrilineal Inheritance and Matrilocal Postmarital Residence

nate periods of occupation and abandonment, in some cases up to several generations. While ecological reasons for such abandonment, such as soil or firewood depletion, have been advanced, from the argument just developed, it is equally probable that social mechanisms delimiting inheritance and land tenure may have been an important factor (something Williams and Shapiro also acknowledge). The occupation, abandonment, and relocation of chiefly centers in the late prehistoric Southeast, it is suggested, was probably related as much to social as to ecological factors.

Ecological Factors and the Stability of Southeastern Chiefdoms

In the South Appalachian area, there is increasing evidence to suggest that the evolutionary behavior of Mississippian societies can be addressed, at least in part, by examining changes over time in the spatial extent and contexts of archaeologically identified Mississippian phases. Given the success that Hudson and his colleagues have had equating sixteenth-century archaeological phases with ethnohistorically documented aboriginal polities, equation of pre-historic Mississippian phases with similar kinds of sociopolitical entities appears to be a viable research option (Hudson, Smith, and DePratter 1984; Hudson et al. 1985; Hally, Hudson, and DePratter 1985; Hally and Rudolph 1986). Following just such a strategy, the existence and evolutionary trajectories of a number of probable local prehistoric Mississippian societies have been examined (Smith and Kowalewski 1980; Rudolph and Blanton 1981; Hally 1984 and 1986; Hally, Hudson, and DePratter 1985; Shapiro 1983; Anderson 1986; Anderson, Hally, and Rudolph 1986). Evidence for cycling behavior has been noted by several authors, particularly in Hally and Rudolph's (1986) overview of Georgia Piedmont Mississippian. That local Mississippian societies appeared, expanded, and then collapsed in the South Appalachian area is thus becoming increasingly recog-nized, as is the existence of apparent unoccupied areas or buffer zones between them (DePratter 1983, 20–43)(Figure 33).

Competition between chiefdoms for agricultural land, hunting territories, and control of raw materials or trading networks or for other reasons has been variously suggested as probable causes for at least some of the organizational fluctuations observed in local prehistoric chiefly societies (Larson 1972; Gramly 1977; Turner and Santley 1979; Wright 1984). It is suggested that buffer zones are also important to chiefly stability and that understanding how these buffers functioned might help us to understand why chiefly cycling and restructuring occurred. Ethnohistoric evidence suggests that Mississippian buffer zones in the Georgia–South Carolina area not only existed but were also aggressively maintained. Individuals from other polities found in these areas were typically subject to attack. Patofa, a war leader from the Oconee Valley, described the nature of this interaction to De Soto during the Spanish army's march to Cofitachequi in 1540:

> . . . the wars waged by these two provinces had never assumed the nature of pitched battles in which one of the two powers invaded enemy territory, but had simply occurred while each hunted and fished in the forests and streams through which the Spaniards had just passed. Meeting thus, they as enemies had slain and captured one another; but since the Indians of Cofachiqui were superior and

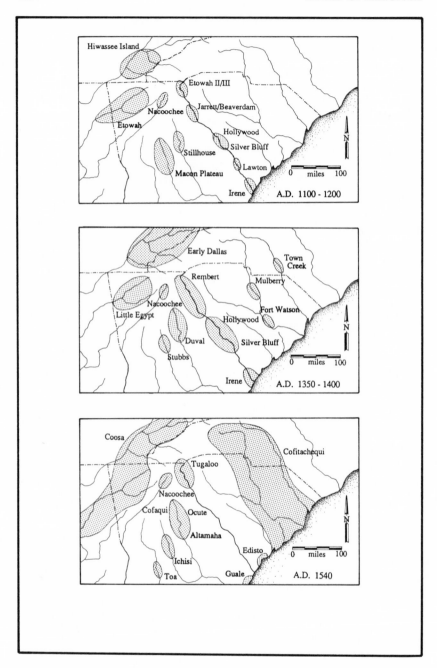

Figure 33. Hypothetical Mississippian Polities in the Vicinity of the Savannah River in A.D. 1100–1200, 1350–1400, and 1540

always enjoyed many advantages in these battles, his own Indians
had become intimidated, and like defeated people had not dared expand or go beyond their own boundaries (Varner and Varner 1962,
284).

This passage contains several interesting pieces of information.
First, local Mississippian polities appear to have occupied fairly
fixed territories that were maintained through indirect warfare. Territories and territorial boundaries, while indistinct, did exist. The
warfare maintaining these territories appears to have been tied to
hunting activity; skirmishes occurred when groups strayed too far
from their own territories. Areas closest to permanent settlements
were thus the safest for hunting and other activities, while increasing danger ensued the farther one went out from this zone. This
behavior appears to be responsible for the formation and maintenance of buffer zones between local Mississippian societies over the
region (DePratter 1983; Anderson 1987).

Terrain closest to permanent settlements thus served as a pro-
curement territory for a range of resources, including farmland (Larson 1972), wild food resources, and animal hides (Hickerson 1965;
Gramly 1977; Turner and Santley 1979). A result of this behavior
was that group boundaries—defined by the unoccupied areas between polities—were infrequently visited. An ecological consequence of this was that buffer zones served as prey reservoirs from
which game animal populations that had been depleted closer to
settlements might replenish themselves (Mech 1977). The maintenance of buffer zones, whether intended or not, appears to have
helped local Mississippian populations avoid severe resource shortages. Mississippian warfare, therefore, may have been linked, in
part, to the necessity of maintaining viable hunting territories
rather than or in addition to the need to control prime agricultural
land (Larson 1972) or as a mechanism offering a means for status
advancement in an nonegalitarian society (Gibson 1974).

Critical areas for investigation are, therefore, to determine where
these buffer zones occurred and how they operated. The existence
of geographically extensive buffer zones is strongly indicated when
Mississippian phase distribution maps from the South Appalachian
area are examined (Figure 33; see also DePratter 1983, 9–13; Hally
and Rudolph 1986), although a range of variables such as survey
coverage bias, population measures, and the utility of temporal indi-
cators all need to be carefully considered when constructing such

maps. It would be important to learn whether the extent of these resource procurement/buffer zones was related to user group population size or density. If a relationship could be shown to exist between a Mississippian polity's population base and the size of its buffer zone (controlling, of course, for variation in gross environmental resource structure), it would suggest that the successful functioning of these buffers was essential to the maintenance of organizational stability. Given this perspective, the collapse of chiefly polities might be as likely to ensue from gradually increasing resource pressure—attrition brought about by the differential success of hunting parties from differing polities in the buffer zones—as from attacks on or threats to actual settlements.

Environmental structure and perturbations are also important factors to consider when examining the stability of chiefly societies. Crop failures brought about by localized or widespread droughts, flooding, or other catastrophes, for example, would have threatened the stability of southeastern chiefly polities. One effective risk minimization strategy might be the dispersal of fields over fairly large areas and in a number of microenvironmental zones (Chmurny 1973; Ford 1980). Such crop dispersal may have also been related to changing social conditions. That is, scattering food sources such as granaries or fields may have been increasingly necessary as warfare and raiding increased or as group political, and hence economic, stability decreased.

Another solution to the problem of periodic crop failure would be the development of larger or more complex organizational networks. Resource shortages in one area could thus be overcome through the chiefly redistribution of stored surpluses from other localities, providing a rationale for increases in social complexity and the growth of ever-larger chiefdoms. As the geographic scale of these entities increased, however, information management would become increasingly difficult, particularly as the number of discrete interacting locales increased (Johnson 1982). As the chiefly elite's administrative burden increased, so too did the possibility of information overload and system collapse, barring the emergence of more effective or efficient decision-making apparatuses. Collapse, rather than reorganization and expansion, appears more typical of the southeastern archaeological record, once complex chiefdoms developed.

Effective information flow is constrained by environmental as well as organizational factors, and the very structure of much of the southeastern landscape, it is argued, hindered the development of complex societies (Blake and Clark 1986). The linear-shaped, often widely separated riverine settlement systems characteristic of many southeastern Mississippian polities, for example, probably made information flow between segments difficult and confined political structure and management largely to within individual valleys. The development of complex chiefly polities may therefore have been possible only in certain areas and precluded or hindered in others by gross regional physiographic structure. In the South Appalachian area, for example, complex Mississippian chiefdoms were present for centuries in northwest Georgia (i.e., Etowah and Coosa) and in central South Carolina (i.e., Cofitachequi). Although the location of the paramount towns in the Mississippian polities occupying these areas shifted about somewhat, strong centralized chiefdoms were present throughout the course of the Mississippian period (Hally and Rudolph 1986; Hally 1987; DePratter 1987). In other areas, in contrast, such as along the Savannah River, highly complex Mississippian polities either never arose or only lasted a few centuries at best. The reasons for these differences in chiefly stability remain unknown and largely unexplored. The possibility that they may be related to ecological parameters needs to be carefully examined.

An Examination of Chiefly Cycling Behavior: Mississippian Political Evolution in the Savannah River Basin

Dramatic evidence for cycling in chiefly polities on the South Atlantic Slope can be seen along the middle and lower Savannah River, which was densely settled by Mississippian populations during the twelfth through fourteenth centuries but was precipitate abandoned around A.D. 1450. Artifacts dating from the interval 1450–1600 are virtually nonexistent, even though analyses of hundreds of collections have been conducted in recent years. About the same time that the Savannah River Valley became uninhabited, there is some evidence that a number of chiefly centers in western South Carolina, along the Broad River, were also abandoned (DePratter 1987). At the time of the De Soto entrada, the middle and lower Savannah River Valley was uninhabited and formed part of an extensive buffer zone separating the rival provinces of Ocute and

Cofitachequi (Figure 33) (Hudson, Smith, and DePratter 1984; Hally, Hudson, and DePratter 1985; Anderson, Hally, and Rudolph 1986). Possible evidence for the emergence of this buffer was observed at Rucker's Bottom, a small agricultural village in the central piedmont portion of the Savannah River Valley. Increasingly complex fortifications appeared there in the last century prior to its abandonment, which occurred at about the same time that the entire lower drainage was depopulated (Anderson and Schuldenrein 1983; 1985). Increasing tension and possibly hostilities between local chiefly polities (i.e., presumably among those along the Savannah River, the Oconee River in central Georgia, and the Santee/Wateree rivers in central South Carolina) is inferred by this appearance and elaboration of fortifications. Minimally, this example demonstrates the importance of a regional perspective when examining local situations.

While the abandonment of the middle Savannah Valley around 1450 is perhaps the most impressive evidence for chiefly cycling behavior in the drainage, considerable additional evidence is available. Several Mississippian ceremonial/political centers emerged along the Savannah River, were used for a century or two, and were then abandoned prior to the final depopulation during the fifteenth century. These sites include the Lawton mound group, occupied circa 1100–1300; the Hollywood mound group, occupied circa 1250–1350; and the Beaverdam Creek mound site, occupied circa 1100–1300 (Rudolph and Hally 1985; Anderson, Hally, and Rudolph 1986) (Figure 34). A marked decline in elaborate goods accompanying the burials in the upper stages of two of these mounds, Hollywood and Beaverdam Creek, was noted. This pattern suggests, following arguments developed by Peebles and Kus (1977, 425, 430), increasing elite impoverishment and concomitant social disruption. Why these centers were abandoned remains unknown, although it appears that the activities undertaken at them were subsumed by other, much larger mound centers elsewhere in the drainage, at the Irene, Silver Bluff, and Rembert sites. This suggests that, locally, the development of increasing social complexity was coupled with increasing centralization of authority at the expense of smaller centers.

Since no obvious evidence for warfare has been found anywhere along the middle Savannah River (although only a few sites have been extensively examined), an immediate question arises about what happened to the people when these centers collapsed and, ultimately, the whole lower portion of the drainage was apparently

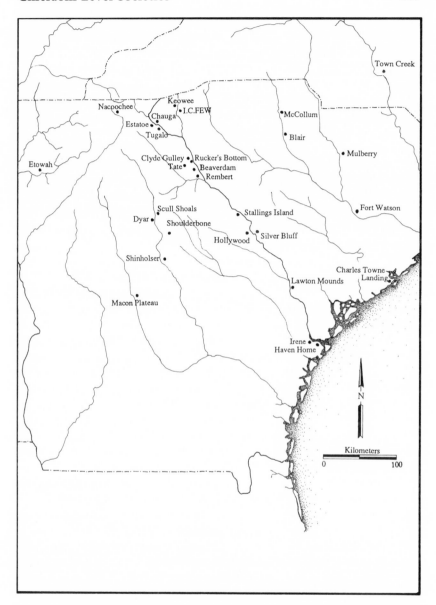

Figure 34. Mississippian Period Archaeological Sites in the Savannah
River Region

abandoned? Where did they go, and why? Were they relocated forcibly or voluntarily? Did they flee to other areas? Did only the organizational structures collapse, with local populations remaining but reverting to more typically "Woodland" settlement patterns, including the use of more traditional ceramic finishes such as cord marking, as has been suggested by Mark J. Brooks (personal communication)? Rudolph and Blanton (1981) have documented a major increase in population in the central Oconee River drainage during later Mississippian times. Some of this increase may be due to population relocation from other areas, including from the Savannah River Valley. Tenuous evidence for the relocation of at least some people into central Georgia is suggested by the appearance of Savannah River–like ceramic assemblages along the upper Oconee River at this time (Ledbetter and Wynn 1987). Comparable questions can be asked about the decline of Macon Plateau, Etowah, and other South Appalachian Mississippian polities.

The depopulation of the lower Savannah River after around 1450 may have been caused, at least in part, by an increasing encroachment on the Savannah Valley polities' traditional hunting preserves by expanding Mississippian populations in central South Carolina and central Georgia. This circumscription appears to have occurred gradually and led to problems for the elites in the Savannah River Basin. About this same time (1400–1450), a general decline in rainfall occurred over the southwestern South Carolina area, as documented in dendrochronological records obtained from bald cypress trees (David W. Stahle and Malcolm R. Cleaveland, Tree Ring Laboratory, Department of Geography, University of Arkansas, personal communication 1987; see also Anderson 1987). By itself, the effects of this decline, which was from an above-average to slightly below-average level of rainfall, would have probably been minimal. In conjunction with other pressures, however, even a slight increase in the probability of crop failure would have likely exacerbated tensions within local political structures.

The populations of Cofitachequi and Ocute observed in the first contact era were extensive and, at least in the case of Ocute, were apparently increasing dramatically (Rudolph and Blanton 1981; Ranjel 1904, 89–102, 140; Elvas 1904, 55–69). Due to the abandonment of the Savannah River Valley, the size of the buffers surrounding these polities were much larger than those in place in this area previously (Hally and Rudolph 1986). One thing is clear: the patterns of chiefly competition that apparently led to the abandonment of the Savannah River Valley do not appear to have been over prime agricultural land, an explanation for Mississippian warfare advanced by Larson (1972). The central Savannah River Valley contains extensive rich farmland but was abandoned for two centuries while complex Mississippian chiefdoms existed in each of the adjoining major drainages. The Savannah River example indicates that investigating local and regional resource structure, in conjunction with an appraisal of the concept of buffer zones, may be an effective means of exploring the relationships between Mississippian warfare, polity size, and stability (see also Anderson 1987).

Conclusions

In this discussion, a number of topics relevant to the study of cycling behavior in chiefly societies have been examined. It has been argued that the stability of chiefly societies, and specifically southeastern Mississippian polities, was related to a number of factors, including: (1) characteristics of primary and secondary chiefdoms; (2) the strength and importance attached to legitimizing ideological structures, including ties with ancestral elites, the occupation of centers of power, and the role of chiefly iconography; (3) scale/time depth–dependent relationships between sacred and secular mechanisms for maintaining authority structures; (4) rules of succession, inheritance, marriage formation, and postmarital residence; and (5) ecological parameters, including both coarse-grained and fine-grained environmental structure, climatic perturbations, and the structure and stability of resource procurement/buffer zones. The investigation of these factors, it is argued, should suggest explanations for organizational change and stability in chiefly polities.

Future work should be concerned with resolving the kinds of cycling behavior that can occur in chiefly societies and the reasons why this behavior occurs. Descriptions of change in the size and organizational properties of chiefly societies need to be examined. Specifically, accounts of events such as societal expansion or collapse, successional events (i.e., leadership changes), and the fission or fusion of polities must be studied. Goals of such research should include resolving what is meant by cycling behavior as well as finding possible explanations for it. Specifically, cases of chiefly cycling should be examined with questions in mind, such as: What specifically is happening? What are underlying triggering/causal mechanisms? And is there any apparent periodicity to the phenomena under study?

Coupled with a search for descriptions and causes of cycling behavior in chiefly polities in general, a detailed examination of ethnohistoric evidence for this kind of behavior in the southeastern United States needs to be conducted. The focus for these investigations should be the recovery of archaeologically testable propositions about the internal organization, operation, and external relations of southeastern chiefly societies. At the time of initial European contact in the Southeast in the early sixteenth century, complex chiefdoms were observed over much of the region. Accounts by early explorers, most notably the records from the De Soto (1539–42), De Luna (1559–60), and Pardo (1565–67) expeditions, contain a wealth of information about these societies. Specific examples of the kinds of information to be found in early contact era sources include: (1) the nature of chiefly succession, (2) descriptions of mechanisms by which chiefly authority was maintained, (3) accounts of chiefly warfare, (4) accounts of tribute flow, (5) descriptions of the ideological structures, (6) descriptions of buffer zones, (7) descriptions of the abandonment of towns and centers, and (8) descriptions of the effects of crop failures or other disasters (Swanton 1946; Hudson n.d. and 1976; DePratter 1983; Hudson, Smith, and DePratter 1984; Hudson et al. 1985 and 1987; Anderson 1985 and 1987). It should be stressed that such ethnohistoric investigations should be directed to early contact era accounts that date prior to the marked organizational changes known to have occurred in southeastern native societies within less than a century after first contact (Ramenofsky 1982; M. Smith 1987).

Topics that can be explored in depth with southeastern Mississippian data include mechanisms for succession in local chiefly polities, how these polities dealt with both environmental and cultural stress, and the nature of secular and ideological authority/power structures and their relationship to chiefly stability. A critical aspect of this kind of research will be the linkage of the archaeological and ethnohistoric data, that is, to justify why the information about Mississippian polities contained in the sixteenth-century accounts has relevance to the study of prehistoric Mississippian societies. A major part of this will be the development of warranting arguments, or arguments of relevance, specifically documenting how information contained in ethnohistoric accounts may be recognized archaeologically.

Acknowledgments

The author would like to thank the following people for their advice and assistance in the preparation of this manuscript: Michael Blake, Mark J. Brooks, John E. Clark, Chester B. DePratter, Richard I. Ford, David J. Hally, John H. House, Charles M. Hudson, Vernon James Knight, Jr., Stephen A. Kowalewski, Gary Shapiro, Marvin T. Smith, John D. Speth, Vincas P. Steponaitis, Paul Welch, Mark Williams, and Henry T. Wright.

11. Conversations with the High Priest of Coosa

Charles M. Hudson

Hernando de Soto first heard of the chiefdom of Coosa in April 1540, when he was in the chiefdom of Ocute, located on the Oconee River in the general vicinity of present Milledgeville, Sparta, and Greensboro, Georgia. He was told that Coosa was a large, wealthy society which lay to the northwest (Elvas in Buckingham Smith 1968, 58). Had he not been intent on going toward the northeast, in search of the chiefdom of Cofitachequi, where he expected to find silver and gold, it is likely that his next stop after Ocute would have been Coosa. From Ocute he would have followed the old Hightower Trail, which lay on or near the present Georgia Railroad. He would have gone to Etowah, at Cartersville, and from there he would have gone north to the main town of Coosa at present Carters, Georgia.

But De Soto went northeast. From Ocute, De Soto led his expedition to Cofitachequi, near present Camden, South Carolina, where the silver and gold he expected turned out to be slabs of mica and pieces of copper. He also learned that Cofitachequi had been struck by an epidemic two years earlier and that many people had died. Perhaps because of this, the supplies of corn in Cofitachequi were not ample.

From Cofitachequi, De Soto led his expedition northward across the mountains and into the Tennessee Valley. Here he came to a town on an island in the French Broad River, which was the center of the chiefdom of Chiaha, a tributary of the chiefdom of Coosa. De Soto and his men had a pleasant stay in Chiaha. It was a beautiful land that perhaps reminded them of their Spanish homeland. There was plenty of food, and the men amused themselves by swimming and fishing in the river.

The people of Chiaha may have been irritated or put out by the Spaniards' demands for food. But when the Spaniards demanded

214

women, the people of Chiaha began to run away and hide. However, there is no evidence that they resisted militarily. De Soto forcibly took some people of Chiaha to serve as burden bearers and as concubines.

De Soto led his expedition southward from Chiaha to Coste, another island town, this one in the mouth of the Little Tennessee River, near present Lenoir City, Tennessee. There the Indians began to show signs of resisting, particularly when De Soto's men began taking food from their corncribs. The Indians of Coste took up arms and made ready to fight, but De Soto used a stratagem to avoid actual bloodshed. Again, De Soto impressed some Indians into service as burden bearers and as concubines.

They continued southward to the main town of Coosa in northwestern Georgia. Here they met a chief who was treated with more pomp than any they had met up to this time. The paramount chief of Coosa came out to meet them seated on a litter, which was carried upon the shoulders of his subjects. He was surrounded by principal men who sang and played upon flutes as the litter was carried along. De Soto and his men remained in Coosa for about a month. Again, the Spaniards enjoyed the ample stores of food, and again the Indians tried to run away and hide to escape being impressed into service by the Spaniards.

When De Soto departed from Coosa, he took the paramount chief and some of his relatives and principal men as hostages. He rounded up and took away some of the people in chains. They moved southward to Etowah and then westward to Ulibahali, at present Rome, Georgia. These people of Ulibahali were tributaries of chief Coosa, and they proved their loyalty by taking up arms and threatening the Spaniards in an attempt to gain their chief's release. But the chief of Coosa told them to lay down their arms, and they did.

When the De Soto expedition departed from Coosa, they left behind a black man named Robles, who had become ill and could not walk. He is described as "a very fine Christian and a good slave" (Varner 1962, 347). After De Soto had traveled downriver from Ulibahali for two days and had come to a small village—probably the King site (Hally 1975)—he discovered that another man was missing. He was Feryada, a Levantine [Garcilaso de la Vega calls him "Falco Herrado . . . a very plebeian person" (Varner and Varner 1962, 346–47)]. According to Garcilaso, this man told the Indians of Coosa that, rather than having to see before him every day De Soto, who had reprimanded and verbally insulted him, he would prefer to live out his life with the Indians. De Soto made an effort to get the Indians to return this man to him, so that he could punish or kill him, but the Indians refused to do so. One wonders whether Feryada would have been emboldened to remain behind at Coosa had not Robles been forced to stay there.

De Soto went on to Talisi, near Childersburg, Alabama. This was the southern limit of the power of the chief of Coosa. Here De Soto released the chief and his principal men, but he refused to release the chief's sister. The chief of Coosa went away weeping. De Soto next went to the territory of Chief Tascaluza, who was an aggressive chief in central Alabama and was much respected and feared by the Indians. De Soto took Chief Tascaluza and some of his principal men hostage just as he had done with Chief Coosa, but Tascaluza and his people reacted differently. They struck the Spaniards in a surprise attack at Mabila. Several of the Spaniards were killed, and almost all of them were wounded, some more than once. The Indians suffered a devastating loss. Perhaps 3,000 of their best fighting men were killed.

After the battle was over, the Spaniards learned that people other than those who were subject to Tascaluza had taken part in this battle. The people of Coosa are not specifically mentioned, but there is other evidence that they probably were participants in the battle. This is one explanation for the many people found buried at the King site who were killed by European weapons. Also, in 1567, Juan Pardo was told that several of Coosa's tributaries whose towns were along the Little Tennessee River had killed some of De Soto's men.

De Soto had gotten a uniformly peaceful reception as he traveled through the chiefdom of Coosa. But Chief Coosa either changed his mind after De Soto had enslaved some of his people, his sister included, or it may be that Chief Coosa had been plotting with Tascaluza from the very beginning. That is, Coosa would give De Soto a peaceful reception and lull the Spaniards into carelessness. Then the two of them would deliver a coup de grace at Mabila.

The De Soto expedition was a failure in that it did not succeed in finding a state-level society with gold and silver and a large and willing supply of labor. But it had established that there was a large continent to the north of the Caribbean. As time went on, the Spaniards grew afraid that their European rivals—particularly France— would found a colony on that continent to the north. If this were to occur, it would make it difficult for Spain to found a colony there. Such a colony might also make it possible for the French to find a road to the fabulously rich silver mines in Zacatecas, and with this they could pose a military threat.

Don Tristan de Luna was selected to found a Spanish colony in North America, or La Florida, as it was called. On August 14, 1559, De Luna's fleet of thirteen ships entered Pensacola Bay, a harbor which he said would be safe in any storm. Five days later a hurricane struck, which sank or damaged all but three of his ships. Most of the food was lost.

Because his colonists were starving, De Luna moved most of them north to a town called Nanipacana on the Alabama River. But they found very little food there. The Indians of Nanipacana had been damaged either directly or indirectly by the De Soto expedition. They ran away from the Spaniards, taking what food they could and destroying some of the rest.

De Luna eventually decided to send a party of men northward to where De Soto had found such ample supplies—Coosa. He sent Mateo del Sauz with 40 cavalry and 100 infantry to go in search of Coosa. This party also included the friars Domingo de la Anunciación and Domingo de Salazar and an Indian woman who could translate Spanish into the language of Coosa. They departed from Nanipacana on April 15, 1560, and they reached Onachiqui, the first town of Coosa, in early June.

This contingent was in Coosa from August until October. Several veterans of the De Soto expedition were among this contingent, and they were at first surprised at how much the place had declined in the 20 years since they were last there. Some of those who had spoken of the country in such grand terms said they must have been bewitched for the country to have seemed so rich and populous.

The power of the chief of Coosa appears to have eroded in the wake of the De Soto expedition. In fact, one of the reasons why the Coosas were willing to feed the Spanish soldiers is that the Europeans had agreed to go with the Coosas on a raid on the Napochies, a tributary people who lived in the vicinity of present Chattanooga, Tennessee. The Napochies had rebelled. Not only were they not paying tribute to the chief of Coosa, they were waging war on him.

From the documents of the De Soto and De Luna expeditions, it is possible to learn quite a bit about the social structure of the

chiefdom of Coosa. Much of this is contained in letters that Fray
Anunciación wrote while he was in Coosa and in an interview he
gave to the historian Dávila Padilla many years later. Anunciación
appears to have had more interest in the ways of the Indians than
did his Dominican brothers. In addition to these documentary
sources, much detailed information on the material and economic
life of the people of Coosa has been accumulated by archaeologists
who have worked in this area for over a century.

But what was the world of the Coosas like from the inside? How
did they conceive of their cosmos? How did they explain why things
happened? How did they regard their first encounter with bearded
people, strangely clothed, who rode upon strange beasts and who
possessed weapons and tools clearly superior to their own?

If only Fray Anunciación had taken full advantage of his inter-
preter, a woman who had probably spent her youth as a Coosa and
who had been enslaved by De Soto and taken to Mexico by the
survivors of the expedition. If only he had interviewed the most
senior or most-respected priest of Coosa.

In what follows, I have tried to imagine what such conversations
might have been like. What follows is either a piece of historical
fiction or else a piece of fictional history. Historical fiction may
be imagined as a fictional bird in a historical cage. The cage may
be large, so that the bird may fly freely about, or the cage may be
small, so that the bird is too confined to show off and cut fancy
capers. In what follows, I have tried to confine my fictional bird
in a pretty small cage. The myths "The Peregrine Falcon's Gift"
and "How Day and Night Were Divided" are adopted from John
Swanton (1929, 2, 194–95).

* * *

To the Illustrious Don Luis de Velasco, Viceroy of New Spain
Illustrious Sir:

I am writing to tell you some of the strange and fantastic things
I learned in Coosa. A man in your position, who has the responsibil-
ity for governing so vast a land, can ill afford to spend time reading
about matters that are small or chimerical. I can well understand
that you would lay these pages aside unread. But even though my
brothers and I have failed in our effort to bring the poor lost sheep
of Coosa within the Christian fold, how long can it be before other
Spaniards more fortunate than we will undertake to build towns
and cities in La Florida and before other friars will undertake to

save the souls of the heathen. It is for these that I have particularly intended these pages.

We knew when we first reached the capital village of Coosa that it was not the rich and fertile province we had been promised. And when our valiant soldiers went with the archers of Coosa to chastise their errant tributaries, the Napochies, we saw that, even with the food we had got from that province, Don Tristan de Luna could not succeed in what he intended. How discouraging it was to have come so far and suffered so much and yet fail to make this a Christian land. But Fray Domingo de Salazar and I did not cease to work to bring the Indians out of the darkness in which they live.

When I first reached Coosa, I wrote letters comparing the people of Coosa unfavorably with the people of Nanipacana. The temples at Coosa were small, excessively rustic, and not much attended by the people. Moreover, I later found that the high priest of Coosa, though in truth he is more a sorcerer or necromancer, dressed not with the best, but with the poorest of his land.

I had frequently seen an old man who was often present when things were happening. He clung to the edges and stood in the shadows. He watched all that occurred, saying nothing. On his bony shoulders he wore an old deerskin mantle on which heathenish designs had been painted, but it was now much worn, and the designs were so faded they could hardly be seen. In his hair, he sometimes wore a tuft of owl feathers.

Had I been more observant, I would have noticed that the people of Coosa paid him deference. But it was an action of his that made us notice him. One day he startled our translator, Teresa de Coosa, by addressing her in Spanish. Then he asked her in the Coosa language what had happened to the Sun Woman whom De Soto had taken from Coosa. When Teresa de Coosa told the priest that the woman had ended up with a cruel master, who in beating her had put out one of her eyes, and that even though Don Tristan de Luna had thought that this woman would be an asset to his venture, she had run away and had hidden herself so that she would not have to return to her birthplace, Teresa said that tears had welled up in the old man's eyes, and he turned his back and walked away.

When I sought the old man out, I learned that twenty years ago he had befriended two men who had been with Hernando de Soto. One was a black slave named Robles, who had fallen ill when De Soto had been in Coosa and could not travel when the expedition continued. The other man was Feryada, a Levantine, who was a deserter. It was from these two that the old man had learned a few words of Spanish and had learned something about our country and our ways. Indeed, we found that the chief of Coosa, even though he had reason to hate the Spanish and to want revenge on them, had commanded the priest to learn as much about them as he could.

Robles and Feryada died 8 or 10 years ago. They died naturally, the old man said, but who can be sure how they died? The priest had long thought about what he had learned from Robles and Feryada. But, strangely, from what they had told him, he had got an idea of what it was about his people that we should know.

If I would come to the temple, he said, he would reveal this to me. But when he realized that Teresa de Coosa, a woman, would have to be present at all times to translate, he said that he could not do it. The Indians are quite as intent on keeping the two sexes separate as were the Israelites. I told him that he could come and talk to me at the hut Salazar and I had built to shelter ourselves and that Teresa de Coosa was not truly a Coosa anymore. In fact, the women of Coosa shunned her most cruelly. When we departed from Coosa, Teresa would surely depart with us. Finally, the old man agreed, and our conversations began. I wrote down what I could as he talked and Teresa translated. Afterward, I would read through my notes, and Teresa, as best she could, corrected and explained what I had written.

This is a true record of what I, Domingo de la Anunciación, have heard and understood. May our Lord guard and give greater increase to the very illustrious person of your Lordship, as I your servant desire. Coosa. October 15, 1560.

First Conversation

What a time of suffering, disorder, and confusion we Coosas have had since you Long Knives first came to our land. I shall never forget that spring when we heard from a man of Ocute that an army of strange men were traveling about. They were not numerous, but they were as confident as a hawk among quail. They walked through Ocute unopposed.

The man said that the Long Knives had wondrous weapons. They were as sharp as a sliver of hard cane or a splinter of fat-lighter pine. But what greatly astonished us was that he said these weapons could not be broken!

Some Coosas said that we had only to wait until these people

were among the wolves of Cofitachequi. The chieftainess of Cofitachequi would drink their very blood. But the strange army walked
through Cofitachequi as easily as one walks through a morning
mist.

News came that they were in Chiaha. It was only a matter of
time when they would be in the capital town of Coosa. Many Coosas
were terrified.

But the Great Chief of Coosa was calm. He talked with his coun-
selors, who were called in from all parts of Coosa. What if we were
to form an alliance with our rival to the south—Tascaluza. Together
we could surely strike the Long Knives a mortal blow. That is the
plan that was made. The Coosas would not resist, no matter how
great the insult or injury. The Long Knives would be lulled into
complacency. Then, in the land of Tascaluza, we would strike with
a vengeance.

But when the blow was struck at Mabila, there followed a day
of slaughter that will never be forgotten. Our blood drenched the
land. We could not understand it. Our warriors are trained in the
art of war from the time they are small boys. They excel in the
art of hand-to-hand combat. The Long Knives had little taste for
it, and little real skill at it. But their weapons were unbelievable,
and their strange clothing made them difficult to kill.

I had many conversations with Robles and Feryada. Both of them
learned to speak the language of Coosa, though neither of them
learned it perfectly. But in time we understood each other well
enough. The questions I asked often exasperated them. They said
that I asked the meaning of things that any child should know.
Their saying this amused me, because they asked the same kind
of questions of me.

I learned much from Robles. He had been born in a province that
was not unlike Coosa. While still a boy, he had been caught and
taken in chains to the land of the Long Knives. What a different
land it was! So many people! And what power their kings had. And
how remarkably their work was divided. Some men did nothing
else but make weapons. They worked constantly to make these
weapons more and more effective.

Robles said that much of the advantage of the Long Knives lay
in their ability to freeze language by making marks on thin white
bark, as you are doing now. This is remarkable to us. Once the
words are placed on that bark, they are there forever, and they always say the same thing. With this, a chief could lay a plan of con-

quest that might take three lifetimes to complete. With this, the
sacred knowledge of a people could be kept forever.

For us Coosas, the only knowledge we possess, or can possess,
is that which we retain in memory. And yet we do try to increase
our knowledge. That is why we were willing to supply food and
shelter to Robles and Feryada for so many years, forgiving them
until they learned to behave and act as true men. We wished to
learn from them, though much of what they said was so extraordinary we doubted that it was true.

Second Conversation

I will tell you some of the things we had to explain to Robles
and Feryada time and time again, either because they could not
grasp it or because when they did grasp it, they could not believe
it.

In all that I say, remember this one thing: *Ours is a mirrored
universe, where time moves in circles.* Forgive me if this sounds
like a puzzle or a paradox. I simply mean that those who are wise
know that relationships in one realm are mirrored in another, just
as a tree is mirrored in a quiet pool of water beneath it.

Thus, in the human realm, women and men are similar beings,
and yet their natures are different—they are opposites. Wherever
you look, the woman-man relationship may be seen. Woman is to
man as the sun is to the moon; as corn is to venison; as red is
to white; as disorder is to order; as the Underworld is to the Upperworld; even as snake is to falcon. Begin wherever you will, as you
move outward, from one realm to another, the same order prevails,
and to understand this is to understand all.

Just as opposites are mirrored everywhere, so are circles. The Sun,
the luminary of the day, moves in a circle. In the morning, the
Sun comes from beneath the edge of the vault of the sky in the
east, and as she does, the day begins to quicken and unfold. Then
the Sun travels her circle across the sky, and as the tired day wanes,
the Sun slips beneath the edge of the sky vault in the west. Then
it becomes dark, and it remains dark while the Sun completes her
circle through the Underworld to the east, where another day begins. And in this circle, day is opposed to night, light is opposed
to dark, east is opposed to west, and, though this may seem obscure,
life is opposed to death.

The Moon, the luminary of the night, also makes a circle each
day, and beyond this it makes a larger circle that takes many days

as it waxes and wanes. There is yet a larger circle as the year waxes and wanes. All of these circles resemble each other. As each begins, life quickens, and things grow in fullness, but then they decline, fall apart, and end in death and disorder. It is for this reason that at the end of each year, we perform our Green Corn Ceremony, in which we cast aside the old worn-out remnants of the year, purify ourselves, and embark on a fresh new year.

Some of the old priests speculate that beyond the year there may be an even larger circle that we do not understand. It is one that takes many years to complete. Some of these old priests say that it is the circle of a chiefdom. At the beginning of this circle, a chief rises in power, and as his domain and influence expand, the circle widens. But then a weakness comes. His tributaries become sullen and restive. Some even refuse to pay tribute, as has lately been the case with our tributaries, the Napochies. His chiefdom may go into decline, and some say that it dies a kind of death. Whether this larger circle exists I do not know for certain. But one thing is certain: In many places in our land, there are large mounds that have been abandoned so long that they have growing on them trees that cannot be encircled within one's outstretched arms.

These mirrored oppositions and circles have not always existed. In ancient time, the world was insanely disordered; no sense could be made of it. It was a time of wonders and extraordinary beings. Ancient time ended, and our time began when order was gradually imposed upon the world and when the rules by which we live were established. We preserve many stories about this change from ancient time to our time, stories about the first man and the first woman, about the origins of corn and game, about how the clever water spider procured fire for man's use, and many others.

It pleased us when we learned that Feryada and Robles believed the world possesses three levels. At last we found something on which we could agree. But in time we saw that this agreement was illusory. The world does exist in three levels, as you know, but for us the levels are different. This earth, the world of familiar things, is much the same for us as it is for you. But we do not believe the Upperworld is filled with the souls of good people. The Upperworld is the place of the First Man and the First Woman, and it is the abode of Thunder and of all the great animals and beings who once lived on earth but who went to the Upperworld when the earth became impure. In the Upperworld all beings are larger and more perfect than beings on earth. Yet because of its perfection, it is a place where few men can enter, and even then not for very long. Only a few priests, such as myself, have themselves attained a purity and a perfection that make them men of the Upperworld. Such men are able to influence the course of things, such as weather and warfare and illness.

Beneath this earth on which we stand, there is an Underworld. But it is not filled with the souls of evil people who there suffer hideous torment. The Underworld is a place of spirits and powerful creatures. The winged serpent is at home in the Underworld (though, in truth, the winged serpent is at home in all three realms). Whereas the Upperworld is a place of perfect order, the Underworld is its opposite. It is a world in which the normal is turned upside down; it is a place of surprising new things; it is a place of frightening disorder. It is possible for certain men to go to visit the Underworld, but first they must fast for several days. And when they are in the Underworld, however hungry and thirsty they become, they must eat or drink nothing, because if they do, they will die when they return to this world.

Our Upperworld is not simply good, and our Underworld is not simply bad. One is a place of order, and the other is a place of disorder. The earth exists in between them, and it is constantly pulled this way and that. Perhaps you can already see that the Underworld is to the Upperworld as ancient time is to our time. The same reality is mirrored everywhere.

This world, the earth on which we stand, is an island that floats upon the waters. It is in the form of a great circle, and Coosa is at the center of it. Even more exactly, the mound upon which the house of the Great Chief of Coosa rests is the center of the earth. From this point, the four directions—two pairs of opposites—radiate to the edges of the earth. The vital, high-spirited, red east is opposed to the wan, dark west, which reeks of death. The peaceful, harmonious, white south is opposed to the cold, blue north, a place of witchcraft and deception. In each of the four directions, different kinds of beings and forces reside, and in our rituals, our priests seek to balance one of them against the other and, on occasion, to invoke all of them at once.

Feryada and Robles used to ask us whether we believed in God, and the truth is, we do and we do not. We believe in many gods, great and small. The greatest is the Sun, the source of all warmth and light and the greatest sustainer of life. But the Sun is not a merciful and loving being as your God is said to be. We have to treat her with respect, because she is notoriously jealous, and if she becomes angry, she can wreak the most terrible punishments. It is for this reason that we never speak her real name, and when we dance or move in most of our rituals, we circle to the right while facing a center. The reason for this is that she circles to the left while facing a center in her transit through the heavens, and she would be furious if we did the same. There is even a story about some people who looked up at the sun, squinting their eyes and screwing up their faces as they did, and she took this to be an insult. She thought they were making faces at her, and she inflicted on them a terrible plague that almost exterminated them. She is an important being like your God, but she is not simply a loving and merciful being.

The Great Chief of Coosa is the Sun's grandchild. They are now many, many generations apart, but she is still grandparent, and the Great Chief of Coosa and his brothers and sisters are her grandchildren, and if she loves anyone, it is them. She sent her grandchildren down to live on earth and to rule here and teach people to live in peace. Had the Sun not sent her kinsmen to earth, we would live no better than the Chiscas.

The Great Chief of Coosa and his kinsmen are of the Sun's lineage. Every Coosa belongs to a lineage, the lineage of his grandmother, and much that is vital to a person comes to him from his lineage. Some lineages are more numerous than others, and some are more influential than others. But none compares to the Sun's lineage.

The Suns do not labor in the fields. Rather, each of us donates a part of his or her produce, as a beloved gift, to the Sun's lineage. But the Suns do not eat all of the produce. The Great Chief is generous, and he sponsors lavish feasts for all of the people, and in this way much of the produce is returned to them.

The Great Chief lives in a house on one of the mounds that you have seen here. Here he is elevated above the mundane, near the superior realm of the Upperworld. From his house, he can look down upon his people, just as the Sun looks down on all the earth. His mound is a mirror of the cosmos. It is elevated, and each of the four directions of the world is plainly to be seen. Our temple is built upon another of the mounds, and in this temple, a sacred fire burns. This is not the ordinary fire that you fair-skinned people use, good only for warmth and for cooking food. Sacred fire is the representative of the Sun on earth, and anything that is done in the presence of sacred fire is instantly known to the Sun. The thin white strand of smoke you see rising from it is our fragile link with the Upperworld.

Members of the Sun's lineage enjoy the best of everything. All Coosas treat them with deference. But it is the Great Chief of Coosa who is most respected. Only he can wear certain garments and ornaments: magnificent feather cloaks, copper ornaments, pearls, and shell gorgets. On some occasions, the Great Chief is carried in procession on a litter, which is borne on the shoulders of his subjects.

When a Great Chief dies, it is a thing we greatly fear and mourn. Upon his good health all of Coosa depends. So when a Great Chief dies, we feel vulnerable and threatened. We raze his dwelling to the ground, lay a thick mantle of earth upon the mound, completely covering it, and on top we build a new dwelling to be occupied by the new Great Chief. And when a Great Chief is buried, it is a great event, on which we expend much wealth. Nothing is too good for this occasion. Because it is a dead Sun, the funeral procession moves in circles to the left. With his body we inter the finest clothing and adornments. His closest retainers are strangled to death to accompany him to the other world. And besides this, some individuals step forward and volunteer to go to the other world with him.

You should not think that only those who are wellborn are the people who are honored in Coosa. Honor and respect is also given to those who earn it through special abilities and achievements. My own lineage—raccoon—is neither large nor powerful. But I am High Priest of Coosa because of my ability to master our traditions and knowledge, and because I have lived with great devotion in accordance with our beloved rules.

And our warriors must earn their place through brave and valiant deeds. The warriors of Coosa, especially the young ones, are the terror of the earth. They are constantly prepared to go out and swoop down upon an enemy. They are to other men as the peregrine falcon is to other birds. Of all the falcons and hawks and eagles, it is the peregrine falcon who is able to speed downward from a great height and to strike and kill a bird in flight. The smaller birds they pluck out of the air; they smash the skulls of the larger birds. They are capable of killing birds that are twice their size. For our warriors, the peregrine falcon—Thunder's falcon—is the most magnificent bird. It is for this reason that the young warriors paint the peregrine eye markings about their eyes, and we emboss likenesses of it on sheets of copper.

When one of our warriors kills an enemy, he does it individually in combat. Even when many warriors are on the field, it is warrior against warrior. We have observed that a few of your warriors enjoy fighting in this way, but for the most part, your warriors prefer to fight in concert with others. And if you will pardon my saying so, they do it with little skill and finesse. Our warriors train all their lives for proficiency in the bow and arrow and in hand-to-hand fighting with clubs. Whereas it seems to us that any clumsy bear could shoot those thunderous weapons of yours, and the same is true of those curious bows you use.

When our warriors kill, they desecrate the slain enemy by cutting off his head or his scalp. When we kill an enemy, it is for vengeance, and vengeance is sweetest when insult is added to injury. In the same way, on those occasions when we have attacked the main town of an enemy chiefdom, when we could enter the town, we have desecrated their temple, defiling all their sacred things.

By now it should be plain to you that one part of the world mirrors another. But if you are not yet convinced of the truth of this, I will give you an example of another kind. It is this: The world of birds mirrors the world of men. I have already told how the peregrine falcon is the warrior of birds.

The woodpecker is another bird our warriors admire, particularly the red-bellied woodpecker and the ivory-billed woodpecker. The red-bellied woodpecker is a bold, aggressive bird. It sometimes happens that birds will come to our houses to eat table scraps. Towhees will come first; then cardinals will come and displace the towhees; blue jays will come and displace the cardinals; but the red-bellied woodpecker will come and displace all other birds. And when the woodpecker, especially the ivory-billed, strikes a tree with his beak, it reminds our warriors of the way they strike an enemy's skull with their clubs. One other thing about woodpeckers: Many of the small timid birds cling to the forest's edge, afraid to go in, but the woodpeckers are at home in the depths of the forests, where our men have to go when they hunt and go to war. Many of our men, moving silently and anxiously through the forest, have been startled by the abrupt, hoarse cry of a woodpecker.

Our warriors also admire the turkey. It is a bird we hunt and eat, but the turkey is a valiant fighter, particularly in mating season.

And it has the sharp senses of a warrior. We say that the turkey carries a scalp lock on its breast.

One of the birds we priests most admire is the kingfisher. Partly it is because the kingfisher is at home in every world. They are birds and therefore are creatures of the air and the Upperworld. But they have the capability of diving into the water and of pulling up small fish. Hence, they are at home in the Underworld, because streams and rivers are paths and roads to the Underworld. Moreover, unlike other birds who build their nests in trees, the kingfisher builds his nest in a small burrow in the face of a steep bank, showing that he is at home in this world. All of this is notable to priests, because we too have to be at home in all of the three worlds. The kingfisher has yet another remarkable ability. Of all the birds, he alone is often able to evade an attack by a peregrine falcon. He does it by repeatedly diving into the water. This infuriates a peregrine, who is so used to success, but there is nothing he can do about it, because he is not at all at home in the watery element.

The crow is a thief and a detractor. You will often see a block of raucous, ugly crows flying about an honest hawk or falcon out hunting for his dinner. Crows will rob the nests of other birds, and they will even rob the nests of hawks and falcons. They steal whatever they can, and they show respect for none.

The horned owl is a witch among birds. They are so peculiar in their appearance that, if the light is bad, one perched on a limb can be mistaken for a cat. They are birds of the night, and their weird cry is never a comfort to anyone. They have the uncanny ability to see in the dark, and with this terrible advantage, they can kill any other bird. They can even kill a peregrine falcon, who can see in dim light but not in darkness. It is a bad sign when a horned owl is heard outside the house of one who is seriously ill. It may be an owl, or it may be a witch who has come to steal the soul of the one who is ill.

Ravens are nearly as frightening as owls, especially when they make that horrid growling sound. Fortunately, they generally keep to the higher mountains, in company with other frightful creatures.

Even small birds mirror the world of men. Hunters, when they are out on the trail, think it lucky when they hear the sound of a chickadee. The chickadee is a pretty bird, and it is a truth teller. But the chickadee's song is easily confused with the song of the tufted titmouse, who is a notorious liar among birds. Is it a chickadee we hear, or only a tufted titmouse? And isn't it the same with men? Old as I am, I am still amazed at how difficult it is to distinguish between truth and falsehood.

Some birds are so beautiful that they are favored by men and gods alike. The Sun, in her vanity, favors the redbird because it is red like she is. We say that the redbird is the Sun's daughter, but this is only a way of speaking.

Please forgive me if I have given you the impression that our beloved knowledge is handed from one generation to another in the way I have tried to explain it to you. Our beloved knowledge lives in stories, dances, and rituals. The sense of it is constantly around us, in everything that we do. Let me tell you one of our bird stories, which you should now be able to understand.

The Peregrine Falcon's Gift

An orphan was traveling about hunting, but he was never successful. His weapon was old, for he was very poor. He killed nothing, and nobody liked him very much. Hungry and desperate, at last he stayed with some people who lived far away. But soon they said, "Go on hunting," and he sadly set out again. He put a pack on his back and walked until nightfall, when he reached a big thicket, and he sat down there. "I do not believe I shall kill anything," he said, as he sat with his legs drawn up. While he was sitting there, he heard a noise. The noise was made by a peregrine falcon, which flew to him, landed, and huddled between his knees. Soon a horned owl came in pursuit, landed, and stood on the other side of the fire, his huge yellow eyes glowing with fury. Then the falcon said to the man, "Take hold of me." So the man laid hold of him and sat there with him. The horned owl said, "Throw him over to me. I want to kill him." "No," answered the falcon, "my way of going about in the light of day is very, very good." But the horned owl kept teasing to have him. Then the falcon said, "This horned owl that talks so is a witch—he who says, 'You will be able to kill something as I do.' Don't throw me over to him, and when day comes, I will give you good hunting." Then the man who could not kill anything, though tempted by the horned owl, protected the falcon until the sun rose. When it was daylight, the horned owl hooted and flew off and sat upon the top of a tree. "Now let me go," said the falcon. The man let the falcon go, and the bird screamed and flew off. He flew up very high, turned, and plummeted down, striking the owl and cutting off his head. The falcon said, "By daylight, my friend, I can whip you." He flew down to the orphan and said, "Now I am very happy. Anything you want, I will do for you," and he disappeared.

After that the orphan picked up his weapon and started on, but after making a very short circuit, he came back. He had killed bear, deer, turkey, and all kinds of game. He brought them to camp and roasted them. Then he was very happy. Now he never had to walk far when he hunted, because he never missed. He stayed there in his camp enjoying all sorts of good things. Then the other people grew angry with him on account of his success.

It should be obvious to you that although this is a simple story about a poor hunter, a falcon, and a horned owl, it is also a story about forthright people who work in the light of day and evil witches who work in the darkness of night. And in passing, it says that people are almost as hard on those who succeed too much as on those who succeed too little.

Need I say that the four-footed animals also reflect the world of men? And lest you think that we people of Coosa are devoid of humor, let me tell you a little story about three of our favorite four-footed animals.

How Day and Night Were Divided

The animals held a meeting and Nokosi, the bear, because he was largest of all the animals, insisted on presiding.

The question was how to divide day and night. Some desired the day to last all the time; others wished it to always be night.

After much talk, Citokoco, the chipmunk, said: "I see that Wotko, the raccoon, has rings on his tail divided equally, first a dark color then a light color. I think day and night ought to be divided like the rings on Wotko's tail."

The animals were surprised at the wisdom of the little chipmunk. They adopted his plan and divided day and night in the same manner as the rings on Wotko's tail, each succeeding the other in regular order.

The bear, beside himself with envy because such a small creature had carried the day, scratched Citokoco's back and thus caused the stripes on the back of all his descendants, the chipmunks.

This is one of the simple, amusing stories we tell our children. But by now you are able to see that there is depth in this simplicity. It is a story about how the chipmunk got his stripes, but it is also a story about how order was imposed on chaos; how ancient time ended and our time began; and how wisdom can come from those who are seemingly small and insignificant. Last of all, it is a story about how time moves in circles, though symbolized in an unusual way—on a raccoon's tail.

References Cited

Abrams, Elliot M.
1986 The Causes of Deforestation and its Role in the Collapse of Copán, Honduras. Paper presented at the 51st Annual Meeting of the Society for American Archaeology, New Orleans, La.
Anderson, David G.
1975 Inferences from Distribution Studies of Prehistoric Artifacts in the Coastal Plain of South Carolina. *Southeastern Archaeological Conference Bulletin* 18:180–94.
1985 The Internal Organization and Operation of Chiefdom Level Societies on the Southeastern Atlantic Slope: An Examination of Ethnohistoric Sources. *South Carolina Antiquities* 17. Columbia, S.C.
1986 The Mississippian in South Carolina. In *Papers in Honor of Robert L. Stephenson*, edited by A. C. Goodyear III. South Carolina Institute of Archaeology and Anthropology and University of South Carolina Anthropological Studies.
1987 Warfare and Mississippian Political Evolution in the Southeastern United States. Paper presented in the "Warfare and the Evolution of Chiefdoms" symposium, 20th Annual Meeting of the Chacmool Conference, Calgary, Alberta.
Anderson, David G., Charles E. Cantley, and A. Lee Novick
1982 *The Matassee Lake Sites: Archaeological Investigations along the Lower Santee River in the Coastal Plain of South Carolina.* Atlanta: Archaeological Services Division, National Park Service.
Anderson, David G., David J. Hally, and James L. Rudolph
1986 The Mississippian Occupation of the Savannah River Valley. *Southeastern Archaeology* 5(1):32–51.
Anderson, David G., and Joseph Schuldenrein
1983 Mississippian Settlement in the Southern Piedmont: Evidence from the Rucker's Bottom Site, Elbert County, Georgia. *Southeastern Archaeology* 2:98–117.
1985 *Prehistoric Human Ecology along the Upper Savannah River: Exca-*

231

vations at the Rucker's Bottom, Abbeville and Bullard Site Groups.
Atlanta: Russell Papers, Archaeological Services Division, National
Park Service.

Baden, William
  1983 Tomotley: An Eighteenth Century Cherokee Village. *Report of In-
    vestigations*, no. 36. Knoxville: Department of Anthropology, Univer-
    sity of Tennessee.

Bandelier, Fanny (translator)
  1964 *The Journey of Alvar Nunez Cabeza de Vaca.* Chicago: Rio Grande
    Press.

Bender, Barbara
  1985 Emergent Tribal Formulations in the American Midcontinent.
    American Antiquity 50:52–62.

Binford, Lewis
  1962 Archaeology as Anthropology. *American Antiquity* 28:217–25.

Blake, Michael
  1986 Status and Power in Chiefs' Residences. Paper presented at the
    "Material Culture and Symbolic Expression" symposium, 11th Con-
    gress of the International Union of Prehistoric and Protohistoric Sci-
    ences, 1–7 September 1986. Southhampton, U.K.

Blake, Michael, and John E. Clark
  1986 Environmental Restrictedness and the Evolution of Complex Socie-
    ties. Unpublished Report.

Bourne, Edward Gaylord (editor)
  1904 *Narratives of the Career of Hernando de Soto in the Conquest of
    Florida.* New York: Allerton.

Boyd, Mark F.
  1951 Fort San Luis: Documents Describing the Tragic End of the Mission
    Era. In *Here They Once Stood: The Tragic End of the Apalachee Mis-
    sions*, by M. F. Boyd, H. G. Smith, and J. W. Griffin. Gainesville: Uni-
    versity of Florida Press.

Bracken, William, Frankie Snow, Chris Trowell, and Nancy White
  1986 *Archaeological Investigations in Telfair County, Georgia, 1985.*
    Douglas, Ga.: University of South Florida and South Georgia Col-
    lege.

Brain, Robert
  1972 *Bangwa Kinship and Marriage.* London: Cambridge University
    Press.

Braley, Chad O.
  1982 Archaeological Survey, Testing and Evaluation of the Pinckney Is-
    land National Wildlife Refuge, Beaufort County, South Carolina. Re-
    port submitted to the U.S. Fish and Wildlife Service, Atlanta.

Braley, Chad O., R. Jerald Ledbetter, and Mark Williams
  1985 Newly Recognized Mississippian Ceremonial Sites in the Oconee

Province. Paper presented at the fall meeting of the Society for Georgia Archaeology, Savannah.

Braley, Chad O., Lisa D. O'Steen, and Irvy R. Quitmyer
1986 Archaeological Investigations at 9MC41, Harris Neck National Wildlife Refuge, McIntosh County, Georgia. Report submitted to the U.S. Fish and Wildlife Service, Atlanta.

Braun, David, and Stephen Plog
1982 Evolution of "Tribal" Social Networks: Theory and Prehistoric North American Evidence. *American Antiquity* 47:504–25.

Brown, James A.
1971 The Dimensions of Status in the Burials at Spiro. In *Approaches to the Social Dimensions of Mortuary Practices*, edited by J. A. Brown. *Society for American Archaeology Memoir*, no. 25. Washington: Society for American Archaeology.
1976 The Southern Cult Reconsidered. *Midcontinental Journal of Archaeology* 1:115–35.
1985 The Mississippian Period. In *Ancient Art of the American Woodland Indians*, by D. S. Brose, J. A. Brown, and D. W. Penny. New York: Harry N. Abrams.

Bushnell, Amy T.
1978 "That Demonic Game": The Campaign to Stop Indian Pelota Playing in Spanish Florida, 1675–1684. *The Americas* 35:1–19.
1979 Patricio de Hinachuba: Defender of the Word of God, the Crown of the King, and the Little Children of Ivitachuco. *American Indian Culture and Research Journal* 3(3):1–21.

Caldwell, Joseph R.
1950 A Preliminary Report on Excavations in the Allatoona Reservoir. *Early Georgia* 1:4–21.
1953 The Rembert Mounds, Elbert County, Georgia. *Bureau of American Ethnology Bulletin* 154:307–20. Washington, D.C.
1955 Cherokee Pottery from Northern Georgia. *American Antiquity* 20:277–80.
1971 Chronology of the Georgia Coast. *Southeastern Archaeological Conference Bulletin* 13:88–92.

Caldwell, Joseph R., and Catherine McCann
1941 *Irene Mound Site, Chatham County, Georgia.* Athens: University of Georgia Press.

Carneiro, Robert L.
1981 The Chiefdom: Precursor of the State. In *The Transition to Statehood in the New World*, edited by G. D. Jones and R. R. Kautz. Cambridge: Cambridge University Press.

Chapman, Carl H.
1980 *The Archaeology of Missouri.* Vol. 2. Columbia: University of Missouri Press.

Chmurny, William W.
  1973 The Ecology of the Middle Mississippian Occupation of the American Bottom. Ph.D. dissertation, Department of Anthropology, University of Illinois at Urbana-Champaign. Ann Arbor: University Microfilms.
Colburn, William B.
  1936 The Use of Beveled Discoidals in Northern Georgia. Papers of the Michigan Academy of Science, Arts, and Letters, no. 21. Detroit.
Cook, Fred C.
  1978 The Kent Mound: A Study of the Irene Phase on the Lower Georgia Coast. Master's thesis, Department of Anthropology, Florida State University, Tallahassee.
  1980 Chronological and Functional Reexamination of the Irene Ceramic Complex. In Excursions in Southeastern Geology, The Archaeology-Geology of the Georgia Coast, edited by J. D. Howard, C. B. DePratter, and R. W. Frey. The Geological Society of America, Guidebook 20. Atlanta: Georgia Department of Natural Resources.
  1986 Origin and Change of Irene Rim Decoration in Coastal Georgia. The Chesopean 24(4):2–22.
Cotton, J. A., L. A. Duncan, G. L. Hickman, and C. F. Montgomery
  1974 Soil Survey of Talladega County, Alabama. Washington: U.S. Department of Agriculture, USDA Soil Conservation and Forest Service.
Covington, James
  1972 The Apalachee Indians, 1704–1763. Florida Historical Quarterly 50:366–84.
Cronin, William
  1983 Changes in the Land: Indians, Colonists, and the Ecology of New England. New York: Hill and Lang.
Crook, Morgan R.
  1978a Mississippian Period Community Organization on the Georgia Coast. Ph.D. dissertation, Department of Anthropology, University of Florida. Ann Arbor: University Microfilms.
  1978b Spatial Associations and Distribution of Aggregate Village Sites in a Southeastern Atlantic Coastal Area. Florida Anthropologist 31(1):21–34.
DeBoer, Warren R.
  1981 Buffer Zones in the Cultural Ecology of Aboriginal Amazonia: An Ethnohistorical Approach. American Antiquity 46:364–77.
Delcourt, Hazel R., and Paul A. Delcourt
  1985 Quaternary Palynology and Vegetational History of the Southeastern United States. In Pollen Records of Late-Quaternary North American Sediments, edited by V. M. Bryant and R. G. Holloway. American Association of Stratigraphic Palynologists Foundation.

DeJarnett, David L., and Asael T. Hansen
   1960 The Archaeology of the Childersburg Site, Alabama. *Notes in An-thropology* no. 4. Tallahassee: Florida State University.
DePratter, Chester B.
   1976 The 1974–75 Archaeological Survey in the Wallace Reservoir, Greene, Hancock, Morgan, and Putnam Counties, Georgia, Final Report. Report on file. Athens: Department of Anthropology, University of Georgia.
   1979 Ceramics. In *The Anthropology of St. Catherines Island: The Refuge-Deptford Mortuary Complex.* Anthropological Papers from the American Museum of Natural History 56(1):109–32.
   1983 *Late Prehistoric and Early Historic Chiefdoms in the Southeastern United States.* Ph.D. dissertation, Department of Anthropology, University of Georgia. Ann Arbor: University Microfilms.
   1987 Cofitachequi: Ethnohistoric Sources and Current Archaeological Knowledge. Paper presented at the 44th Annual Meeting of the Southeastern Archaeological Conference, Charleston, S.C.
DePratter, Chester B., Charles M. Hudson, and Marvin T. Smith
   1983 The Route of Juan Pardo's Explorations in the Interior Southeast, 1566–1568. *Florida Historical Quarterly* 62:125–58.
DePratter, Chester B., and Christopher Judge
   1986 Regional and Temporal Variation in Material Culture: Wateree River. Paper presented at the LAMAR Institute Conference on South Appalachian Mississippian, Macon, Ga.
Dickens, Roy
   1976 *Cherokee Prehistory: The Pisgah Phase in the Appalachian Summit Region.* Knoxville: University of Tennessee Press.
Dobyns, Henry F.
   1983 *Their Number Become Thinned.* Knoxville: University of Tennessee Press.
Drennan, Robert D., and Carlos A. Uribe (editors)
   1987 *Chiefdoms in the Americas.* Lanham, Md.: University Press of America.
Duncan, Gwyneth A.
   1985 A Morphological Analysis of the Tugalo Phase Vessel Assemblage. Master's thesis, Department of Anthropology, University of Georgia, Athens.
Earle, Timothy K.
   1977 A Reappraisal of Redistribution: Complex Hawaiian Chiefdoms. In *Exchange Systems in Prehistory,* edited by T. K. Earle and J. E. Ericson. New York: Academic Press.
   1978 The Economic and Social Organization of a Complex Chiefdom: The Halelea District, Kaua'i, Hawaii. *Anthropological Papers of the*

Museum of Anthropology, no. 63. Ann Arbor: Museum of Anthropology, University of Michigan.

Elliott, Daniel T.
    1981 Finch's Survey. *Early Georgia* 9(1–2):14–24.

Elvas, Fidalgo de
    1904 *True Relation.* Translated by Buckingham Smith. In *Narratives of the Career of Hernando de Soto in the Conquest of Florida,* edited by E. G. Bourne. New York: A. S. Barnes and Company.

Fairbanks, Charles
    1950 A Preliminary Segregation of Etowah, Savannah, and Lamar. *American Antiquity* 16:142–51.
    1952 Creek and Pre–Creek. In *Archeology of Eastern United States,* edited by J. B. Griffin. Chicago: University of Chicago Press.

Feinman, Gary, and Jill Neitzel
    1984 Too Many Types: An Overview of Sedentary Prestate Societies in the Americas. In *Advances in Archaeological Method and Theory,* edited by M. B. Schiffer. New York: Academic Press.

Ferguson, Leland G.
    1971 *South Appalachian Mississippian.* Ph.D. dissertation, Department of Anthropology, University of North Carolina. Ann Arbor: University Microfilms.

Ferguson, Leland G., and Stanton W. Green
    1984 South Appalachian Mississippian: Politics and Environment in the Old, Old South. *Southeastern Archaeology* 3:139–43.

Fish, Paul R., and David J. Hally
    1983 The Wallace Reservoir Archaeological Project: An Overview. *Early Georgia* 11(1–2):1–18.

Flannery, Kent V.
    1972 The Cultural Evolution of Civilizations. *Annual Review of Ecology and Systematics* 3:399–426.

Ford, James A., and Gordon R. Willey
    1940 An Interpretation of the Prehistory of the Eastern United States. *American Anthropologist* 43:325–63.

Ford, Richard I.
    1980 *The Color of Survival.* Santa Fe, N.M.: Discovery, School of American Research.
    1981 Gathering and Farming before A.D. 1000: Patterns of Prehistoric Cultivation North of Mexico. *Journal of Ethnobiology* 1:6–27.

Frankenstein, Susan M., and Michael J. Rowlands
    1978 The Internal Structure and Regional Context of Early Iron Age Society in Southwestern Germany. *Bulletin of the Institute of Archaeology* 15:73–112.

Fried, Morton H.
1967 *The Evolution of Political Society: An Essay in Political Anthropology.* New York: Random House.

Gallup, J. R.
1980 Climatic Features and Length of Growing Season in Alabama. *NOAA/National Weather Service Agricultural Experiment Station Bulletin,* no. 517. Auburn, Ala.: Auburn University.

Gameson, A. L. H.
1957 Weirs and the Aeration of Rivers. *Journal of the Institute of Water Engineers* 11:477–90.

Garrow, Patrick H., and Marvin T. Smith
1973 *The King Site (9F15) Excavations—April, 1971 through August, 1973: Collected Papers.* Rome, Ga.: Dennis Hodges.

Gibson, Jon L.
1974 Aboriginal Warfare in the Protohistoric Southeast: An Alternative Perspective. *American Antiquity* 39:130–33.

Goldman, Irving
1970 *Ancient Polynesian Society.* Chicago: University of Chicago Press.

Goldstein, Lynne G.
1976 *Spatial Structure and Social Organization: Regional Manifestations of Mississippian Society.* Ph.D. dissertation, Department of Anthropology, Northwestern University. Ann Arbor: University Microfilms.

Gramly, Richard Michael
1977 Deerskins and Hunting Territories: Competition for a Scarce Resource of the Northeastern Woodlands. *American Antiquity* 42:601–5.

Griffin, James B.
1952 Culture Periods in Eastern United States Archeology. In *Archeology of Eastern United States,* edited by J. B. Griffin. Chicago: University of Chicago Press.

1967 Eastern North American Archaeology: A Summary. *Science* 156:175–91.

1984 Changing Concepts of the Prehistoric Mississippian Cultures of the Eastern United States. In *Alabama and the Borderlands: From Prehistory to Statehood,* edited by R. R. Badger and L. A. Clayton. University: University of Alabama Press.

Haggett, Peter
1966 *Locational Analysis in Human Geography.* London: Edward Arnold.

Hally, David J.
1970 Archaeological Investigations of the Potts' Tract Site (9MU103) Carters Dam, Murray County, Georgia. *University of Georgia Laboratory of Archaeology Series Report,* no. 6. Athens, Ga.

1975 Introduction to the Symposium: The King Site and Its Investigation. *Southeastern Archaeological Conference Bulletin* 18:48–54.

1979 Archaeological Investigations of the Little Egypt Site (9MU102), Murray County, Georgia, 1969 Season. *University of Georgia Laboratory of Archaeology Series Report*, no. 18. Athens, Ga.

1980 Archaeological Investigations of the Little Egypt Site (9MU102), Murray County, Georgia, 1970–72 Seasons. Report submitted to the Heritage Conservation and Recreation Service, U.S. Department of the Interior.

1982 The Late Mississippian Period in North Georgia. Paper presented at the 39th Annual Meeting of the Southeastern Archaeological Conference, Memphis, Tenn.

1983a Use Alteration of Pottery Vessel Surfaces: An Important Source of Evidence for the Identification of Vessel Function. *North American Archaeologist* 4:1–25.

1983b The Interpretive Potential of Pottery from Domestic Contexts. *Midcontinental Journal of Archaeology* 8:163–96.

1984 Vessel Assemblages and Food Habits: A Comparison of Two Aboriginal Southeastern Vessel Assemblages. *Southeastern Archaeology* 3(1):46–64.

1986 The Cherokee Archaeology of Georgia. In *The Conference on Cherokee Prehistory*, edited by D. G. Moore. Swannanoa, N.C.: Warren Wilson College.

1987 Abandoned Centers and Change in Mississippian Societies. Paper presented at the 44th Annual Meeting of the Southeastern Archaeological Conference, Charleston, S.C.

Hally, David J., Charles M. Hudson, and Chester B. DePratter

1985 The Proto–Historic along the Savannah River. Paper presented at the 42d Annual Meeting of the Southeastern Archaeological Conference, Birmingham, Ala.

Hally, David J., and James L. Rudolph

1986 Mississippi Period Archaeology of the Georgia Piedmont. *University of Georgia Laboratory of Archaeology Series Report*, no. 24. Athens, Ga.

Hann, John H.

1985 The Visitation of the Provinces of Apalachee and Timucua Made by Domingo de Leturiondo in 1677–1678. Report on file. Florida Bureau of Archaeological Research, Tallahassee.

1986 Translation of Governor Redolledo's 1657 Visitation of Three Florida Provinces and Related Documents. *Florida Archaeology* 2:81–145. Florida Bureau of Archaeological Research, Tallahassee.

1987a Political Organization among Southeastern Indians in the Early Historic Period. Paper presented at "A Program on Atlantic History,

Culture, and Society" symposium, Johns Hopkins University, Baltimore.

1987b Apalachee: The Land between the Rivers. *Ripley P. Bullen Monographs in Anthropology and History*, no. 7. Gainesville: University Presses of Florida.

Harper, R. M.

1943 Forests of Alabama. *Geologic Survey of Alabama Monograph*, no. 10. University, Ala.

Hatch, James W.

1974 Social Dimensions of Dallas Mortuary Practice. Master's thesis, Department of Anthropology, Pennsylvania State University.

1975 Social Dimensions of Dallas Burials. *Southeastern Archaeological Conference Bulletin* 18:132–38.

1976 *Status in Death: Principles of Ranking in Dallas Culture Mortuary Remains.* Ph.D. dissertation, Department of Anthropology, Pennsylvania State University. Ann Arbor: University Microfilms.

Heidenreich, Conrad

1971 *Huronia.* Ontario: McClelland and Stewart Limited.

Helms, Mary W.

1979 *Ancient Panama: Chiefs in Search of Power.* Austin: University of Texas Press.

Hesse, Brian, and Susan K. Henson

n.d. Faunal Remains. In *Archaeology of the Rodgers–CETA Site, A Lamar Village Site on Talladega Creek, Central Alabama,* by C. R. Nance, J. Bergstresser, L. Haikey, S. K. Henson, B. Hesse, K. A. Kirk, and E. Morgan. Report on file. Department of Anthropology, University of Alabama at Birmingham.

Heye, George G., F. W. Hodge, and George H. Pepper

1918 The Nacoochee Mound in Georgia. *Museum of the American Indian, Heye Foundation Collections*, no. 66(3). New York.

Hickerson, Harold

1965 The Virginia Deer and Intertribal Buffer Zones in the Upper Mississippi Valley. In *Man, Culture, and Animals*, edited by A. L. and A. P. Vayda. AAAS Monograph.

Holmes, William H.

1903 Aboriginal Pottery of the Eastern United States. *Bureau of American Ethnology Annual Report*, no. 20. Washington, D.C.

Howard, James H.

1968 The Southeastern Ceremonial Complex and Its Interpretation. *Missouri Archaeological Society Memoir* no. 6.

Hudson, Charles M.

n.d. The Juan Pardo Expeditions: Exploration of the Carolinas and Tennessee, 1566–1568. Paper submitted for publication.

1976 *The Southeastern Indians.* Knoxville: University of Tennessee Press.

Hudson, Charles M., Marvin T. Smith, and Chester B. DePratter
1984 The Hernando de Soto Expedition: From Apalachee to Chiaha. *Southeastern Archaeology* 3(1):65–77.

Hudson, Charles M., Marvin T. Smith, David J. Hally, Richard Polhemus, and Chester B. DePratter
1985 Coosa: A Chiefdom in the Sixteenth Century United States. *American Antiquity* 50:723–37.
1987 Reply to Boyd and Schroedl. *American Antiquity* 52:845–46.

Hurst, G. A.
1981 Effects of Prescribed Burning on the Eastern Turkey. In *Prescribed Fire and Wildlife in Southern Forests,* edited by G. W. Wood. Belle W. Baruch Forest Science Institute, Clemson University, Georgetown, S.C.

Hynes, H. B. N.
1970 *The Ecology of Running Waters.* Toronto: University of Toronto Press.

Jennings, Jesse, and Charles Fairbanks
1939 Pottery Type Descriptions. *Southeastern Archaeological Conference Newsletter* 1(2).

Johnson, Gregory A.
1982 Organizational Structure and Scalar Stress. In *Theory and Explanation in Archaeology: The Southampton Conference,* edited by C. Renfrew, M. J. Rowlands, and B. A. Segraves. New York: Academic Press.

Jones, B. Calvin
1972 Colonel James Moore and the Destruction of the Apalachee Missions in 1704. *Bureau of Historic Sites and Properties Bulletin* 2:25–33.
1982 Southern Cult Manifestations at the Lake Jackson Site, Leon County, Florida: Salvage Excavation of Mound 3. *Midcontinental Journal of Archaeology* 7:3–44.

Jones, B. Calvin, and Charles Ewen
1987 Did De Soto Sleep Here? We Think So. Paper presented at the 44th annual meeting of the Southeastern Archaeological Conference, Charleston, S.C.

Jones, B. Calvin, and John T. Penman
1973 Winewood: An Inland Fort Walton Site in Tallahassee, Florida. *Bureau of Historic Sites and Properties Bulletin* 3:65–90.

Jones, B. Calvin, Mark Williams, Katharine Bierce–Gedris, John H. Hann, Rebecca Storey, Randolph J. Widmer, and John F. Scarry
1987 San Pedro y San Pablo de Patale: A 17th Century Spanish Mission in Leon County, Florida. Report on file. Florida Bureau of Archaeological Research, Tallahassee.

Jones, Grant
  1978 The Ethnohistory of the Guale Coast through 1684. In *The Anthro-pology of St. Catherines Island: Natural and Cultural History*, edited by D. H. Thomas, G. Jones, J. Durham, and C. Larsen. Anthropological Papers of the American Museum of Natural History, vol. 55(2):178–210.

Kalleburg, H.
  1958 Observations in a Stream Tank of Territoriality and Competition in Juvenile Salmon and Trout (Salmo salar L. and S. trutta L.). *Report of the Institute of Freshwater Resources* 39:55–98.

Kelly, Arthur R.
  1935 Exploring Prehistoric Georgia. *Scientific American* 152(3):117–20, (4):184–87, (5):244–46.
  1938 A Preliminary Report on Archaeological Exploration at Macon, Georgia. *Bureau of American Ethnology Bulletin*, no. 119. Smithsonian Institution, Washington, D.C.
  1970 Explorations at Bell Field Mound and Village: Seasons 1966, 1967, 1968. Report submitted to the U.S. National Park Service, Atlanta, Ga.
  1972 The 1970–1971 Field Seasons at Bell Field Mound, Carters Dam. Report submitted to the U.S. National Park Service, Atlanta, Ga.

Kelly, Arthur R., and Clemens de Baillou
  1960 Excavations of the Presumptive Site of Estatoe. *Southern Indian Studies* 12:3–20.

Kelly, Arthur R., and Robert S. Neitzel
  1961 Chauga Mound and Village Site (38OC1) in Oconee County, South Carolina. *University of Georgia Laboratory of Archaeology Series Report*, no. 3. Athens, Ga.

Kelly, Arthur R., Frank Schnell, Don Smith, and Ann Schlosser
  1965 Explorations at Sixtoe Field, Carters Dam, Murray County, Georgia. Report on file. Department of Anthropology, University of Georgia, Athens.

Kelly, H. D.
  1985 Letter from H. D. Kelly to Roger Nance, 19 June 1985.

Knight, Vernon James, Jr.
  1981 *Mississippian Ritual*. Ph.D. dissertation, Department of Anthropology, University of Florida. Ann Arbor: University Microfilms.
  1985a Symbolism of Mississippian Mounds. Paper presented at the 42d Annual Meeting of the Southeastern Archaeological Conference, Birmingham, Ala.
  1985b Tukabatchee: Archaeological Investigations at an Historic Creek Town in Elmore County, Alabama, 1984. *Report of Investigations*, no. 45. Office of Archaeological Research, Alabama State Museum of Natural History, University of Alabama, Tuscaloosa.

1986 The Institutional Organization of Mississippian Religion. *American Antiquity* 51: 675–87.

Knight, Vernon J., Jr., and Tim S. Mistovich
1984 Walter F. George Lake: Archaeological Survey of Fee Owned Lands, Alabama and Georgia. *Report of Investigations*, no. 42. Office of Archaeological Research, Alabama State Museum of Natural History, University of Alabama, Tuscaloosa.

Kofele-Kale, Ndiva
1981 *Tribesmen and Patriots: Political Culture in a Poly–Ethnic State.* Washington, D.C.: University Press of America.

Kormareck, E. V.
1981 History of Prescribed Fire and Controlled Burning in Wildlife Management in the South. In *Prescribed Fire and Wildlife in Southern Forests*, edited by G. W. Wood. Belle W. Baruch Forest Science Institute, Clemson University, Georgetown, S.C.

Landers, J. L.
1981 The Role of Fire in Bobwhite Quail Management. In *Prescribed Fire and Wildlife in Southern Forests*, edited by G. W. Wood. Belle W. Baruch Forest Science Institute, Clemson University, Georgetown, S.C.

Larson, Lewis H., Jr.
1955 Unusual Figurine from the Georgia Coast. *Florida Anthropologist* 10(1–2):37–52.
1971a Archaeological Implications of Social Stratification at the Etowah Site, Georgia. In *Approaches to the Social Dimensions of Mortuary Practices*, edited by J. A. Brown. Society for American Archaeology Memoir, no. 25. Washington, D.C.
1971b Settlement Distribution during the Mississippian Period. *Southeastern Archaeological Conference Bulletin* 13:19–25.
1972 Functional Considerations of Warfare in the Southeast during the Mississippi Period. *American Antiquity* 37:383–92.
1980 *Aboriginal Subsistence Technology on the Southeastern Coastal Plain during the Late Prehistoric Period.* Gainesville: University Presses of Florida.

Lawson, Samuel J.
1987 La Tama de la Tierra Adentro. *Early Georgia* 15.

Ledbetter, Jerald, and Lisa D. O'Steen
1986 Late Mississippian Settlement North of the Oconee Province. *The Profile* 54.

Ledbetter, R. Jerald, and Jack Wynn
1987 An Archaeological Assessment of Three Sites in the Oconee National Forest, Greene County, Georgia. Gainesville, Ga.: U.S. Department of Agriculture, Forest Service.

Lee, Chung Ho
  1977 *Settlement Pattern Analysis of the Late Mississippian Period in Georgia*. Ph.D. dissertation, Department of Anthropology, University of Georgia. Ann Arbor: University Microfilms.
Lewis, Thomas, and Madeline Kneberg
  1946 *Hiwassee Island: An Archaeological Account of Four Tennessee Indian Peoples*. Knoxville: University of Tennessee Press.
Lineback, N. G., and C. T. Traylor
  1973 *Atlas of Alabama*. University: University of Alabama Press.
Linton, Ralph
  1936 The Study of Man. New York: D. Appleton-Century.
Marotti, Frank, Jr.
  1985 Juan Baptista de Segura and the Failure of the Florida Jesuit Mission, 1566–1572. *Florida Historical Quarterly* 63:267–79.
Martinez, Carlos A.
  1975 Culture Sequence on the Central Georgia Coast 1000 B.C.–A.D. 1650. Master's thesis, Department of Anthropology, University of Florida, Gainesville.
Mech, L. David
  1977 Wolf–Pack Buffer Zones as Prey Reservoirs. *Science* 198:320–21.
Michie, James
  1980 An Intensive Shoreline Survey of Archeological Sites in Port Royal Sound and the Broad River Estuary, Beaufort County, South Carolina. *Research Manuscript*, no. 167. University of South Carolina, Columbia.
Milanich, Jerald T.
  1977 A Chronology for the Aboriginal Cultures of Northern St. Simons Island, Georgia. *Florida Anthropologist* 30(3):134–42.
Mobley, H. E., and W. E. Balmer
  1981 Current Purposes, Extent, and Environmental Effects of Prescribed Fire in the South. In *Prescribed Fire and Wildlife in Southern Forests*, edited by G. W. Wood. Belle W. Baruch Forest Science Institute, Clemson University, Georgetown, S.C.
Mohr, C.
  1901 Plant Life of Alabama. *USDA Contribution to the US National Herbarium*, no. 6. Washington, D.C.
Monk, C. D.
  1968 Successional and Environmental Relationships of the Forest Vegetation in North Central Florida. *American Midl. Nat.* 79(2): 441–57.
Moore, Clarence B.
  1897 Certain Aboriginal Mounds of the Georgia Coast. *Journal of the Academy of Natural Sciences of Philadelphia* 11(1):1–138.

Moorehead, William K. (editor)
1932 *Etowah Papers.* Andover, Mass.: Phillips Academy.

Morgan, Eddie
n.d. Paleobotanical Remains from Midden Deposits: Simple Composition and Representativeness in Relation to Archaeological Context. In *Archaeology of the Rodgers–CETA Site, A Lamar Village Site on Talladega Creek, Central Alabama,* by C. R. Nance, J. Bergstresser, L. Haikey, S. K. Henson, B. Hesse, K. A. Kirk, and E. Morgan. Report on file. Department of Anthropology, University of Alabama at Birmingham.

Morrell, L. Ross
1965 The Woods Island Site in Southeastern Acculturation 1625–1800. *Notes in Anthropology,* Vol. 11. Tallahassee: Florida State University.

Morse, Dan F.
1977 The Penetration of Northeast Arkansas by Mississippian Culture. In *For the Director: Research Essays in Honor of James B. Griffin,* edited by C. E. Cleland. Museum of Anthropology, University of Michigan, Anthropological Papers, no. 61.

Morse, Dan F., and Phyllis A. Morse
1983 *Archaeology of the Central Mississippi Valley.* New York: Academic Press.

Myer, William E.
1928 Indian Trails of the Southeast. *Annual Report of the Bureau of American Ethnology,* no. 42. Washington, D.C..

Neitzel, Robert S.
1965 Archeology of the Fatherland Site: The Grand Village of the Natchez. *Anthropological Papers of the American Museum of Natural History,* vol. 51, no. 1. New York.

Nelson, D. J., and D. C. Scott
1962 The Role of Detritus in the Productivity of a Rock Outcrop Community in a Piedmont Stream. *Limnology and Oceanography* 7:396–413.

Otto, John S., and Russell L. Lewis, Jr.
1974 A Formal and Functional Analysis of San Marcos Pottery from Site SA16–23, St. Augustine, Florida. *Bureau of Historic Sites and Properties Bulletin,* no. 4. Florida Department of State, Tallahassee.

Padgett, Thomas
1975 Some Observations on Mossy Oak. Paper presented at the 32d Annual Meeting of the Southeastern Archaeological Conference, Gainesville, Fla.

Paulk, Herschel L.
1973 *Soil Survey of Montgomery, Toombs, and Wheeler Counties, Georgia.* Washington, D.C.: U.S. Department of Agriculture, Soil Conservation Service.

Payne, Claudine

1981 A Preliminary Investigation of Fort Walton Settlement Patterns in the Tallahassee Red Hills. *Southeastern Archaeological Conference Bulletin* 24:29–31.

1982 Farmsteads and Districts: A Model of Fort Walton Settlement Patterns in the Tallahassee Red Hills. Paper presented at the 39th Annual Meeting of the Southeastern Archaeological Conference, Memphis, Tenn.

Paynter, Robert W.

1981 Social Complexity in Peripheries: Problems and Models. In *Archaeological Approaches to the Study of Complexity*, edited by S. E. van der Leeuw. Universeit van Amsterdam, Amsterdam.

Pearson, Charles E.

1977 Analysis of Late Prehistoric Settlement on Ossabaw Island, Georgia. *University of Georgia Laboratory of Archeology Series Report*, no. 12. University of Georgia, Athens.

1979 *Patterns of Mississippian Period Adaptation in Coastal Georgia.* Ph.D. dissertation, Department of Anthropology, University of Georgia. Ann Arbor: University Microfilms.

Peebles, Christopher S.

1974 *Moundville: The Organization of a Prehistoric Community and Culture.* Ph.D. dissertation, Department of Anthropology, University of California, Santa Barbara. Ann Arbor: University Microfilms.

1978 Determinants of Settlement Size and Location in the Moundville Phase. In *Mississippian Settlement Patterns*, edited by B. D. Smith. New York: Academic Press.

Peebles, Christopher, and Susan M. Kus

1977 Some Archaeological Correlates of Ranked Societies. *American Antiquity* 42:421–48.

Peterson, Alvah

1956 *Fishing with Natural Insects.* Columbus, Ohio: Sparr and Glenn Company.

Phillips, Philip

1970 Archaeological Survey in the Lower Yazoo Basin, Mississippi, 1949–1955. *Papers of the Peabody Museum of Archaeology and Ethnology*, no. 60. Harvard University, Cambridge.

Piatek, Bruce J.

1985 Non–Local Aboriginal Ceramics from Early Historic Contexts in St. Augustine. *Florida Anthropologist* 38.

Polhemus, Richard

1985a *The Toqua Site, 40MR6: A Late Mississippian, Dallas Phase Town.* Knoxville: Tennessee Valley Authority.

1985b Mississippian Architecture: Temporal, Technological, and Spatial Patterning of Structures at the Toqua Site (40MR6). Master's thesis,

Department of Anthropology, University of Tennessee, Knoxville.

Ramenofsky, Ann F.

  1982 *The Archaeology of Population Collapse: Native American Response to the Introduction of Infectious Disease*. Ph.D. dissertation, Department of Anthropology, University of Washington. Ann Arbor: University Microfilms.

Ranjel, Rodrigo

  1904 A Narrative of De Soto's Expedition Based on the Diary of Rodrigo Ranjel. In *Narratives of the Career of Hernando de Soto*, translated by Buckingham Smith, edited by E. G. Bourne. New York: A. S. Barnes and Company.

Reyher, Rebecca

  1952 *The Fon and His Hundred Wives*. Garden City, N.Y.: Doubleday and Company.

Reynolds, Henry

  1894 Notes on the Hollywood Mound. In *Report of the Mound Explorations of the Bureau of Ethnology*, edited by C. Thomas. *Bureau of American Ethnology Annual Report*, no. 12. Washington, D.C.

Ritzenthaler, Pat

  1966 *The Fon of Bafut*. New York: Thomas Y. Crowell Company.

Rudolph, James L.

  1983 Lamar Period Exploitation of Aquatic Resources in the Middle Oconee River Valley. *Early Georgia* 11(1–2):86–103.

Rudolph, James L., and Dennis B. Blanton

  1981 A Discussion of Mississippian Settlement in the Georgia Piedmont. *Early Georgia* 8:14–36.

Rudolph, James L., and David J. Hally

  1985 *Archaeological Investigations of the Beaverdam Creek Site (9EB85), Elbert County, Georgia*. Russell Papers, Archaeological Services Division, National Park Service, Atlanta, Ga.

Sahlins, Marshall D.

  1958 *Social Stratification in Polynesia*. Seattle: University of Washington Press.

  1981 Historical Metaphors and Mythical Realities: Structure in the Early History of the Sandwich Islands Kingdom. *ASAO Special Publications*, no. 1. University of Michigan Press, Ann Arbor.

Sanders, William T., and Barbara J. Price

  1968 *Mesoamerica: The Evolution of a Civilization*. New York: Random House.

Scarry, John F.

  1984 *Fort Walton Development: Mississippian Chiefdoms in the Lower Southeast*. Ph.D. dissertation, Department of Anthropology, Case Western Reserve University. Ann Arbor: University Microfilms.

  1985 A Proposed Typology for the Mississippian Period Ceramics of the

Fort Walton Area: A Type–Variety Approach. *Florida Anthropologist* 38:199–233.

1987 Mississippian Emergence in the Fort Walton Area: The Evolution of the Cayson and Lake Jackson Phases. In *Mississippian Emergence: The Evolution of Ranked Agricultural Societies in the Eastern United States*, edited by B. D. Smith. Washington, D.C.: Smithsonian Institution Press (in press).

Scarry, John F., and Claudine Payne
1986 Mississippian Polities in the Fort Walton Area: A Model Generated from the Renfrew–Level XTENT Algorithm. *Southeastern Archaeology* 5:79–90.

Schnell, Frank, Vernon J. Knight, Jr., and Gail S. Schnell
1981 *Cemochechobee: Archaeology of a Mississippian Ceremonial Center on the Chattahoochee River*. Gainesville: University Presses of Florida.

Schroedl, Gerald
1985 Overhill Cherokee Archaeology at Chota-Tanassee. *Report of Investigations*, no. 38. Knoxville: Department of Anthropology, University of Tennessee.

Sears, William H.
1950 Preliminary Report on the Excavation of an Etowah Valley Site. *American Antiquity* 16:137–42.
1952 Ceramic Development in the South Appalachian Province. *American Antiquity* 18:101–10.
1955 Creek and Cherokee Culture in the 18th Century. *American Antiquity* 21:143–48.
1956 *Excavations at Kolomoki: Final Report*. Athens: University of Georgia Press.

Service, Elman
1962 *Primitive Social Organization: An Evolutionary Perspective*. New York: Random House.

Setzler, Frank M., and Jesse D. Jennings
1941 Peachtree Mound and Village Site, Cherokee County, North Carolina. *Bureau of American Ethnology Bulletin*, no. 131. Washington, D.C.

Shapiro, Gary
1981 Archaeological Investigations at Site 9GE175. *Wallace Reservoir Project Contribution*, no. 13. University of Georgia, Athens.
1983 *Site Variability in the Oconee Province: A Late Mississippian Society of the Georgia Piedmont*. Ph.D. dissertation, Department of Anthropology, University of Florida. Ann Arbor: University Microfilms.
1984 Ceramic Vessels, Site Permanence, and Group Size: A Mississippian Example. *American Antiquity* 49(4):696–712.

1987 Archaeology at San Luis: Broad–Scale Testing 1984–1985. *Florida Archaeology*, no. 3. Florida Department of State, Tallahassee.

Shennan, Stephen

1982 Exchange and Ranking: The Role of Amber in the Earlier Bronze Age of Europe. In *Ranking, Resource, and Exchange: Aspects of the Archaeology of Early European Society*, edited by C. Renfrew and S. Shennan. Cambridge: Cambridge University Press.

1986 Central Europe in the Third Millennium B.C.: An Evolutionary Trajectory for the Beginning of the European Bronze Age. *Journal of Anthropological Archaeology* 5:115–46.

Smith, Bruce D.

1978 Variations in Mississippian Settlement Patterns. In *Mississippian Settlement Patterns*, edited by B. D. Smith. New York: Academic Press.

1984a Mississippian Expansion: Tracing the Historical Development of an Explanatory Model. *Southeastern Archaeology* 3(1):13–32.

1984b Mississippian Patterns of Subsistence and Settlement. In *Alabama and the Borderlands: From Prehistory to Statehood*, edited by R. R. Badger and L. A. Clayton. University: University of Alabama Press.

Smith, Buckingham (editor)

1968 *Narratives of De Soto*. Gainesville, Fla.: Palmetto Books.

Smith, Hale G.

1948 Two Historical Archaeological Periods in Florida. *American Antiquity* 13(4):313–19.

1973 *Analysis of the Lamar Site Materials at the Southeastern Archaeological Center*. Tallahassee, Fla.: Southeastern Archaeological Center.

Smith, Marvin T.

n.d. A Preliminary Site Report for Archeological Salvage Undertaken at 9GE5. *Laboratory of Archeology Manuscript*, no. 229. University of Georgia, Athens.

1981 Archaeological Investigations at the Dyar Site, 9GE5. *Wallace Reservoir Project Contribution*, no. 11. University of Georgia, Athens.

1983 The Development of Lamar Ceramics in the Wallace Reservoir: The Evidence from the Dyar Site, 9GE5. *Early Georgia* 11(1–2):74–85.

1984 *Depopulation and Culture Change in the Early Historic Period Interior Southeast*. Ph.D. dissertation, Department of Anthropology, University of Florida. Ann Arbor: University Microfilms.

1987 *Archaeology of Aboriginal Culture Change in the Interior Southeast*. Ripley P. Bullen Monographs in Archaeology and History, University of Florida Press, Gainesville.

Smith, Marvin T., David J. Hally, and Gary Shapiro

1981 Archaeological Investigations at the Ogeltree Site, 9GE153. *Wallace Reservoir Project Contribution*, no. 10. University of Georgia, Athens.

Smith, Marvin, and Stephen Kowalewski
  1980 Tentative Identification of a Prehistoric "Province" in Piedmont Georgia. *Early Georgia* 8:1–13.
Smith, Robin E. L., Chad O. Braley, Nina T. Borremans, and Elizabeth J. Reitz
  1981 Coastal Adaptations in Southeast Georgia: Ten Archeological Sites at Kings Bay. Report submitted to the U.S. Department of the Navy.
Snow, Frankie
  1977 An Archaeological Survey of the Ocmulgee Big Bend Region. *Occasional Papers from South Georgia*, no. 3. South Georgia College, Douglas.
  1978 Detection of an Indian Trade Path. *The Profile* 20.
  1984 Auchenehatchee: A Creek Indian Camp in Telfair County. *The Profile* 46.
South, Stanley
  1982 Exploring Santa Elena 1981. *Research Manuscript*, no. 184. South Carolina Institute of Archaeology and Anthropology, Columbia.
Steinan, Karl
  1984 Coastal Occupation of the Georgia Coastal Marsh. *Southeastern Archaeology* 3(2):164–72.
Steponaitis, Vincas P.
  1978 Location Theory and Complex Chiefdoms: A Mississippian Example. In *Mississippian Settlement Patterns*, edited by B. D. Smith. New York: Academic Press.
  1983 *Ceramics, Chronology, and Community Patterns: An Archaeological Study at Moundville.* New York: Academic Press.
Storey, Rebecca
  1985 Lake Jackson Skeletal Material. Report on file. Florida Bureau of Archaeological Research, Tallahassee.
Stransky, J. J., and R. F. Harlow
  1981 Effects of Fire on Deer Habitat in the Southeast. In *Prescribed Fire and Wildlife in Southern Forests*, edited by G. W. Wood. Belle W. Baruch Forest Science Institute, Clemson University, Georgetown, S.C.
Swanton, John R.
  1922 Early History of the Creek Indians and Their Neighbors. *Bureau of American Ethnology Bulletin*, no. 73. Smithsonian Institution, Washington, D.C.
  1929 Myths and Tales of the Southeast Indians. *Bureau of American Ethnology Bulletin*, no. 88. Smithsonian Institution, Washington, D.C.
  1931 Source Material for the Social and Ceremonial Life of the Choctaw Indians. *Bureau of American Ethnology Bulletin*, no. 103. Smithsonian Institution, Washington, D.C.
  1939 *Final Report of the United States De Soto Expedition Commission.*

U.S. House of Representatives Document 71, 76th Congress, 1st session. Washington, D.C.

1946 The Indians of the Southeastern United States. *Bureau of American Ethnology Bulletin*, no. 137. Smithsonian Institution, Washington, D.C.

Thomas, David Hurst

1987 The Archaeology of Mission Santa Catalina de Guale: Search and Discovery. *The American Museum of Natural History Anthropological Papers*, vol. 63, no. 2. New York.

Tilley, Christopher

1982 Social Formation, Social Structures and Social Change. In *Symbolic and Structural Archaeology*, edited by I. Hodder. Cambridge: Cambridge University Press.

Trimble, Stanley

1974 *Man Induced Soil Erosion on the Southern Piedmont, 1700–1970*. Ankery, Iowa: Soil Conservation Society of America.

Trinkley, Michael

1981 *Studies of Three Woodland Period Sites in Beaufort County, South Carolina*. Columbia: South Carolina Department of Highways and Public Transportation.

Turner, E. Randolph, and Robert S. Santley

1979 Deer Skins and Hunting Territories Reconsidered. *American Antiquity* 44:810–16.

U.S. Geological Survey

1973 *State of Georgia*. Slope map, scale 1:500,000.

Van Doren, Mark (editor)

1955 *Travels of William Bartram*. New York: Dover Publications.

Varner, John G., and Jeanette J. Varner (translators)

1962 *The Florida of the Inca*. Austin: University of Texas Press.

Ward, Trawick

1965 Correlation of Mississippian Soil Types. *Southeastern Archaeological Conference Bulletin* 3:42–48.

Waring, Antonio J.

1968 *The Waring Papers: The Collected Works of Antonio J. Waring*, edited by S. Williams. *Papers of the Peabody Museum of Archaeology and Ethnology*, no. 58. Harvard University, Cambridge.

Waselkov, Gregory A.

1980 Coosa River Valley Archaeology. 2 vols. *Auburn University Monograph*, no. 2. Auburn, Ala.: Auburn University.

Wauchope, Robert

1948 The Ceramic Sequence in the Etowah Drainage, Northwest Georgia. *American Antiquity* 13:201–9.

1950 The Evolution and Persistence of Ceramic Motifs in Northern Georgia. *American Antiquity* 16:16–22.

1966 Archaeological Survey of Northern Georgia with a Test of Some Cultural Hypotheses. *Society for American Archaeology Memoir*, no. 21. Menasha, Wis.

Webb, Clarence H.
1977 The Poverty Point Culture. *Geoscience and Man* 17.

Webster, David
1975 Warfare and the Evolution of the State: A Reconsideration. *American Antiquity* 40:464–70.

Wharton, Charles
1978 *The Natural Environments of Georgia*. Atlanta: Georgia Department of Natural Resources.

White, John R.
1983 Early Nineteenth Century Blast Furnace Charcoal: Analysis and Economics. *Conference on Historic Archaeology Papers* 15: 106–22.

Willey, Gordon R.
1939 Ceramic Stratigraphy in a Georgia Village Site. *American Antiquity* 4:140–47.

Willey, Gordon, Charles DiPeso, William Ritchie, Irving Rouse, John Rowe, and Donald Lathrap
1956 An Archaeological Classification of Culture Contact Situations. In *Seminars in Archaeology: 1955*, edited by R. Wauchope. Society for American Archaeology Memoir, no. 11. Menasha, Wis.

Willey, Gordon R., and Jeremy A. Sabloff
1980 *A History of American Archaeology*. 2d ed. San Francisco: W. H. Freeman and Company.

Williams, Mark
1975 Stubbs Mound in Central Georgia Prehistory. Master's thesis, Department of Anthropology, Florida State University, Tallahassee.
1976 WPA Excavations at Stubbs Mound. *Southeastern Archaeological Conference Bulletin* 19:6–7.
1982 Indians along the Oconee after De Soto: The Beginning of the End. *Early Georgia* 10:27–39.
1983 *The Joe Bell Site: Seventeenth Century Lifeways on the Oconee River*. Ph.D. dissertation, Department of Anthropology, University of Georgia. Ann Arbor: University Microfilms.
1984 Archaeological Excavations at Scull Shoals Mounds, Georgia. *U.S. Forest Service Cultural Resources Report*, no. 6. Gainesville, Ga.
1986 The Origins of Macon Plateau. Paper presented at the 50th Anniversary Celebration, Ocmulgee National Monument, Macon, Ga.
1988 Scull Shoals Revisited. *U.S. Forest Service Cultural Resources Report*, no. 1. Gainesville, Ga.

Williams, Mark, and Gary Shapiro
1985 The Antiquity of Lamar Centers in the Oconee Province. Paper

presented at the 42d Annual Meeting of the Southeastern Archaeological Conference, Birmingham, Ala.

1987 The Changing Contexts of Political Power in the Oconee Valley. Paper presented at the 44th Annual Meeting of the Southeastern Archaeological Conference, Charleston, S.C.

Williams, Stephen

1982 The Vacant Quarter Hypothesis. Paper presented at the 39th Annual Meeting of the Southeastern Archaeological Conference, Memphis, Tenn.

Winters, Howard D.

1968 Value Systems and Trade Cycles of the Late Archaic in the Midwest. In *New Perspectives in Archaeology*, edited by S. R. and L. R. Binford. Chicago: Aldine Publishing Company.

Wood, G. W. (editor)

1981 *Prescribed Fire and Wildlife in Southern Forests*. Georgetown, S.C.: Belle W. Baruch Forest Science Institute, Clemson University.

Wood, W. Dean, and Chung Ho Lee

1973 A Preliminary Report on Archaeological Reconnaissance in Green, Morgan, and Putnam Counties, Georgia. Report on file. Department of Anthropology, University of Georgia, Athens.

Woodruff, J. F., and E. J. Parizek

1956 Influence of Underlying Rock Structures on Stream Courses and Valley Profiles in the Georgia Piedmont. *Annals of the Association of American Geographers* 54:129–39.

Worth, John E.

1988 Mississippian Occupation on the Middle Flint River. Master's thesis, Department of Anthropology, University of Georgia, Athens.

Wright, Henry T.

1984 Prestate Political Formations. In *On the Evolution of Complex Societies Essays in Honor of Harry Hoijer 1982*, edited by T. K. Earle. Malibu, Calif.: Undena Publications.

Index

253